The Temporal Path

Presented by: Ly Cam Ha
Illustration: Dz & Hannah
Cover artists: Tomy
Published by: WuWei Press
California, USA

ISBN: 979-8-9878147-2-7

John NT

The Temporal Path

Introduction
The Temporal Path of John Nguyễn & Our Shared Journey

When John Nguyễn invited me to pen an introduction for his book, I approached the task with a sense of duty. Yet, after immersing myself in the manuscript of *The Temporal Path*, I found that my ambition to craft a conventional introduction dissolved. What unfolded before me was not just a book, but an experience - one so profound that it left me compelled to share the deep and unexpected emotions it stirred within me.

The Temporal Path is a work that transcends mere narrative, offering instead a journey into new, profound, and startling ideas that I had never encountered before. Upon finishing the author's preface, I felt the need to prepare myself - both mentally and physically - for the journey ahead. I sought to create a quiet, solitary space to fully engage with the text. Yet, as soon as I began reading, life itself seemed to intervene, with distractions clamoring for my attention. It was as if "hunters" from outside my peaceful space were intent on disrupting my focus. But, fortified by my own experiences and by John Nguyễn's words, I found the strength to maintain that quiet space, protected from the noise of the outside world.

In this space, I discovered a resonance between my own poetic sensibilities and John Nguyễn's prose - a shared dramatic spirit that urges us not to flee from fear, but to confront it. This connection reminded me of a verse from my poem, "Declaration of Dream," where I wrote:

More and more birds of prey are gathering above.

They circle around, staring with unblinking eyes.

They bring the sound of death from high above,

Sharp claws scratching coldly along our spines,

Waiting for our warmth to fade, for our eyes to dim,

Then, descending like the hungriest beings on earth,

Our frightened love becomes a feast.

Yet love must be great and defiant,

Even in the darkest corners where we dwell,

Even as we sleep in our small beds.

In our dreams, we must never surrender.

In reading *The Temporal Path*, I chose not to delve into the author's biography, preferring instead to meet John Nguyễn through his words. Language, no matter how artful, can never fully mask the truth it seeks to convey. Through his writing, I glimpsed a multifaceted man - vulnerable and strong, puzzled and enlightened, both empty and full. These contradictions shape a portrait of John Nguyễn as complex as the human experience itself, and they form the essence of *The Temporal Path*.

The manuscript, spanning 505 pages, distills into a set of fundamental questions: "Who am I? Why am I here? Where am I heading?" The answers to these questions are woven throughout the text, sometimes emerging directly and at other times subtly, as questions become answers in themselves. John Nguyễn's preface hints at a truth he has discovered, a truth not merely of intellectual realization but of lived experience. He has spent his life honing his ability to approach and understand this truth, a truth that resonates with the common human condition.

As I continued to read, each page felt like a new day, a new life unfolding. This progression - this continuous discovery - mirrors the nature of life itself. Living, as *The Temporal Path* suggests, is a constant challenge, a relentless pursuit without the promise of satisfaction. Some passages reveal moments of enlightenment, only to be followed by deeper abysses and greater trials. Such is the nature of existence: a ceaseless journey toward truth, where the destination is not a final resting place but a perpetual path of growth and self-discovery.

This journey, which John Nguyễn calls *"The Temporal Path,"* is not without its hardships. There are moments of sadness, exhaustion, and doubt, where the author contemplates running away from himself. Yet, despite these trials, he embraces life with an intensity that is both awe-inspiring and relentless. His words rise and fall like the waves of a stormy sea, embodying the spirit of a never-ending song. Some pages brim with life, with seeds bursting through their shells toward the light, while others depict a profound emptiness, where renewal seems impossible.

And yet, despite the challenges presented in *The Temporal Path*, the book never leaves me feeling hopeless. Instead, it teaches us that each new day brings the same difficulties, but also the same opportunities for insight, inspiration, and determination. Though John Nguyễn's reflections may resemble the meditations of a Zen master, he is not a sage, but a witness to the moral transformations within himself. He is an action, a breath - a reflection of you and me, in another form. We are, in his words, both one and countless, and our time on this earth is a sacred gift.

It is not uncommon for works of prose to end with a poem, but the poems of John Nguyễn are unlike any I have encountered. They evoke images of a woodcutter, a beggar, a monk - figures who traverse this world with songs that echo the misfortunes, dreams, and revelations of life. These poems resonate with the spirit of the universe itself, offering us glimpses of something greater, something divine.

In sharing my thoughts here, I aim not only to discuss this book but also to reflect on the nature of life itself - a life that exists within each of us. This world contains everything the universe has to offer: all its sorrows, all its joys, all its darkness, and all its light. Yet, the choice of what we embrace lies not with some external force, but with each of us individually.

Nguyễn Quang Thiều

Writer

Chairman of the Việt Nam Writers' Association

Ha Noi, November 2021

" Lingering sorrow with deepest emotion,

A journey through this world's terrain,

Pausing, hesitant, to pour into each page,

My love for humanity, profound and unspoken. "

Preface

1.

The Buddha has illuminated the nature of human existence through the concept of Panca-skandha - the five aggregates of attachment that constitute our being. These five components - form (Rupa), sensation (Vedana), perception (Samjna), mental formation (Samskara), and consciousness (Vijnana) - are the essence of our experience in this world. Rupa is the body, Vedana is our emotional response, Samjna is our capacity for imagination, Samskara represents our will and deliberate actions, and Vijnana is our consciousness. Though interpretations may vary, Panca-skandha is essentially a model of human existence, a reflection of our Body, Feelings, Understanding, Interactions, and Mind.

Buddha teaches that we are nothing beyond these aggregates, and the myriad ways in which they combine create the diversity of human experiences. These five components are interdependent, each influencing the other, and they form the ego - a construct born from unstable elements, ever-changing in response to the laws of cause and effect and the cycles of samsara.

As the Buddha Sutra describes:

Form is like foam, appearing and dissolving like fleeting encounters.
Feelings are as fragile and transient as bubbles, shifting between joy and sorrow.
Perception is like a mirage, an illusion that deceives the traveler in the desert.
Mental formations are like the tender banana tree, easily swayed by the winds of karma.
Consciousness is akin to magic, unpredictable and mutable, ever subject to change.

2.

In recent years, sleepless nights have become my companion, driven by the weight of responsibilities and the inevitable approach of age. Often, I return home to the loyal greeting of a dog by the gate, its wagging tail a small comfort. No matter how late it is, I must read a few pages before sleep takes over, though often I find myself waking in the midst of chaotic dreams.

In those dreams, I encounter vivid scenes - a beautiful woman just out of reach, an acquaintance waving from across an impassable road, or an old friend's smile from years past. The faintest noise - a dog's bark, a truck's horn - brings me back to reality, reminding me that I am still in this world, still walking the path of life.

Jalāl ad-Dīn Rumi, the great Sufi poet, once wrote:

> *"This being human is a guest house. Every morning, a new arrival*
>
> *A joy, a depression, a meanness, some momentary awareness*
>
> *Comes as an unexpected visitor. Welcome and entertain them all!*
>
> *. . . Be grateful for whoever comes, because each has been sent*
>
> *As a guide from beyond."*
>
> **(Jalaludin Rumi, The Guest House)**

3.

It has been more than 30 years since I left university and embarked on the journey of life's hardships. I can no longer count the roads I've traveled or the friends I've made along the way. Seven passports, filled with visa stamps, are now a testament to my wanderings, and I am onto my eighth. I remember the sound of train whistles from my youth, echoes that still startle me today.

In 1990, I visited Switzerland, meticulously preparing for my first foray into the West - armed with maps, instant noodles, a Russian water boiler, and $200. Yet, despite my preparations, I found myself starving for two days on a train due to a misunderstanding of the schedule. I thought I would arrive the same evening, but the journey took a full day and night longer. As the Berlin Wall crumbled and East Germany ceased to exist, my plans to return home through Berlin were foiled. Instead, I journeyed through Austria, Hungary, and Yugoslavia, catching glimpses of nomads by flickering flames, and wondering if I shared some of their gypsy blood.

4.

Reflecting on those early 1990s, I recall doing business in Poland while pursuing scientific research in Trieste, Italy. Returning to my country, I traversed the northern provinces, crossed rivers into China, mingled with smugglers, and shared nights under the stars. Life was an adventure, one that took me to the edge of the world and back.

5.

We all harbor dreams of the future. As children, our dreams are pure and beautiful, but as life's worries, love, and disappointments pull us in different directions, we find ourselves drifting. At times, a sudden turning point - like a resounding inner call - awakens us to our true path.

Even as we strive to turn our dreams into reality, we may feel lost, wondering how we arrived at this place. When I wake abruptly from a dream, I often find myself suspended between imagination and reality, between being and nothingness, between deep memory and fleeting moments. There exists within me a man different from the one I know, or the one others expect. This is the new self, with a fresh "operating system" and a new "general model." It might be the ego I lost in my pursuit of happiness, or the one I have yet to discover… or perhaps the ego that is still awaiting its awakening.

6.

The 1990s were a time of great change across the world, in every country, every family, and within each individual. After years of wandering abroad, enduring life's ups and downs, I returned to Vietnam to settle down. It was time to close the door on social affairs, to retreat into books and the solace of nature. I lost my direction, unsure of where to go next. In the dead of night, I would start my motorbike and ride off into the darkness, sometimes sleeping on the road, drenched by rain. At dawn, I would return home, greeted by the sight of buffaloes on the roadside, signaling the start of a new day.

7.

I lived in a humble, tile-roofed house by the Red River, surrounded by a garden of yellow chrysanthemums and shady trees. Whenever I saw a butterfly fluttering by, I thought of Zhuangzi and his dream. Was it I who dreamt of the butterfly, or the butterfly who dreamt of being me? As the river rose and the lake overflowed, I was reminded of Walt Whitman's words:

"Flow on, river! Flow with the flood-tide, and ebb with the ebb-tide!

Frolic on, crested and scallop-edged waves!

Gorgeous clouds of the sunset! Drench me with your splendor...

These and all else were to me the same as they are to you,

I loved well those cities, loved well the stately and rapid river, ...

The time will come, though I stop here to-day and to-night."

(Walt Whitman, *Crossing Brooklyn Ferry*)

Whenever I wake in the middle of the night, I am transported back to the familiar roads and rivers of my homeland, haunted by the fundamental questions: "Who am I?" "Why am I here?" "Where am I heading?"

8.

There are moments when I lose faith, unsure of my purpose. Why do I pursue my trade? Is it pride that drives me? Why do I work so hard? In these times, I visit universities, drawn to the echoes of my past. Perhaps it is there that I will find the answers. Yet, even as I grapple with the stresses and illnesses of daily life, I remember my schooldays - the relentless pursuit of knowledge, the sleepless nights in libraries, the drive to earn my PhD. I defended my thesis on a summer day in 1989, and though it was a beautiful day, filled with the scent of birch blossoms, I stepped out of the room with an empty head, unsure of my next step. Everyone congratulated me, my teachers praised me, but all I wanted was to go home, homesick after six long years.

9.

Life continues to flow, bringing new worries and challenges. What should I do now? How long can I evade life? My connections, friends, and colleagues are waiting. When we reach the boundary of meditation, faced with decisions, there are only two possibilities: if we find earth beneath our feet, we can walk; if it is empty space, we must learn to fly.

In enlightenment, we gradually face reality. The question "Why have I come here?" is replaced by "What should I do? Which way should I go?" This is the process of awakening.

10.

There is a story of a young Buddhist monk who followed two older monks to a lawn by a lake to meditate. When they had just sat down, one older monk stood and said, "I need to fetch a cushion." He ran across the water's surface as fast as lightning and returned the same way. The young monk, astonished, kept silent. Later, the other older monk rose, saying, "I need to fetch a palm-leaf hat." He too ran across the water to the pagoda and back. The young monk, eager to emulate them, tried to cross the water but fell in repeatedly. Seeing his struggle, one older monk said to the other, "Should we tell him where the rocks are?"

If only someone would reveal the hidden rocks on the temporal path! They might guide us toward our desires and help us achieve our goals. As the Bible says: *"Everyone who hears these words of mine and puts them into practice is like a wise man who built his house on the rock.*

The rain came down, the floods came, and the winds blew and beat on that house; yet it did not fall, because it had its foundation on the rock.

But everyone who hears these words of mine and does not put them into practice is like a foolish man who built his house on sand.

The rain came down, the floods came, and the winds blew and beat against that house, and it fell with a great crash." (Matthew 7:24–27, Bible)

For generations, our predecessors have written about love, power, and happiness, yet humanity continues to stumble and suffer. Who should I ask? Whom should I trust? Which path should I follow? Or should I rely solely on myself?

11.

Life rarely unfolds as we expect. Unexpected events are always on the horizon. After a period of retreat, I moved from my dilapidated house to my office, which became both a meeting room and my bedroom. The metal roof leaked during rainstorms, drops of water startling me awake. After much persuasion, I agreed to take on a new role, leading an organization. In less than a year, the sinking ship began to rise, escaping danger. Yet, old friendships turned to enmity, and close friends became deceitful. I left with a heavy heart.

My journey into business and real estate was accidental. A friend and I offered consultancy services for a project in a high-tech park, searching for prime plots of land. This led us to a poor countryside where we began developing an urban area. The high-tech park transformed into a new quarter, and the business expanded to coastal cities, the Central Highlands, and even the southernmost islands. Life became like a military march - newcomers joined, some lagged behind, and a few deserted, but the march continued.

12.

Someone once wrote, "There are moments when you think everything has ended, but it is just beginning." I would add, "When we are elevated in victory, an abyss may lie ahead."

In recent years, the financial markets have been unpredictable. Bank shares, once seemingly worthless, soared in value, and land prices skyrocketed. I reinvested my profits into banks and established a securities company. Now, investment hopes are on the brink of collapse. Patience and perseverance are my mantras.

13.

Throughout my life, I have been a perpetual student, always seeking something new. Perhaps I will travel to neighboring countries or distant lands in South America. The future is uncertain, but I am certain that I will learn something valuable from people and cultures along the way. The best way to learn is to teach. By sharing knowledge, I gain deeper understanding and learn from my students. Helping others, especially young people and colleagues, to avoid the mistakes I made is a worthy endeavor. Though I cannot pave the way for them, I can show them where the rocks lie beneath the surface, guiding them across the lake.

,, Understand, I'll slip quietly away from the noisy crowd

when I see the pale

stars rising, blooming, over the oaks.

I'll pursue solitary pathways through the pale twilit meadows, with only this one dream:

You come too. " (Rainer Maria Rilke, *Pathways*)

14.

The musician Trịnh Công Sơn wrote:
"Through years and years still on the go
To nowhere 'til life's worn out.
On my shoulders the sun and moon
Shed through my heart eternal light."

From the moment we are born, we embark on a journey. No matter where it takes us, the ultimate destination is a return to ourselves. We wander through life with countless plans, but in the end, all we seek is peace of mind and the essence of our true self. Life moves in cycles, from the smallest cells to the vast cosmos. We begin in the first house - our mother's womb - and life unfolds through the cycles of seasons, the rising and setting of the sun and moon, and the ebb and flow of tides.

I have read thousands of books and traveled tens of thousands of roads. Now, I stand before my mother, feeling the same childlike purity as in my youth.

We understand that space is not flat but curved; life is not a straight path but a magical dance of creation. The route to the future is not a broad highway but a winding path that leads us deeper into the mysteries of the self. Only by completing the cycle of learning does life become whole.

"It's the circle of life

And it moves us all

Through despair and hope

Through faith and love

'Til we find our place

On the path unwinding

In the circle

The circle of life"

(Elton John, *Circle of Life*)

15.

The enigmatic Persian poet Rumi wrote of the "formless realm," a place where one returns to oneself. Time may add threads of silver to our hair, but the fire of life's experiences continues to burn brightly within. As Pablo Neruda beautifully expressed:

"Time adds

its threads

to your hair, but in my heart your honeysuckle

fragrance

is living fire.

It is beautiful,

as we have done, to grow old living life to the full." (Pablo Neruda, *Ode to Time*)

Let time be the true test. Reaching the formless meditative realm reminds us that life cannot be defined by external events but by the consciousness within us. In this realm, we find equilibrium, embracing suffering, loss, and disappointment without identifying with them. It is here that we spread our arms and sing, celebrating life's trials and triumphs.

16.

With greater enlightenment, I have come to understand that I am no longer defined by external circumstances but by the internal transformations I have undergone. I do not define myself by life's hardships, but by the courage I have found to chart a new course. I do not define myself by sadness and misery, but by the resilience and faith that allow me to begin anew. I do not define myself by the duration or depth of relationships, but by their sincerity, trust, and affection. After enduring challenges and becoming who I am, I have been forged in the flames of time on the journey back to my true self.

Through the successes and failures that have tempered my soul, I have discovered a formless meditative realm within me - a place of peace and freedom, the home of the ego I have long sought.

17.

Human life is often measured in a span of a hundred years, yet our physical form, reduced to ashes, endures beyond time. The essence of our existence, housed in impermanence and the non-ego, may begin anew from a speck of dust somewhere in this world.

You will sing the song of life, feeling the vastness of human existence in the universe:

"To see a World in a Grain of Sand

And a Heaven in a Wild Flower

Hold Infinity in the palm of your hand

And Eternity in an hour"

(William Blake, *Auguries of Innocence*)

18.

Or you may awaken suddenly, overwhelmed with the joy of perception and enlightenment, like the great poet Tagore, who walked through the endless stream of life with arms wide open, singing:

"I feel that all the stars shine in me.

The world breaks into my life like a flood.

The flowers blossom in my body.

All the youthfulness of land and water smokes like an incense in my heart;

And the breath of all things plays on my thoughts as on a flute."

(Rabindranath Tagore, *Verses - Fruits - Gathering, 83*)

This is the potential within each of us. Yet, I believe that you and I will find our formless realm in this world, achieving enlightenment as we return to our true selves and discover the essence of our being.

Autumn 2021

Part 1: Walking Alone

At the last minute, I decided to leave all my work behind to visit my children. I bought my plane ticket just a day before departing. On the same day, two of our high-ranking managers handed in their resignations, leaving a mountain of work at the office. As I sat on the plane, I couldn't shake off the worry.

But as the plane took off, I sighed in relief. It was the right decision. Work would never be finished, and the most important thing now was to see my children.

*

Meeting my son in New York filled me with joy, though we didn't openly show it - men don't, after all. We shared a bedroom, rearranging a table and chair so one of us could sleep on the floor. I insisted on taking the floor, leaving the bed for my son.

That night, the cold seeped into my bones, making sleep difficult. There was only one blanket, and my son snored softly beside me. I sat up, wrapped my coat around myself, and eventually drifted off. But the chill kept waking me. Finally, I slipped into the bed, careful not to wake him, though he took up most of the space as he always did. I clung to the edge, just glad to be near him.

Before dawn, I woke and sat in meditation, the city slowly coming to life outside the window. When I finished, the sun was rising, casting light over the tall buildings.

I waited for my son to wake, checking in with the office to give some guidance. When he finally got up, he put on some music and sat at the table to study. No breakfast was forthcoming, and it was dinnertime back in Vietnam. He hurried off to school, promising we'd have lunch together.

Feeling the pangs of hunger, I rummaged through the kitchen. All I found were some vegetables and eggs. I threw everything into a pot, adding whatever spices I could find, and made myself a simple meal.

My son shares the flat with friends, so I was wary of someone walking in on me. Thankfully, they were all at school. I enjoyed my makeshift meal - a bowl of vegetable soup, a salad, and a boiled egg - content with my New York breakfast and Hanoi dinner.

I couldn't resist sending my son a picture of my breakfast by the window, overlooking Wall Street. His reply made me laugh, but also panic: "Have you eaten cauliflower from a can? Oh, my God..." I quickly spat it out, texting back, "Is it for the dog or cat?" "No, it's my roommate's," he replied. Good heavens. I made a mental note to buy a bag of cauliflower to replace it.

After a quick nap, I caught up with work from Hanoi on the phone. When I waved my hand, my ring slipped off - how thin I had become! That evening, I had dinner with my son and his friends, a group of bright, driven young people. Can Vietnam rise alongside the world's leading nations? It depends on this new generation.

As I observed New York from the 49th floor, I realized I was higher than thousands of buildings but still lower than dozens. It's just like my company - a mix of highs and lows.

*

The next morning, I was up early again, sending messages, emails, and preparing to leave for Vancouver. My son took me to a place with good food, better than the sushi from the night before. After school, we explored the city, ending the day with a sad opera on Broadway. Despite having visited New York twice before, I hadn't seen the museums - always closed or too crowded.

For dinner, my son chose a Japanese restaurant once frequented by writer Murakami. Then it was time for me to head to the airport. But as I sat in the waiting room, I dozed off, only to wake up and realize the plane to Vancouver had already left. I had been so tired, having traveled and explored all day, but I was disappointed to miss the flight - I wanted to be closer to my daughter this time.

As I returned to my son's apartment, the day's weight pressed down on me - work pressures, family quarrels, the disillusionment with unfaithful employees. The rain fell lightly, blurring the streetlights, and I couldn't help but think that maybe everything happens for a reason. Perhaps it was Heaven's way of giving me one more night with my son or protecting me from something amiss with the plane.

It was a dark day, and as I returned to the apartment, I found my son playing with his friends. If I had known, I might have stayed at a hotel. Connecting to the Wi-Fi, I saw messages from my wife about issues in Hanoi, adding to my frustration. I understood then why some choose to escape - to board a train far from home or, like a man I once read about, to live in a station for years after constant quarrels with his wife.

Family is like a nation - there are always problems to solve, some of which can never be fully resolved. No matter the development level, every family has its own struggles.

*

Today, I'll go to the airport early, just in case. My son asked if I needed him to see me off, but I declined. I can manage on my own. He had plans to attend a friend's birthday party. As he helped me into a taxi, he turned away quickly, and I watched the bustling stream of cars move on.

I've been to New York several times, and every city feels the same after a while. Emotions, friendships, possessions, affections - they're all like shadows on water, fleeting clouds in the sky. Life, too, is like that.

The Buddha was right. He left the palace, sought enlightenment, and found peace. Perhaps we are like donkeys, tied to a stake, walking in circles - accepting life as it comes. Yet, even though we may not all become enlightened like the Buddha, we should find contentment in our purpose, whatever it may be.

For the Buddha, the purpose was enlightenment, peace, and the sustenance of life. For King Trần Nhân Tông, it was fulfilling his duties as a king, seeking enlightenment, and helping others. For me, it's about fulfilling my family obligations, cultivating my mind and body, seeking positive changes, helping others, and finding peace.

*

This morning in Vancouver, the sun bathed the city in light. I showered, ironed my clothes, and waited for my daughter. Last night, I had arrived late at her university hostel - more luxurious than any hotel. Yet, it was so large that it took me a while to find her room.

Nearly 40 years ago, I was a student like my daughter. Half a lifetime has passed, and the river of life continues to flow, branching into new paths.

We spent the day wandering the streets, searching for old books, watching short films, and enjoying the vibrant energy of youth. My daughter fulfilled my wish by taking me to a ballet performed by young talents and a charity auction. I even had the chance to see a Cirque du Soleil performance, which made me think about the performance of my own life's memories.

Traveling halfway around the world to be with my daughter, sharing such beautiful moments with her, filled me with emotion. The dances, the faces, the footsteps - all so full of life, yet so fleeting.

*

I left Canada yesterday morning, the rain and cold making the wet trees sparkle outside the window. The airport was crowded with Chinese and Asian travelers, bustling about. When I woke up, I found myself in Europe, surrounded by tall Germans speaking in their heavy accents. A customs officer questioned me, reprimanding me for saying my purpose was to visit my children when I also planned to travel. It left me annoyed and nervous.

The airports in Frankfurt and Paris always depress me - too vast and confusing. Traveling for ten days through so many large airports left me exhausted. Or perhaps youth had left me, and I was no longer in the right frame of mind. The seasons change, and so do we.

I returned to Switzerland after a long time. This small country has accomplished great things. Vietnam, with its limitless potential, can learn much from such nations. The future is still ahead of us. It's up to us to decide whether we want to learn or not.

I spent two days with my daughter, visiting her university and having dinner with her friends. Before checking on her living conditions, I stopped by a music shop to buy some records. I've passed my love for music on to my children, buying them gramophones, phonographs, and amplifiers.

Early in the morning, still dark, I set off once again, alone. No one was there to see me off. Walking in the dim light of an autumn morning, I realized that my children are growing up, finding their own paths, while their mother and I continue our journey alone.

*

There's something profoundly moving about spending time with my children. I enjoyed delicious meals with my son, shared his messy apartment, and felt the romantic connection with my youngest daughter, who is dedicated to her studies and passionate about the arts. She reminded me of my own student days. My oldest daughter, on the other hand, invited me to stay in a five-star hotel and treated me to fine dining at a Michelin-starred restaurant. She's carving out her own style in a wealthy Western world.

In the end, I traveled around the world only to find myself again.

1. WHO LEARNS FROM WHOM?

After the meeting, I returned to the office to find only milk and nuts left. Not much of a lunch. So, I decided to step out for a proper meal. As luck would have it, I ran into one of the company drivers, who kindly invited me to join him for lunch. We ended up at a place that had run out of food, leaving us with nothing but beer. The beer was good - sweet even, perhaps because we were both hungry.

As we drank, the driver mentioned that he had learned a lot from me. I was taken aback. "Oh, have you driven me occasionally?" I asked, curious. "No," he replied, "I've learned from H, your regular driver." I couldn't help but laugh. "So, you've learned how to put up with me, then?" I thought to myself, though I didn't say it out loud. The beer was good - so we **had another**

.

I started to wonder: Do the drivers learn from each other and share everything? My thoughts drifted back to something my daughter once said. She jokingly called Uncle H, my driver of over 20 years, my second wife. When I asked her why, she explained, "Because he takes care of everything for you - from your clothes and shoes to your medicine and food."

Oh, my God...

> "I want to talk endlessly; my mind is flooded with words, but my mouth is silent - voiceless and speechless."

2. MUTE DESIRE

There are days when he sits at the table, eating the same meal he's had every day for what feels like an eternity. The room often sinks into silence, the only sound being the methodical chewing of his food. Especially after long meetings or a grueling day at work, he comes home utterly exhausted, teetering on the edge of wanting to explode. He fantasizes about walking away from it all - abandoning his work, shaving his head, retreating to a solitary place where he can live in obscurity and find peace of mind and body. Such is life!

This lunch was no different. It was the beginning of the week, in the last month of the year, and he was buried under a mountain of work. A tray of rice sat on the table; the dining room felt cold despite the sunshine streaming through the window. Only his heart remained lonely.

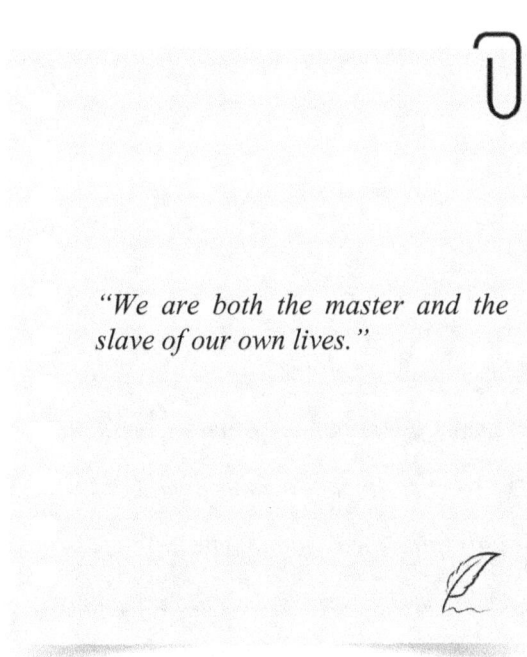

"We are both the master and the slave of our own lives."

3. SEASONAL CHANGE

Summer rains and breezes carry the scent of fresh grass and damp earth, the wet courtyard blanketed in green moss, stirring moments of loneliness and quiet trembling. The changing seasons transform the natural world around us, yet they also bring a sense of peace and calm to our minds.

Emptiness

In whom do we confide when we are sad?

The room is empty - no music, no books, no glass.

We dive into meditation, lamenting in our hearts.

The universe is vast, yet we too are empty.

4. PATH OF LIFE

You continue walking on a road dusted by the passage of time,

Through sudden bends and tangled roundabouts.

On either side, rise barriers of preconception,

Of deceitful power and the scream of loneliness.

You tread along desolate, forgotten streets,

Passing men and women lost in the shadows

From a past steeped in squalor to a future teetering on chaos,

Wandering through a present of trivial intentions.

Where are the glorious royal dynasties with their magnificent palaces?

Where are the dazzling dreams that once danced on the waves of the blue sea?

There are only fragments of memory, broken bricks, and shattered tiles.

The dust of time cloaks history in a mossy shroud.

You gaze at silhouettes of illusion,

Lonely at sunrise, fading at sunset.

The solitary sun blazes with the ambitions of dynasties,

While night descends, cold, with distant flickering stars.

You remind yourself to endure, to pass through the narrow gate,

Knowing that all animosity and forgiveness will be forgotten.

Recorded in the books stained by time, you have not yet opened the page with sacred hope.

You have wandered aimlessly, led by the call of impermanence,

Save for the sunrise and sunset in their disordered light.

Restless nights bring vague sounds and figures,

Leisurely walking, intentionally waiting.

Let go of willful waiting - surrender to Him.

5. INNOCENCE

You, a being with thoughts and a purpose in life, will only achieve the greatest work of your existence when you let go of calculation and thought. True innocence arises after many years of wandering through life, forgetting the self. When you reach this state, you may find yourself both thoughtful and thoughtless.

Thoughts are like rain falling from the sky, like waves dancing in the sea, like stars shining in the night, like green leaves sprouting in the warmth of spring. In truth, you are the rain, the sea, the stars, and the leaves. When you realize this, you become innocent and pure, and you merge with all that surrounds you.

6. FRAGRANCE OF THE NIGHT

Each day, he is consumed by the demands of the world,

Lost in a maze of calculations and worries.

Each night, he descends into the depths of solitude.

The garden, bathed in the stillness of night,

Slumbers in sweet, fragrant dreams.

A bell tolls gently, as if in welcome

Soft footsteps - could it be her?

How lovely is this lingering fragrance,

Stirring memories of a love from another life.

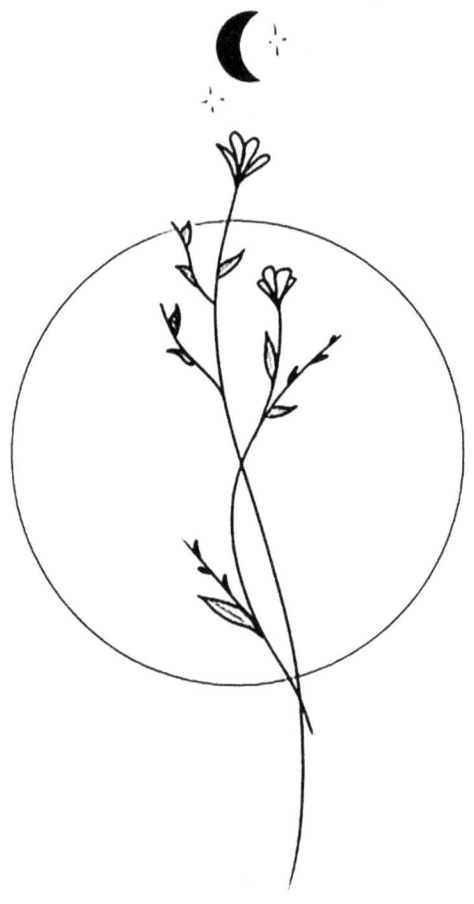

7. A MULTICOLORED FLOWER

From a delicate, thin little girl, she blossomed into a young woman of incomparable beauty. She was captivated by books, her wide eyes always eager to take in the world around her. She was like a multicolored flower, exuding a seductive fragrance that drew others near.

Beneath her elegant appearance, sparkling intelligence, and sharp speech, lay a heart that lived with unbridled passion. She loved fiercely, experienced life fully, and ultimately perished in the flames of her own intensity.

Men were drawn to her irresistible charm, yet they proved unfaithful or weak, unable to cherish her with the depth she deserved. Her eyes, deep and vast, were filled with a sense of wonder - and yet, also with a profound loneliness. Life, for her, was both a miracle and a solitary journey.

She relentlessly pursued love, knowledge, and fleeting vanities, seeking solace in the emptiness of night until the break of dawn. In the end, she was like a candle burning itself away, melting into nothingness.

Intelligent women

Many beautiful women may start without much intelligence, but over time, they learn and grow, becoming more clever and wise. Those who recognize that they lack beauty often strive even harder to cultivate intelligence and achieve success.

Women can accomplish anything men can, and often do it better. How admirable and deserving of respect they are. Yet, it seems that for women, success is often equated with happiness.

A woman's intelligence is most powerful when subtly hidden behind an air of naivety. The highest form of intelligence for a woman lies in knowing how to enhance her beauty and charm.

"Simply because - beauty is intelligence," she once said to me.

Regretfully, she was so smart that she never found her own happiness.

8. LONELINESS

My dear Him, where should I go now?

My heart is heavy with dim suspicions…

I leave behind the years of drifting in the stream of life,

The days spent struggling just to exist,

The fleeting moments of hope that briefly flickered,

The torment of love that seared my soul,

The melting dreams and aspirations,

Dissolving in the constant, infinite changes.

This question returns, smitten with remorse,

Tearing my heart into shreds like a tattered palm-leaf hat.

I feel like a dead leaf on a rainy afternoon, a traveler

Wandering aimlessly into the fading light of the sunset…

Suddenly, the vast silent emptiness

Resounds from some distant place, encircling me.

Perhaps there are men and women

And spirits lurking in the shadows.

Do we all silently run through the stream of life

With wordless affection buried deep in our hearts?

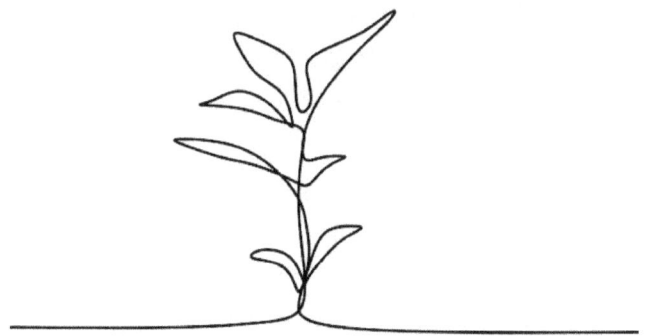

9. THE FATHER'S HEART

My dear daughter is setting off tomorrow to study abroad, stepping into a new chapter of her life. As a father, I will prepare the most delicious meal to send you off with love. No matter what life has in store for you out there, this home will always welcome you back. I've wandered through life's trials and triumphs and learned that a man's heart is as fleeting as mist. Happiness and sadness are both transient, but you must savor and live fully in every moment you're given.

Remember, your father and mother are always with you. Remember the sound of the flowing water, a gentle reminder of time's passage. The round-eyed dog will always wait for you, the frogs will croak their familiar tune, and the flowers will sway in the breeze, their petals softly falling on the flagstones. I will follow every step you take on your journey…

I love you… with a soft, sweet, silent, and protective love… please come back to me, whether you are happy or sad… I have walked this path too… full of eagerness, yet also full of loneliness… go ahead, my dear… May Buddha bless you…

I love you.

Talk to myself

A tree rises to the sky and does not remember its root.

The soil silently nurtures and gives everything it has,

Receiving the sorrowful yellow leaves as they fall.

I am One with many lives.

10. PERSISTENCE – KNOWLEDGE – PATIENCE

Life stretches out in a series of hard days and long months. Yet, he finds solace and enlightenment in books. The spacious house feels empty - his wife is on the mountain, and his children are far away, studying.

Daily work brings a mix of good and bad news. Each day feels much like the last. For the past 35 years, he has pushed himself forward, continually encouraging himself to keep going.

His health fluctuates, some days better than others, but he always reminds himself to live with joy in each day. Uninterrupted trips attempt to fill the void, and carefully laid plans help console his mind.

No matter what happens, he knows he must live each day with equanimity and kindness. And so, he commits to living with persistence, knowledge, and patience. Persistence to climb the steep slopes and reach his goals; clear-sightedness through the pursuit of knowledge to face life's dangers; and patience to endure and overcome hardships.

11. SOLITARY

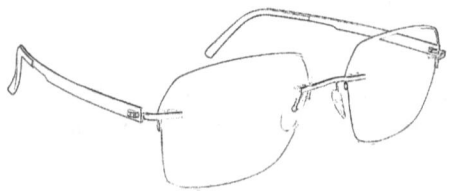

When you're passionate about something or someone, you long to hold onto them forever. But that's just the wishful thinking of the human mind. Everything is in constant flux, like the ceaseless flow of life. Eventually, you come to realize that everything you've done and everything you will do is carried out by you alone.

"The trees tremble, their shadows flicker and blur.

At night, my mind stills, and clarity emerges.

This world reveals itself as an illusion,

As I drift from morning to night, between fleeting joy and sorrow."

12. RESTLESSNESS

Innermost feelings rise like lingering mist,

Drifting from the lake of the mind,

From rivers and streams isolated in this world,

From the dim ocean of desire.

They curl into grey clouds,

Gathering and dispersing with the winds of life,

Only to fall as drops of sadness upon this world.

The rain divides souls, if only for a moment

Some panic, others turn away,

Loneliness stands beside desolation,

Passing through the long, sorrowful nights.

Yet when the sun rises, plants and flowers greet

Sparkling drops of loneliness,

Melting into the earth's embrace, returning to their source.

13. MEANS

When you attain the level of an "unprejudiced, innocent heart," you become a Zen master of life. You no longer require the colors, canvas, or brush of a painter. You need no external means or techniques to grasp or rely on. There is no target outside of yourself, and no opponent to aim at. You have legs and arms, body and mind - everything you need.

Yet, to express your thoughts, you may still require certain means. Your life is revealed through these "means," as essential as your own body. Your legs and arms are your paintbrush, and the whole universe is your canvas. On it, you paint the 70, 80, or 90 years of your life, and this painting is titled "Life."

14. STOICISM

Reading *Meditations* by Marcus Aurelius, I realize that in the solitude of power and understanding, a clear-sighted king reveals the hidden corners of the human heart. A true leader is profoundly solitary. Everyone looks to him, relies on him, watches him closely, harbors animosity, and envies him.

What is my stoicism?

Like lotuses rising from a swamp of stinking mud,

Surrounded by frogs, fish, and birds, whether foul or pure,

Lotuses remain unaffected by their surroundings;

They silently blossom, needing only sunlight.

Your mind is the same. No matter how noisy and chaotic its surroundings, it can still rise in silence and awaken, guided only by the light of wisdom.

Wisdom is to see all living beings and humans as they truly are,

For the appearance of everything has its reason.

In a single glass of water, you can see the ocean, a word, matter, and all forms containing thoughts, history, and fate.

This is when wisdom begins to shine.

15. ASPIRATIONS

Oh, aspirations,

Both noble and trivial,

Quietly nestled in your heart,

Lingering through the years

Of struggle, longing, and loss.

These burning aspirations,

Forged in life's smelting furnace,

Often entangled in the murky grasp

Of covetous desires,

Or driven by the need for revenge,

Born of deep-seated insecurities.

Oh, the unfinished aspirations,

Leaving behind sad, dull clouds

And grey mist in your mind,

Drifting like the dim smoke of nostalgia.

Yearning for tranquility, yet touched by fear,

Of the deceitful schemes of others.

Please, be still. Please, let go.

Soothe your mind. Gently. Calmly.

Please, show gratitude. Please, forgive.

For your enemies, for yourself,

And immerse yourself in the cool stream of love,

Flowing from a heart filled with the simple joy of life.

16. BEHIND

One day I will set off and leave forever. What will I leave behind?

I have not yet imagined. As time passes, the vibrant and emotional events of the past

fade into faint memories. The colorful images of yesterday now linger only as vague lines.

Many old, isolated objects gather the dust of oblivion. The bookcases hold worn, yellowed pages, bearing the weight of time. I acquired them over the years, each book a testament to a fleeting moment in the endless span of a human life.

This long journey in human existence feels as brief as a flash of light in the vastness of the universe. Why? The difference between the minuscule and the immense is merely relative.

Earth is but a tiny speck in boundless space.

And I, only a microbe in the Milky Way, my body teeming with billions upon billions of living cells.

So what did I come into this world for?

To chase after fame and fortune, to nurture plans, to achieve fleeting accomplishments,

To drown in love, to experience happiness and sadness, the inevitable ups and downs of life.

But in the end, what does this life truly mean?

Take Heart

My heart hardens in the silence of loneliness.

Without love, I won't embrace melancholy.

No wine, no flowers await tomorrow.

I'll leave it all behind and journey far away.

17. HARDSHIPS

He waited for his flight for four long hours, downing five glasses of juice, a pear, and an apple, trying to fill the emptiness. He arrived in Chengdu, China by train, with plans to fly to Hà Nội. Then, the news came - his son was ill in New York, and he realized he could fly there directly from Chengdu. Desperation gripped him as he bought the ticket, eager to reach his son, feeling life unravel before his eyes.

The night before, his daughter, who was in New York caring for her brother, had sent a message, reproaching him for neglecting the family, for being too consumed by work. How those words stung - they were true, perhaps, but no one had ever spoken to him like that before. He always believed he was living and working for the good of many, for his employees, for his family. But perspectives differ, shaped by one's angle, circumstances, time, and need.

During his week in China, he was busy, always meeting and entertaining guests. Meals were heavy, his body weary from years of stress. He's been on medication for a long time, a consequence of his relentless worrying over the business.

Why does he worry so much? Couldn't he just live for himself, for his family? It's easy to say, but impossible for him to do. When his parents were ill, he only visited once or twice - his older brother, with more free time, was the one who cared for them daily.

So, *who do we really live for? And why?* We're always caught in a whirlwind of work, crushed by the weight of endless anxieties.

Buddha taught to conquer anger, passion, and greed to attain enlightenment. Now, he eats vegetarian meals to heal, and his days are consumed by the endless stream of social obligations. He doesn't even have time to think about desires, fame, or fortune anymore. There's nothing left to command.

The world feels so unreal. When his parents expressed their simple wishes, he'd say he only hoped to age as gracefully as they did. When his daughter asked him to care for himself, he'd insist he could manage, despite being ill and growing older. Whenever he feels lost, he recalls Buddha's words: *"We are but small islands in an immense ocean."* *But how, then, will he care for himself?*

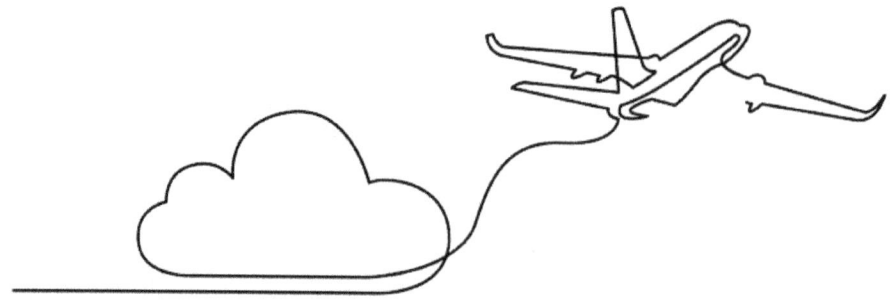

His children live far away, and he's left to battle his illness alone. His health is fading, his face gaunt and pale. He has his secretary, driver, guide, and housekeeper. His relatives check in occasionally, and his subordinates seem oblivious, turning a blind eye to his struggles. *So, does he live for his employees and his organization?* Nonsense. For his relatives? Irrational. *Should he live for himself and let everything else go?*

Retreat to the forest or the mountains? Perhaps he'd find peace for a few days, but soon, the weight of responsibilities, duties, and the ties of love and gratitude would pull him back. It's difficult, if not impossible, to live as Buddha taught.

"I become clear-sighted because I can see the dim light of the Moon in the black night.

I think of love when I fall into a snare of deceitfulness in the bright sunshine."

18. BITTER VOICE

You despise those lofty, empty titles,

Yet you dread the thought of dying alone, in dull isolation.

Who are we, but a bunch of arrogant fools?

Eagerly clawing our way through life, chasing petty dreams,

Private ambitions, and the pursuit of some fleeting prize.

Do we not realize we're teetering on the edge of a cold, dark grave?

Who are we to crave glory?

We strive for grand, illusory achievements,

Yet we can't appreciate the simple, little joys

Laughter, affection, sharing, love

For our families, our friends, our country.

Instead, we haul around a heavy rucksack,

Filled with worthless trinkets we treat like precious gems.

But when death comes knocking tomorrow,

These so-called treasures will turn to dead weight,

Dragging our skeletons deeper into the earth's embrace.

And you, you pray to the Gods for protection.

As the sun slowly fades,

You hope for the flickering light

Of morning and evening stars

To guide you to a peaceful end.

19. HURT

When we confront failure, emptiness, and misery, we slow down, sometimes even stop, to learn the painful art of acceptance and adaptation. It's in these moments we realize we've been running alone. We gradually grow accustomed to the void, pushing ourselves to keep moving forward. Yet, there remains a faint hope that we might achieve something meaningful, leaving behind an imprint so that someone might remember us after we're gone.

Every day brings unexpected challenges, making it difficult to lead the simple, peaceful life we once desired. Our original dreams - finding a soulmate, building a happy family, having a nice home, and gaining a little recognition - seem so modest. But then we start running faster and faster, swept away by time itself. In the rush, we forget what we're doing, what we're pursuing, and why.

Letting Go

A speck of dust in my eye makes me blink endlessly,

Anxieties swirl, unsettling my mind.

One day, I will leave this world, perhaps becoming dust myself.

Letting go of these fleeting thoughts, all else dissolves into nothingness.

20. INTERNAL CONFLICT

Religion is understood as a unique way of living, but living itself is a matter of life and death, often manifesting as a struggle within thyself. This struggle is not something to be taken up reluctantly, but rather it forms the foundation of all external conflicts - such as a struggle against an opponent in the flesh. It is within this internal conflict that the true essence of the art reveals its hidden secret. Thus, the teachings of this art are no different from those of a Zen master, whether thou art living peacefully in solitude or engaging in a battle with an opponent.

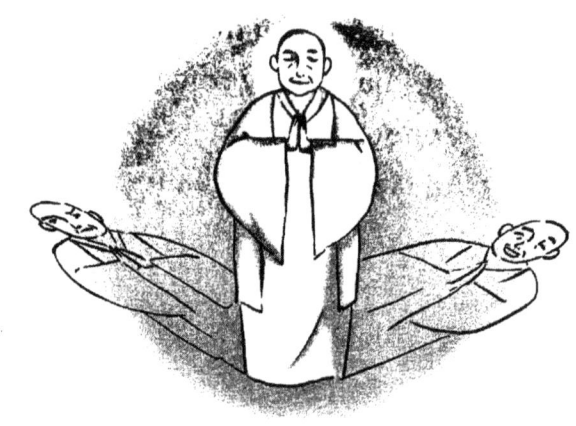

21. DOSAGE

People often criticize undesirable traits when viewed through the negative lens of human nature. For instance, they may judge someone for being overly feminine, dictatorial, reckless, or conniving. But consider these traits from a different perspective:

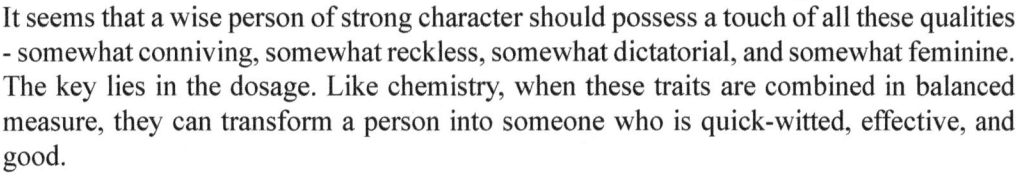

Femininity: Possessive and erratic

Dictatorial: Authoritative and superior

Reckless: Fanatic

Conniving: Calculating, ingenious, and cautious

It seems that a wise person of strong character should possess a touch of all these qualities - somewhat conniving, somewhat reckless, somewhat dictatorial, and somewhat feminine. The key lies in the dosage. Like chemistry, when these traits are combined in balanced measure, they can transform a person into someone who is quick-witted, effective, and good.

Predestined by the Creator

By day, we toil; by night, we cherish.

Love between partners may ignite only desire,

Yet passion for thought and seeking births creativity and art.

Ambition and power can kindle conspiracy and war,

But reverence for the divine guides us to enlightenment and peace.

In the darkest night, the sun will rise,

Illuminating the mind with its radiant light,

Whether you find solace in stillness or depths of meditation.

22. GLIMPSE

Leaning my head back on the chair, I gazed at the sky and wondered what it would be like to step onto the balcony, climb over, and let go - leaving behind all the anxieties and sorrows. It seemed, for a fleeting moment, that it might be a way to escape, to leave everything behind.

Why did this thought arise? Perhaps it was because the last few days had been filled with hardships, worries, and sadness. A wave of nostalgia washed over me as I listened to old Russian songs. The music, once comforting, now felt unsettling, stirring memories of a youth long gone. Life, with all its torments and unfinished aspirations, felt heavy.

I suddenly thought of my student days, so full of energy and promise. How quickly time passes. One song mentioned that the soul is like a mirror - if it remains bright, the hair will not turn white. I wondered if my soul had kept its purity.

Then, I deeply missed my children. I thought of the years when I was too busy to be close to them, and now they are far away. There was a pang of sadness when I sent a message to my youngest, asking her to come home and share a meal. But she didn't respond.

I felt a touch of self-pity, alone in a strange city, surrounded by the myriad sounds of life. The room, once filled with music and lyrics that had begun to feel oppressive, now fell into silence.

In the end, everything is only a glimpse.

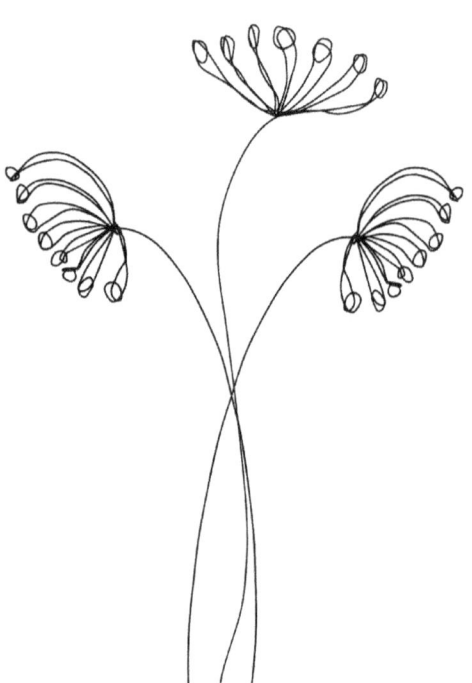

23. TRUTH

There's always a struggle within me,
As relentless as a heartbeat,
Between the seductions of the mind.
I find myself torn,
Between what I want and what I can't have,
Between what's right and what's wrong in this life.
I see impermanence everywhere
In the cities I pass through, the countries I visit, the people I meet.
They remain unchanged, even as millions of footsteps tread upon them.
I've had grand dreams,
And I've poured everything into realizing them,
Yet I've seen statues gazing sadly at the passing reality.
I've longed to dedicate my life to something beautiful,
To noble pursuits, through years of relentless effort,
But still, I strive to keep my mind in check, not indulging in fleeting pleasures.
If only I could be like a bee
A worker bee, tirelessly gathering nectar to make honey and build a hive.
A drone, indulging in the pure act of copulation.
A queen bee, choosing a well-matched partner,
And managing the hive until it's exhausted.
To live like this would be a life complete with passion,
And the sweet honey I've made would eventually fall into the hands of others.
There's always a struggle within me,
As relentless as a heartbeat,
Between the seductions of the mind.
I find myself torn,
Between what I want and what I can't have,
Between what's right and what's wrong in this life.
I see impermanence everywhere
In the cities I pass through, the countries I visit, the people I meet.
They remain unchanged, even as millions of footsteps tread upon them.
I've had grand dreams,
And I've poured everything into realizing them,
Yet I've seen statues gazing sadly at the passing reality.
I've longed to dedicate my life to something beautiful,
To noble pursuits, through years of relentless effort,
But still, I strive to keep my mind in check, not indulging in fleeting pleasures.
If only I could be like a bee
A worker bee, tirelessly gathering nectar to make honey and build a hive.
A drone, indulging in the pure act of copulation.
A queen bee, choosing a well-matched partner,
And managing the hive until it's exhausted.
To live like this would be a life complete with passion,
And the sweet honey I've made would eventually fall into the hands of others.

24. WHY?

We pass each other by, or walk side by side for just a brief moment on the road of life. It's rare, almost impossible, to cross paths again.

Yet, even knowing this, why can't we let go of the mistakes others have made toward us, or the ones we've made that have hurt someone else? Why do we cling to what's already gone, even when we know it can't be held onto? What is it that keeps us feeling so melancholy?

Be Ardent Today

Pour another cup, let yourself float,

This body is fleeting, impermanent

Why the melancholy?

We don't know where tomorrow leads, but living fully today is enough.

25. ISOLATION

The Covid-19 pandemic was a profound event. Originating in China, it spread across the globe, leaving the world in a state of panic. At first, European countries and America dismissed it, but soon it reached their shores, forcing them to shut their doors and isolate from the outside world. Every day, the number of infected and dead grew, a stark reminder of how fragile human life is in the face of nature.

Following his friends' advice, he retreated to a deserted coastal area for several days. There, he ate and drank in moderation, sunbathed, exercised, read books, and held meetings with colleagues via video calls. And he felt much better. Life is short; perhaps he has only ten good years of effective work before age catches up. So, he resolved to make the most of it, striving to complete two or three more significant works.

What do we bring with us?

1. In our body: exercise, patience.

2. In our heart: forgiveness, gratitude.

3. In our spirit: sympathy, compassion.

4. In our mind: thirst for knowledge, the drive to learn.

26. COMING HOME

After 45 days of quarantine to avoid the pandemic, he finally returned home. How hard life can be! For the last 20 to 30 years, he has lived with a sense of pessimism, always fighting. He has faced countless challenges and has had to continually overcome adversity, pushing himself to improve.

His approach has been:

- Negative present.

- Pessimistic thoughts.

- Fighting to reach a target.

Whether he reaches his goal or not depends on patience, luck, or the help of a patron. But today, he realizes that life's nature is one of unending hardship. As long as we are alive, new difficulties will continue to arise. Joy, happiness, and pleasure exist, but only in fleeting moments - perhaps 10 to 20 percent of life. So why not create happiness and optimism for ourselves and seek out the positive aspects of life?

From today, no matter how difficult the situation, he resolves to live differently:

- Finding the positive in everything.

- Thinking with humor.

- Sharing optimism.

- Fighting with wisdom.

The Covid-19 pandemic struck the world like a blow, plunging many countries into crisis and damaging economies. Hearts were divided, some nations isolated, while others sought connection. This has happened many times throughout human history. The solution, then, is to fight with optimism and positivity, to seek opportunities and happiness for ourselves and those around us. Keep moving forward, toward the finish line.

Bitter Wine

Empty room, deserted garden, noise beyond the walls.

Longing to share a cup of wine with you.

If loneliness tastes bitter,

Why not drink deeply from this cup of bitter wine?

27. LOOKING BACK

For those we have shared life with, we can see that there are phases of time:

- We loved each other.

- We were angry with each other.

- We felt lonely, even while side by side.

And then, inevitably, there comes a time of separation.

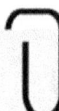

Exhausted

Lips brush rosy cheeks, hands smooth the hair.

Caressing waist, breast, and hip with tender care.

What remains after these fleeting moments?

Love, when the body is exhausted and bare.

28. MOTIONLESSNESS

For Zen masters, action arises from stillness, for it is a struggle both with and without the self. In this way, one might aim at a subject outside or at oneself, yet never truly confront oneself. Thus, you become both the initiator and the target. As Zen masters often say, "Though the student acts within the flow of life, they must always maintain a motionless center."

29. DILIGENCE

Though we know:

- *Our bodies are fleeting and unreal.*

- *Human life is filled with sorrows and anxieties.*

- *Existence is impermanent.*

Still, we strive to:

- *Live wholeheartedly.*

- *Do useful things.*

- *Realize our dreams.*

Therefore:

- *Be patient every day.*

- *Perfect ourselves.*

- *Give as much as we can.*

- *And pray diligently.*

30. COME BACK

Gray hair turns softly,

What do we seek?

Blossoms found at last,

On the old path.

Return to green mountains,

Birdsong each morning,

Streams flow gently by,

Under a light sky.

One meal, one heart,

Simple vegetables, nuts too,

Find peace within,

Kindness guides you.

Silent day and night,

Clouds gather, disperse,

Every path leads home,

Come back soon.

31. MIND TRAINING

Reflecting on the art of living, one might define it in simple terms, yet it invites deeper contemplation. Through mind training, life's skills become an art, and ultimately, they transform into a 'non-artistic art.'

Life is not merely external movements with tools and techniques, but an internal harmony with oneself. Tools and techniques are only a means to an end, not the end itself. They are pathways that guide us, but they are not the final destination. They serve as aids for the last decisive leap.

32. BUDDHA

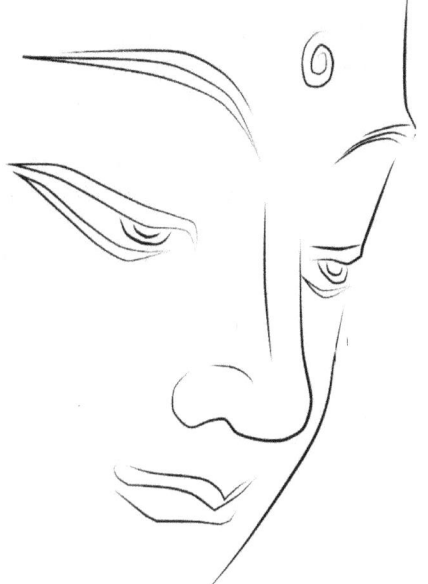

He has sat there, silent, for a long time.

I approach Him, bow my head, and pray softly.

He seems to listen, both near and far,

With light beams darting from an immense galaxy.

His eyes radiate a deep tranquility.

Is He looking at me, or beyond?

In prayer, I find peace of mind,

And my thoughts flash like a star

In this lonely life. He is the universe.

I flee the realm of unconsciousness and come to Him,

Seeking Him through many incarnations, caught in the wheel of life.

Who remembers, who forgets, who is lost in this world?

I return here, kneel before Him, and meditate.

33. OLD AGE

I told my older brother to take our father to the south, to escape the cold of winter in Hà Nội. So I traveled to Sài Gòn to see them both. We shared meals together whenever I had free time. The sight of two white-haired sons scooping rice, wiping our father's mouth, and gently advising him in a restaurant moved me to tears.

Father constantly complains of pain in his legs, shortness of breath, and coughing at night. I wonder how my own health will be in 30 years. Will there be anyone beside me?

I tell myself not to complain if I must live alone. I must learn to accept dissatisfaction.

In the Present Moment

When nostalgia stirs, I become yesterday.

When wishes arise, I dwell in tomorrow.

Let go of the past and the future,

Find peace in the present moment.

34. INCOMPREHENSION

One day, he encountered an unexpected moment that felt like a weight lodged in his chest. It was then he realized he was living in a city, in a world, he did not truly understand. Each day, he traversed the familiar streets with indifference, disconnected from their emotions, their sorrows, their stories.

Life became unbearable as he saw the roads he walked lined with traps, deceit, ingratitude, and resentment. He longed to build a life of good values, but the relentless current of existence pulled him along, forcing him to struggle and drift with the flow.

The stream of life flowed ceaselessly - sometimes gently, sometimes with violent force - until it reached a turn of fate. He was carried along, sinking into that stream, yet still, he could not comprehend why. Disgrace, fear of failure, dead ends, and illness appeared suddenly and fatefully.

Misfortune came quietly, dealing a death-blow at the peak of tragedy, then left just as silently and indifferently. He often felt lonely, as if the tie between him and life was either too loose or entirely absent. The old stories, old friends, and old connections faded with time, memories becoming vague and gradually slipping into oblivion.

In certain moments, the world around him seemed colorless, odorless, tasteless, and space felt motionless. There was no world, no time, no human life. Were these moments nothingness and emptiness?

Dust of the World

You are the clear voice within the heart,

I am the shadow that sways with the world.

In a life of ups and downs, joy and sorrow entwine,

Do not be arrogant, for you too will turn to dust of the world.

35. GOOD WINE

Every joyous feast eventually ends, and fresh flowers wither. Nothing lasts forever, so do not cling to anything. Everything flows impermanently, like water.

Knowing this, we should refrain from making promises we cannot keep. As our hair turns white with time, we can still savor a cup of good wine, steeped in the joys and anxieties of days gone by.

Blossom

Close your eyes, let tomorrow bring an end to sorrow.

Yesterday's sadness, last month's worries - nothing new.

Set aside contemplation, embrace the joy of living.

New beginnings, new love - blossom every day.

36. SEEKING A WAY

If one begins from the origin of the mind, finding a way inward and approaching the nameless yet profound competence within, he may hope for guidance from a Zen master toward the path's end. This journey is for true seekers, not for the merely curious. In the first steps of this quest, perfection cannot be expected. One must overcome countless obstacles and traverse many paths before finally knocking at the door of truth. Along the way, there will be moments of deep loneliness, when it seems you are seeking the impossible, yet the truth feels just within reach.

37. TEND DUCKS

Listening to the conversations around him on the flight to Koh Samui Island, he realized how remarkably similar they were.

At an age past 50, when their children had grown and gained independence, many couples find themselves traveling to distant lands, drifting through life, spending time on journeys, or even seeking medical care in foreign countries.

Don't be arrogant like a goose holding its head high,

But humble like a flock of ducks following their herder.

It seems that my wife is the only one with a flock of just one duck.

38. SILENCE

For the past several months, he had confined himself to a coastal house, seeking refuge from the pandemic. Yet, even in isolation, he continued to work with his team, envisioning new products and nurturing a dream - a vision of building a great future for his country.

In the quiet, he immersed himself in learning and meditation.

The one who is driven by a passion for greatness,

Striving for sacred significance,

Will dig through mountains of challenges,

Avoiding futile gatherings

And the empty flattery of inferiors.

39. CONFESSION

Among millions, only tens of thousands nurture the will to achieve great things. Yet, of those, only a few thousand reach their goals, and perhaps a few hundred find true success in their fields. The number of truly exceptional individuals is less than a hundred, and those who reach the pinnacle are fewer still - less than ten.

To achieve such heights, these ten must sweat blood and tears. Yet, when they pass away, their names often fade into oblivion.

Who led the country centuries ago? Who built this land, expanded its borders, commanded strong armies, and achieved glorious feats? Today, we remember very few of them.

Likewise, a hundred years from now, no one will know who we were - not even our descendants. Will anyone light incense on our altar or tend to our grave? In troubled times, our graves may be forgotten, and even in peaceful times, we cannot expect the homage of future generations.

So, let us not be consumed by ambition and countless desires. Doing hundreds of things is not better than doing a few things we truly enjoy. Knowing thousands of people is not as valuable as being close to a few who matter.

Why, then, do we busy ourselves with endless plans and schemes?

Is it not better to care for ourselves and our loved ones? Long-term aspirations and thousand-year legacies are but illusions.

What we need is peace and joy every day.

Death begins a new cycle of life, with no right and wrong or good and bad.

Every love leads to separation and loneliness.

Every word, emotion, sound, and image is only an aftertaste

Of a figure who left and vanished.

Only emptiness and silence remain.

40. A SMALL GARDEN

His office is in a tall building surrounded by skyscrapers. The space is quiet, filled only with the hum of air-conditioners, the soft shuffle of footsteps, and the murmurs of the staff. Even the plants in the office seem silent.

But since he created a small garden on the balcony, he has found peace in the sight of colorful flowers and leaves swaying gently in the breeze, the murmur of flowing water, and the soft chime of wind bells.

Only when he steps out the door does he encounter a world that is much more lively and animated.

Flowers and Leaves

Footwear and carpets of all kinds make our feet callous and insensitive. Looking back on a lifetime, there were only roads, mountain passes, and hardened footsteps.

But one day, in the dawn's sunlight, with a slight chill in the wind and dew still clinging to the grass, you walk barefoot. You feel the cool earth, the soft leaves, and the hard pebbles beneath your feet. Take a deep breath, spread your arms, and gaze at the sky. In that moment, you'll feel connected to both earth and sky.

On another day, instead of wearing perfume, immerse yourself in an oak bathtub filled with warm water, colorful flowers, leaves, and herbs. Suddenly, you'll realize - you are also flowers, leaves, and grass.

41. ESOTERIC MEANING

Why does a Zen master avoid speaking of himself and his spiritual journey? It's not modesty, but a respect for the esoteric nature of the mind. The path to enlightenment is deeply personal and beyond words. True understanding comes through direct experience, not explanation.

For the Zen master, even discussing meditation requires care, as the most profound truths are felt, not spoken. Silence and simplicity guard these truths, inviting each seeker to discover them within.

42. PENITENCE

Yesterday morning, I went to the hospital for a general check-up since I'd had a lingering cough for quite some time. After a blood test, a scan, and a doctor's examination, the results were just as unclear as before. The advice was vague, leaving me to figure out the cause on my own.

A few days ago, I'd been reading a lot about various diseases, which only added to my worry. But on the way back to the office, I resolved not to dwell on it too much and to live happily, as if each day were my last.

When I returned to the office, I remembered I had an appointment with an old friend. I treated him to a fine lunch, complete with delicious food and wine. As the wine flowed, so did the conversation. The wine started off harsh, became acrid, and eventually turned sweet. By the end, we had polished off six bottles.

Perhaps my spirits had lifted after the hospital visit because I found myself savoring each cup of wine, reminiscing about the good old days, and cherishing every drop of that aromatic drink.

Strangely, my mind remained clear, showing no signs of inebriation. My friend, however, was swaying side to side, delivering grand, chivalrous speeches. I nodded along, encouraging him, and poured more wine. We clinked our glasses together, and whatever my friend desired, I was happy to oblige. In that moment, my heart grew quiet, and I glimpsed a reflection of my younger self.

This morning, I approached the Buddhist altar, bowed my head, and struck the bell. I performed my penitence for the indulgences of the past few days, praying for kindness for myself, for today and tomorrow, so that I might take better care of myself, love life, and grow wiser.

As I delved into meditation, I thought of my friend, whose hair had turned completely white. I, on the other hand, still had only a few white strands hidden among the black. Oh my God! My youth isn't over yet. There are still many temptations ahead. I prayed to Buddha, stroking the bell for peace of mind, and silently begged to be filled with compassion.

Ephemerality

Pour the first cup, and the dry heart softens.

Pour the second, and the blood warms.

Drink the third, and realize life is fleeting.

Let everything go - human life is ephemeral.

43. DEPRESSION

He never expected to fall into depression. Today, after a simple and satisfying meal prepared by his driver, he played a CD of old songs. With his face buried in his hands, he meditated to the music, letting the memories of the distant past wash over him. A sudden wave of depression hit him, as if he had lost something precious.

Time passes so quickly. The university doors closed behind him long ago, yet it feels as though he just left. It seems he has never fully lived with anyone, at any time. His eyes grew wet with tears.

Was it the sweetness of these melodies that brought them on?

Being Nice Drunk

My life feels like a long incarnation of a slave,

Burdened with daily sorrows and anxieties.

Sometimes I escape the weariness in drunkenness,

Finding fleeting comfort in the company of beauties.

44. APHORISM THAT WARMS THE HEART

In loneliness, who shares our inmost feelings? Who do we confide in?

Thinking too much in solitude only deepens our depression. Dwelling on difficulties leads to unhappiness, for overthinking stifles the mind, leaving no room for fresh air.

When worry consumes you, sit in silence, cease the thoughts, and let the mind calm. To quiet mistaken thoughts, focus on your breath, counting each inhale and exhale. Gradually, the mind will find peace.

Reading books often is also a balm for the soul. God places certain books in our hands, offering guidance and insight. The writings of great minds, drawn from their life experiences, can provide precious lessons, enlightening and warming us when we feel mentally cold.

45. SCHOOL FOR MEDITATION

You must meditate and allow the essence of meditation to illuminate, in its own way, the art of living. This illumination may not be enlightenment in its fullest sense, but it can reveal what lies behind the fog that clouds our vision. It is like a distant flash of lightning, briefly piercing the darkness.

If you understand this, then any art, game, or profession becomes a primary school of meditation. Through the introspective movements of arms, legs, or mind, we can see more clearly what is happening around us. Yet, the events themselves often remain beyond full comprehension.

Each path of artful living, each movement in life, can be a gateway to meditation.

46. SPICES

When cooking, women often skillfully blend spices, creating dishes that are not only delicious but aromatic as well. They also have a knack for arranging a tray of rice with appetizers, main courses, side dishes, and desserts so that it looks both beautiful and nutritious.

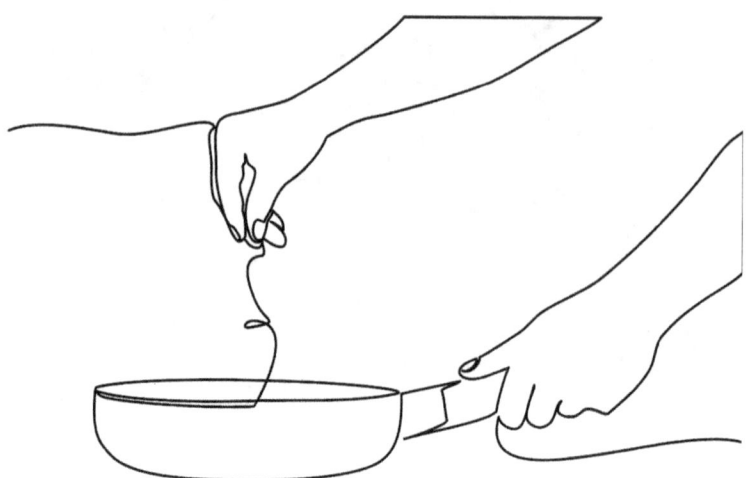

Regrettably, though, women sometimes forget to apply this talent to other areas of life. Perhaps that's why men often take the top spot in cooking contests and rise to the ranks of professional chefs. It seems men not only know how to cook but also how to master the art of service. For them, service is an art - a noble form of dedication - while women tend to focus more on savoring the food itself.

So, gentlemen, it wouldn't hurt to take a page from the culinary book: learn to cook, and more importantly, learn the art of dedication.

47. REAL PLEASURE

You go to the spa to be pampered, massaged, and comforted. Similarly, you find joy in playing with dogs and cats because they are lovable, devoted, and exude charm in every gesture and glance. You adore children for their innocence, warmth, and radiant smiles.

These genuine, sincere, and natural feelings are what we all crave deep in our hearts because they bring us true pleasure. But as we grow up, that carefree joy seems to fade, burdened by relationships, responsibilities, obligations, and countless ties.

So, if you want to find real happiness and keep your soul fresh and your heart sweet, you need to untangle those ties and embrace a free, interesting life. Keep a naive smile, a bright look, and an honest expression. Let your soul reflect nature, and your emotions flow naturally, like a wild animal. In doing so, you return to your primal instincts.

Dogs and Cats

In my opinion, dogs are loyal, sentimental, and a bit stubborn, while cats are smart but delightfully unpredictable. When we're young, we're more like cats - playful and unpredictable. As we age, we become more like dogs - steadfast and loyal.

However, old cats tend to get lazy, fat, and slow, while old dogs grow wise, clear-headed, and flexible.

So, if we're wise, we should aim to be like a clever dog or a loyal cat as we grow older.

48. READING ALOUD

You enjoy thinking and making associations. Yet, every thought often leads to countless vague ideas that sometimes stray far from the subject at hand. Even when reading a book, you might find yourself easily lost in thoughts.

It's no coincidence that many people chant in chorus in churches or pagodas. There's something wonderful about singing a song aloud, reciting a poem, or even reading a few pages with feeling, each word imbued with sweet imagery.

By raising your warm and familiar voice from the depths of your heart, you awaken the quiet parts within you, allowing you to dive deeply into perception. This simple act can fill you with a glowing feeling, letting your heart blossom with positive emotions.

Zen Hall

I favor reading over meditating,

For a library is my Zen hall, and I, its student.

Each day, I devour books,

As diligently as monks in meditation.

49. LETTING GO

Throughout life, you encounter many kinds of people. Some you meet only once but remember forever, while others, despite working with them day and night, leave no lasting impression. A fleeting glimpse of a stranger may etch a strong memory, yet many regular companions fade into obscurity. But with time, most old stories are forgotten.

Within a year or two after someone passes away, they are remembered only by a few close relatives. It's clear that when we leave this world, even our own kin will soon forget us.

So, let go of today's anxieties. Live like the birds, singing joyfully each day, flying to beautiful gardens to greet the first rays of dawn. Don't burden yourself with the worries of this world, for they do little to improve our lives.

Tell Ourselves

Life can be tough - no doubt about it.

We work hard, we overthink, and still, nothing seems quite right.

But hey, tell yourself - it's all just nothingness.

Be happy now, because who knows if tomorrow will show up?

50. REALIZATION

After several hours of playing together, his youngest son grew quiet, lost in his computer. The father, adrift in memories, let the instrumental music carry him away. Suddenly, his son stood up, saying goodbye as he prepared to leave with his mother, who waited outside the door. The father asked his son to invite her in - he hadn't seen her in weeks since being discharged from the hospital. A few minutes later, his son returned, saying that mother was tired and didn't want to come in.

The son lowered his head, gently rubbed his dad's head, and looked at him with quiet, unspoken sadness.

Ephemeral Thoughts

He finds happiness fleeting, brief,

Loneliness a constant companion.

Aspirations rise high, unattainable,

Reality, stark and unadorned.

Then one day,

His beloved departs, sighing.

His beautiful women grow restless,

For his mind drifts too deep,

Lost in thoughts, endlessly swirling.

Heaven and earth dance on,

Their rhythm eternal, unbroken.

Fate brings both parting and reunion.

Left with echoes, faint and fading,

Dissolving into the stream of thought.

Without past or future, just now

Time but a string of moments.

All things are mere concepts, fleeting.

Life is birth and death entwined.

Let your emotions find peace, gently.

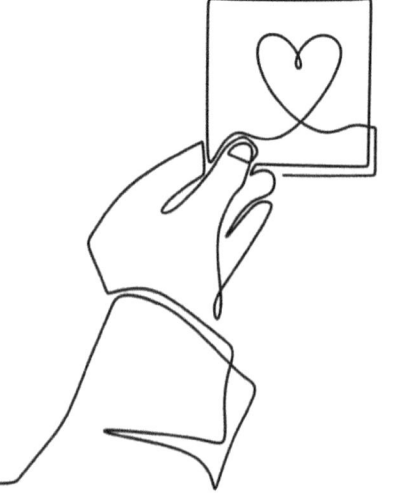

51. OCEAN OF SUFFERINGS

He observes the endless stream of people,

Each one moving with purpose, yet burdened.

Worry etched on every face,

Their minds tethered to unseen burdens.

In that sea of faces, he sees a common thread - sorrow.

Buddha's words resonate deeply: life is an ocean of suffering.

Indeed, all of humanity is adrift in its depths.

With this understanding, he feels a profound compassion,

For himself and for the world,

Knowing that beneath our struggles, we all share this journey.

> **Tomorrow**
>
> *I don't know what tomorrow holds,*
>
> *Life is short, full of untold mishaps.*
>
> *Love may not bridge every divide,*
>
> *But let us at least refrain from causing pain.*

52. WAITING

The crowd is noisy, divergent, and divided. Without unity, it may be better to walk alone. Yet, loneliness can easily breed unhappiness, discouragement, and negativity.

Sometimes, you travel as a backpacker with a group of friends. On these journeys, you've seen young and kindred spirits emerge from different people, transforming long paths into shorter, happier, and more meaningful experiences.

Thus, when a group shares passion, empathy, and common ideals, they can achieve great and significant things. Knowing this, you still wait patiently for companions who share your vision. Let fate unfold as it will.

Better That

Life is a struggle, demanding all we can give.

Yet, let it be engraved in our hearts:

Better to endure an insult than seek revenge,

Better to walk alone than to make rash friends.

53. MYSTERIOUS INNER FEELINGS

From childhood to the time when his hair turned white, there has always been a quiet, enigmatic pull within him. This deep, almost mystical connection to spirituality has lingered, a subtle thread woven through the fabric of his life. Yet, despite this profound interest, life's demands have kept him from fully exploring this path, as the daily grind of making a living has taken precedence.

Still, in quiet moments, he feels that mysterious presence, gently reminding him of the spiritual realms beyond the material world. It is a call to pause, to reflect, and to reconnect with the inner self that seeks more than the transient.

54. NATURAL LIGHT

Our lives often feel confined by doors and thick walls. Speedy travel distances us from direct contact with fresh air, as we spend our days moving in and out of small or large boxes.

Yet, when we venture far from the cities, there are moments when we pause along the road to admire the simple beauty of wildflowers, a serene lake reflecting the sky, cows ambling slowly along dyke slopes, or bright orange clouds at sunset. These scenes nourish the soul.

On weekends, a visit to a Zen monastery nestled deep in the mountains offers a chance to reconnect. There, within a vast forest, you might watch a stream flow, see blossoms in bloom, and spend a night under the sweet light of dawn. As you ride through the mountains from dawn to dusk, pausing to gaze up at a sky filled with twinkling stars and distant galaxies, you may feel the echoes of the universe itself.

The world around us is bathed in natural light, day and night. Open your heart to welcome it.

55. LED BY BELIEF

He has lived between two centuries,

Witnessed a nation emerge from a war,

A century-long struggle with countless losses,

But now, forgiveness has made old enemies friends,

While comrades of yesterday become rivals today.

He, with a small stream of hopefuls,

Steps forward, eager to revive the nation.

A new generation, austere yet ambitious,

Spends its youth reclaiming what was lost,

In the relentless pursuit of fame and fortune.

They struggle not just with the world outside,

But with the shadows within their own hearts.

He has seen the wealthy,

Puffed up with arrogance,

blocking the path of the vulnerable.

And wars of religion continue,

Keeping distant nations from drawing near,

In a world gone mad with conflict.

Many times, he has felt the weight of weariness,

Like a traveler on a long road,

Glancing around with indifferent eyes,

Letting life's stream carry him away,

To mix with the sands until the ocean calls,

And he drifts into the universe of nothingness.

Yet, he continues to change,

Keeping pace with the shifting times,

Striving to do things differently.

He learns each day,

By observing life and reading books,

Realizing that he is like a fish out of water,

Once cloaked in arrogance and ignorance.

But in those moments of realization,

He understands that only the truly preeminent,

Those who can lead with belief,

Can inspire the weary to press on.

For belief, after all, is often kinder than reality.

Belief

Every era experiences its ups and downs, with history constantly in motion, like a river that never ceases to flow. Humanity drifts upon the vast sea of life, uncertain of when the world will find peace, whether in times of war or tranquility. Yet, in the midst of chaos, talented individuals rise to the occasion, and exceptional souls emerge, leaving their mark on both the world and their nation. Today, we may call them sages; tomorrow, they will be revered as holy men.

56. ELEGANCE

Defining elegance can be tricky, but perhaps it's that charming blend of indifference and patience that carries a certain depth. If greatness feels out of reach or transformation seems a bit too challenging, simply aim to be elegant. It's a graceful fallback plan.

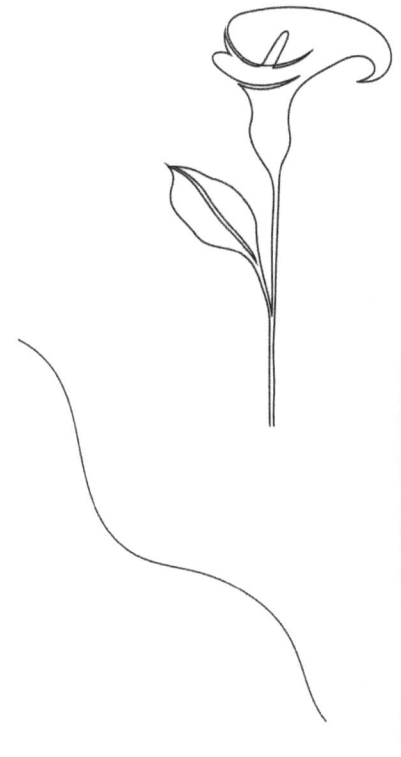

Wharf of Enlightenment

Sparkling foam beckons ephemeral clouds,

Dewdrops surrender to predestined sunlight.

Petals drift in the wind of non-doing,

In a fleeting moment, the lotus throne of Nirvana shines.

57. REASSURE OURSELVES

Don't dwell on fear; embrace the challenge.

Don't focus on danger; seek the solution.

Don't fear failure; see it as training.

Don't chase triumph; find the path forward.

Don't worry about death; view it as an experience.

Don't fret over hardships; cultivate patience.

Smoldering Loneliness

After a string of endless meetings, he found himself having a late lunch on the office balcony. The winter sunlight offered a gentle warmth, a brief reprieve. Over the past 30 years, he had grown accustomed to eating alone, sometimes in the solitude of his car. His latent aspirations, however, remained just that - smoldering quietly, unable to ignite into the great flame he once envisioned.

58. GOOD SLEEP

Work overload seems to follow me right to bed. The phone buzzes with messages - Viber, Telegram, WeChat, Skype - along with music apps, movies, and sports, all of which feel inseparable from my daily life. I often carry my anxieties, joys, and sorrows into the night, making it hard to rest. But to truly sleep well, all we need to do is put the phone away, create a silent, dimly lit space, and allow the mind to unwind.

Think of bygone days, but only recall the happy moments. Be thankful for life and the people we've encountered. Let go of sorrows, allowing the breath to soften and the heart to ease. When the mind becomes peaceful and relaxed, sitting in meditation for just ten minutes can help. Relax quietly, and then gradually sink into a good sleep.

Enjoying

When we recognize that everything is impermanent and ever-changing, we begin to see that there's no need to dwell in sadness or worry over the things that don't satisfy us. Youth is fleeting, beauty fades, and nothing remains the same - so why not find happiness in the simple things around us?

True joy lies in a peaceful mind, and true peace is found in nature. The sunlight filtering through the trees, the sound of rain, the dance of clouds, the rustle of wind, the vibrant colors of flowers, the songs of birds, the gentle movement of fish - these are the things that bring us closer to tranquility. A cup of tea, a shared smile, a fleeting glance, a familiar melody - these moments are what make life rich.

All we need to do is walk slowly, observe closely, listen with intent, and reflect on the beauty of nature. In doing so, we allow ourselves to relax, embracing the pure enjoyment of life in every moment.

59. HOW TO LIVE IN SOLITUDE?

In the books of religions and their methods, it is not easy to find what you are truly seeking. Over time, you may become disappointed, lose inspiration, and eventually conclude that only those who genuinely live in solitude can understand the meaning of 'lonely.' It seems that this understanding is reserved for those who practice self-abnegation in meditation, those who lose their ego and 'merge' with the Almighty - those we know as monks.

At this point, you might think that there is no other way, that it is impossible to find a path to enlightenment unless you verify it through your own suffering and solitude. You realize that without this essential experience, all words of enlightenment feel hollow.

But how does one become a meditator? How does one truly live in solitude? Is there a path for you to follow while your life today is disturbed by endless daily information and weighed down by worries? This way of life seems so different from that of a Zen master.

For these questions, you may find no satisfactory answer, even though you have read descriptions of steps that promise to lead you to some form of enlightenment in religious texts.

60. YOUNG AND FRESH

She's in her twenties, radiating youth and freshness with a sparkle that catches the eye. Her sturdy shoulders, full chest, and graceful figure give her a presence that's hard to ignore. When she laughs, it's as if her entire being joins in - her eyes, her cheeks, even her body sways lightly like a young blade of grass in the sunlight. She may not be the sharpest mind in the room, but there's an innocence in her sweet voice and twinkling eyes that's utterly charming. She carries the natural scent of grass, flowers, and leaves, a fragrance that's as fresh as her spirit.

She hasn't found happiness yet, but she's curious and full of life, eager for what's to come. I can't help but admire her - coddling her with a gentle compassion, reminding myself to stay grounded, not to get lost in the past or future. Just the present.

And then, I sit for meditation.

Love

Love is a lion, hungry and fierce,

A lover, a deer, carefree and swift.

After hours of tracking, the thrill of the chase,

A feast is shared, both heart and grace.

In the end, who's the lion, who's the fawn?

In love's wild dance, the roles are gone.

> ***Picking flowers***
>
> *Dahlias stand tall, splendid yet indifferent,*
>
> *Roses, exquisite and charming, but with a chill.*
>
> *Gladioluses, so elegant, keep their distance,*
>
> *And countless other blooms, each with its own grace and fragrance.*
>
> *Plant them in your garden for contemplation,*
>
> *Or arrange them in vases for decoration.*
>
> *But remember, when cutting, use a knife or shears with care,*
>
> *For a rose's thorn can prick and draw blood unaware.*
>
> *Camellias, grapefruit flowers, or magnolias - sweetly scented,*
>
> *Can be picked gently, with just the touch of a bare hand.*

61. ELEGANT RESILIENCE

This world seldom offers care or favor to anyone; rather, it often resembles the caprices of unfavorable weather. We must accept its erratic and ungrateful nature.

If we recognize that we are destined to carry burdens as we navigate this wandering life, what is there to grieve? Instead, let us continue our journey with grace and an elegant spirit.

In the Embrace of Night

The dark roofs bow, surrendering to sleep,

While my soul roams through dreams vast and deep.

Deserted streets, where solitary lights gleam,

A distant figure hastens, lost in a dream.

On the lotus throne, the Buddha rests still,

Enfolded in calm, exuding a tranquil will.

Faint floral fragrances drift through the night,

As whispered prayers rise, taking graceful flight.

From afar, the soft chants of scriptures resound,

While white jasmine blooms in joy unbound.

62. SLAVERY

We are mere servants

To countless pursuits in life,

Yet we fool ourselves into thinking we're masters.

Born into the tangled web of family, society, and ties,

We spend our lives depending on others,

Hoping to make someone stay.

Among us servants, sparks of hidden hatred flare

Sometimes whispered, sometimes shouted.

And so, society splinters into havens

For lonely, resentful souls.

Were it otherwise, revolutions would be endless,

For too many hearts unite in quiet rebellion.

But alas, as we tend our sheep,

Life as a servant drifts on

Until the day we awaken,

No longer wishing to be slaves to desire.

63. FIVE SENSES

You have spent much time realizing that your pursuit of meditation goes beyond mere academic reasoning. In every profession, people rely on specific tools - carpenters with saws, painters with brushes and paint, musicians with instruments, cooks with kitchen utensils, and so on. No matter the field, our hands, body, and mind are essential. As we engage in our work, there is a constant flow of movement within and around us, connecting us with the tools of our trade, whether it be an opponent in a game, a vehicle we drive, a colleague with whom we negotiate, or a goal we aim to achieve. This interaction creates a unified whole, where you and the objects of your focus merge seamlessly, requiring skill and practice.

As you engage with these objects, your five senses come alive, registering sounds, smells, colors, tastes, and emotions. These interactions are profoundly unique, leaving a lasting imprint on your senses, with a powerful, almost magical grip that lingers long after the experience. The process is both extraordinary and inevitable, as these sensory impressions become an integral part of your being, shaping your perceptions and responses.

Ultimately, this engagement is not just about the external tools or the tasks at hand but also about the internal harmony that emerges from this union. It is in the merging of you and your objects of focus that the true essence of meditation begins to reveal itself, guiding you toward a deeper understanding of both the world around you and your place within it.

64. TRANSITIONAL PERIOD – INNOVATION

Nature is the ultimate trendsetter, constantly updating its look like the four-season runway model it is. It has its ups and downs but generally knows how to pick the best makeover strategies. Especially during those seasonal transitions, there seems to be an unexpected twist - like an internal debate between honoring past fashions and unveiling the latest styles. These influences mingle and tussle, creating nature's miraculous nuances.

Just when you sense spring knocking, you're greeted with dreary, windy, and icy days.

Then autumn rolls in, carpeting the streets with yellow leaves, turning everyone into poets. Suddenly, a week of bright sun and heavy showers barges in, pretending it's still summer, leaving you scrambling for both sunglasses and umbrellas.

Civilizations and humans aren't much different. A nation teetering on decline suddenly blossoms in culture and art. People chased from everywhere somehow produce exceptional individuals. A handful of exiles in foreign lands morph into outstanding leaders, bringing fame to their new homes. It's like life's way of saying, "When the going gets tough, the tough get going."

Similarly, before wars or during the downfall of old eras prepping for a revolution, great leaders often emerge, as if answering a cosmic casting call.

Our personal lives also have these theatrical moments. Phases filled with hardships, confusion, and mishaps eventually bow out, making way for a new, brighter, and better act. It's as if the previous drama queen within us decides to retire.

At such times, what once screamed, burned, and tormented us suddenly vanishes. The hidden strength within ushers in a fresh breeze, tearing down and sweeping away the cobwebs of the past. A warm, cheerful, and lively belief permeates us, much like that first sip of morning coffee.

There's a peculiar joy in watching flames devour countless reports and documents that have squatted in filing cabinets for the last twenty years. Those dirty, yellowed papers seem all too eager to embrace oblivion.

You pause. Then move on. Let go. And you set foot on a new path.

PART 2: COMMITMENT

There are matters that take time to understand from new angles.

*

Yoga

I've been at this yoga business for over 20 years, mainly to stay limber. Then, one day, I stumbled upon the fact that children's bones are soft while those of us with a bit of seasoning have bones that are, shall we say, less forgiving. It hit me - I'm actually more flexible than many of my peers. While friends flaunt gray hairs and wrinkles, I've only got a sprinkling of white strands and skin that still garners compliments at the spa. I can't help but touch my face... Ah, maybe yoga does more than just stretch muscles.

*

Lao Tzu

For years, Lao Tzu's "Tao Te Ching" was just homework to me. I even dabbled in writing about Taoist leadership and crafted a booklet on "The Tao of Longevity and Sex" for my friends. The takeaway? Water beats fire, softness trumps hardness. So, approach others humbly, and when necessary, put yourself below them. If your partner's content, you'll find happiness too.

Lately, my desires have mellowed. I've turned vegetarian, sworn off alcohol, and steered clear of parties. If someone nudges me to drink, I'll politely decline, and if they push, I might just slip away mid-event, leaving them puzzled.

Revisiting Lao Tzu, I finally grasp the Three Jewels of Taoism: Jing (Essence), Qi (Breath), and Shen (Spirit). Master your breath, preserve your essence, and cultivate your spirit - basically, qigong. Keep the blood flowing, and the spirit stays sharp. Ah, so the dance between softness and hardness is about timing and preserving that Jing. No wonder Shou Lao, the God of Longevity, had that prominent forehead.

*

Mantrayana

Poor health often starts in the mind, from worrying too much about work. I took up "Light Meditation" to heal myself. It's fascinating - imagining each cell in my body as a tiny universe, shimmering with light, in a warm space filled with joy. It's the energy of "Spirit – Heat – Happiness." Sometimes, I feel like I'm living in the world of "Avatar."

I realized we are beings of light. In health, we shine; in sickness, dark spots appear. That's why the elderly often seem dimmer, colder, sadder. When we die, only a faint soul light drifts away... just as Buddha said, nothing is permanent.

*

Fresh

I headed to the beach to soak in the sky, clouds, and waves. There was just one man, probably older than me, with half-gray hair, reclining a few rows away, staring thoughtfully into the distance. The wind was strong, the sun bright, yet it felt cold.

Suddenly, a young girl in a short skirt appeared, cheerfully talking and dancing around him. With oversized heart-shaped sunglasses, she snapped photos, then sat beside him, singing softly, her voice blending with the waves. The man seemed to come alive, shedding his jacket to bask in the sun and wind. I realized, a youthful mind brings joy to the heart and warmth to the body.

*

Yab-Yum

The ancients said life requires both talent and virtue. Easier said than done. But virtue is a slippery concept - different for everyone, depending on culture and time. It's abstract but sounds good, so people nod along. Lately, buzzwords like talent, mind, and vision have become trendy - grand yet vague. What do they mean? Just nod knowingly and move on.

Mantrayana goes deep. They say men represent strength, hardness, roughness, patience - symbolizing compassion. Women embody softness, flexibility, creativity, mystery, birth, and death - symbolizing wisdom. When one unites compassion and wisdom, they achieve the pinnacle of "Unsurpassed Yújiā" or "Vajrayana." And to master "Mantrayana," you must practice Yab-Yum.

*

Nirvana

Yújiā is Yoga. Vajrayana is qigong through yoga, or "Qigong Yoga" in Mahayana Buddhism.

Yoga aims to open the 7 chakras, the body's energy centers, awakening the source of "Spirit – Heat – Happiness," from the base to the crown. Preserve this energy, reach the crown, and you achieve "Great Bliss" or "Nirvana." Vajrayana says, at this point, you become a Buddha.

That's why Buddhas often have towering crowns. Mantrayana goes beyond Lao Tzu. Masters of immortality strive for longevity, gathering essence in their foreheads. Buddhas, reaching Nirvana, accumulate at the crown, passing through the forehead, opening the third eye, then the Divine eyes. Impressive.

Finding balance in practice is hard; maintaining it is even harder. Achieving Great Bliss? Well, good luck with that...

*

Detoxify

I'm in the middle of a detox, flushing out bad cells. Eleven days of just liquids. Not too tired, but light exercise helps. I've paused Yoga, opting to watch sunrises and sunsets by the sea. The sun shifts from yellow to bright to purple, waves crash endlessly, the wind is relentless. My mind is sharp, eyes clear. Everything feels...right.

Body and mind.

Then, out of nowhere, a girl with long legs strolls along the waves, tight pants held by tiny strings, hips swaying, breasts bouncing rhythmically like the waves.

To keep my composure, I look down, sipping my porridge. Recovery takes time, I remind myself.

*

I return to my room, prepping for tomorrow. It's been a long day of writing. Understanding is a journey, sometimes spiraling back to revisit old thoughts but from a higher vantage point.

1. ALRIGHT

The day's highlight was settling matters with a leader who had suddenly resigned. They both parted ways content, each wiser for the experience.

That night, back home, a friend who had just finished reading his manuscript offered some intriguing suggestions. He reflected on the feedback, appreciating the value of another's perspective. He went to bed early, a book open on the pillow, and drifted into a peaceful sleep, knowing that wisdom comes not just from action, but from reflection.

Tomorrow, a new journey awaits - heading South once again, with the quiet understanding that every step forward brings its own lessons.

"Such a field of illusions the world is

It expands vast when dreams take flight,

Yet narrows tight when jealousy roots,

For in jealousy lies the seed of pain,

And countless reasons to be consumed by it."

2. OVERLOAD

On the way to the airport for yet another trip to the Central cities, he replayed the past week in his mind.

Monday kicked off with a briefing, quickly followed by a trip to the North city that afternoon. Tuesday was a blur of endless internal meetings. Wednesday had him sitting down with Japanese partners to discuss production projects. By Thursday, he was on a plane to Saigon, meeting with investors. Friday brought him back to the Head Office, straight from the airport to the Training Institute, where he spent the entire day teaching. Saturday morning was consumed by a long session with the creative team, and now, off to DN city to meet a partner, then on to HA city to inspect the construction site. And Sunday? Another meeting, this time with city officials.

...He was running on fumes. The week had drained him completely. Family felt like a distant memory, and each day seemed like an endless loop of fatigue.

He made a sudden decision to turn the car around and head home. The familiar road felt like a lifeline. At home, his youngest son was waiting by the door, eager to go out with friends.

And that was enough. He opted for a sauna to melt away the stress.

He fired off a few texts to his team, calling for backup.

"I can't keep going forever. Time to let me rest while you guys take the lead," he thought, smiling at the irony of finally asking for help.

"The mountains tremble,

The oceans moan,

The woods whisper secrets unknown."

3. POWERLESS

Generally speaking, we often admit to being powerless in the face of lustful desires. No matter how much we try to suppress or control them, we remain passive, as if something inevitable has already occurred.

In the beginning, it's all about suppression, fiery intensity, frantic urgency, and a sense of something violent and unstoppable. The heart races, everything feels constricted, and there's an aching that demands release.

By the end, the scene shifts - weariness sets in, the body heaves a sigh, loosens up, and starts sweating. What once felt intense now feels subdued. You might feel light-hearted, restless, and perhaps fall into a fitful sleep, only to wake startled, the memory already fading as you sink back into the routine of life.

Mirror

Always carry a mirror with you,

To reflect on what you see.

After gentle comes connection,

After care, reciprocity.

After sweetness, pursuit,

After sincerity, deceit.

And see

After frugality, sharing,

After simplicity, self-respect.

After poverty, we rise,

After falling, we grow.

4. ENLIGHTENMENT

In any profession or game, even though one must use their legs, arms, or entire body, it is never merely about training muscles. When a part of your body is engaged - legs, arms, shoulders, chest, head - you must learn not to exert all your strength from that part or any other part of your body. Instead, let that specific part work while the rest of the body remains at ease, uninvolved in the action. Only then can you begin to approach the Zen state where the movement of that part aligns seamlessly with the object, leading to "enlightenment."

To reach this state, years of dedicated practice in your field are required. And in the quiet moments of reflection, you must admit that to become mature in your profession, in your interactions with colleagues, partners, or competitors, whether in life or in any game, you have faced countless failures. Despite diligent practice and learning, the path to "enlightenment" remains elusive.

5. MOODY

He started the day on a high note, feeling quite pleased as he headed to the office. He managed to solve a few tricky problems and then rewarded himself by retreating upstairs to read, listen to some jazz, and soak in the calm of a relaxing weekend. He even stumbled upon some materials that promised healing - a nice bonus.

After lunch, while enjoying a well-deserved rest, the phone rang. An important call, it seemed. He had no choice but to go.

Ten minutes into the meeting, he was hit with bad news - superiors asking for the impossible, yet again. This wasn't the first time he'd heard such news; in fact, it had made him ill over the past two or three years. Here it was again. He stayed calm at first, but once the guest left, the weight of it began to press on him, ruining what had been a peaceful afternoon.

And then, as if on cue, a few more groups of guests arrived, one after another. Oh no.

His stomach began to ache, his whole body sagged under the sorrow.

He chuckled to himself - health really does seem tied to mood. After all, it's the habit of clinging to delusions and the inability to let go that does the damage.

He'd read countless books, listened to numerous Buddhist teachings, all in the hope of finding peace, of shedding his ego...

But, as he reminded himself with a wry smile, it's easier said than done.

Heartbreaking moment

Far and near, loved ones gone,

Echoes of old songs carry me back,

Into memories, distant and fading,

Where only shadows remain.

6. INSECURITY

Insecurity is like that odd feeling you get when you can't quite remember if you locked the front door. It sneaks up on you, born from vague worries about things that did or didn't happen - or maybe never will. As the years roll by, you start to wonder: Will anyone remember me when I'm gone? What will they recall? Will my legacy be meaningful, or just another footnote?

These thoughts don't arrive like an organized to-do list; they hit like random bursts of thunder on a sunny day. What have you missed? What's been gnawing at you all your life, still left unchecked? Youth has a funny way of slipping by, leaving a trail of unfinished business and forgotten victories. So why does this insecurity cling on like a stubborn stain?

You've faced down fears of honor, money, even the proverbial devils, and discovered that they're not as permanent as they seemed. They can be forgotten or reclaimed. But the meaning of life? That's the slippery fish that refuses to be caught. Insecurity is just the mind's way of reminding us that life isn't all sunshine and roses - it's also about not having enough, or fearing we don't.

But here's the twist: Insecurity brings with it a quiet, nagging pain - a little like a pebble in your shoe. It's that lack of love, the missing harmony, the absence of shared laughter. Reality is never quite enough, and like a small stream of love, it often dries up before it even reaches the ocean. Love is scarce because, let's face it, we're all just solitary creatures at heart.

So, what to do? You've got two options:

1. Take the Western approach: Fix the problem head-on, endure the discomfort, and move on.

2. Or go Eastern: Soothe the pain, be patient, and let time do its thing.

Either way, let go of the restless wandering, and focus on the now. Think of insecurity as:

A bird soaring freely in the sky,

A fish diving deep into the sea,

Wild animals darting through the forest,

And the wind dissolving into the air.

And remember, one day you and your soul will return to the void. That, my friend, is where peace lies.

7. HANGING ON

The world is a swirl of ambiguity, life a tangle of chaos, and feelings as fleeting as thin air. Long journeys and big dreams weigh heavily on your shoulders, yet the mind feels lonelier by the day. In these moments, it's tempting to cling to old memories for comfort, or to seek solace in brief distractions.

But if you're stronger, you might choose to face it all in silence, turning inward to explore the depths of your thoughts. You begin to ask: where, why, and how? And slowly, you uncover the roots of renunciation, giving, and the true essence of joy.

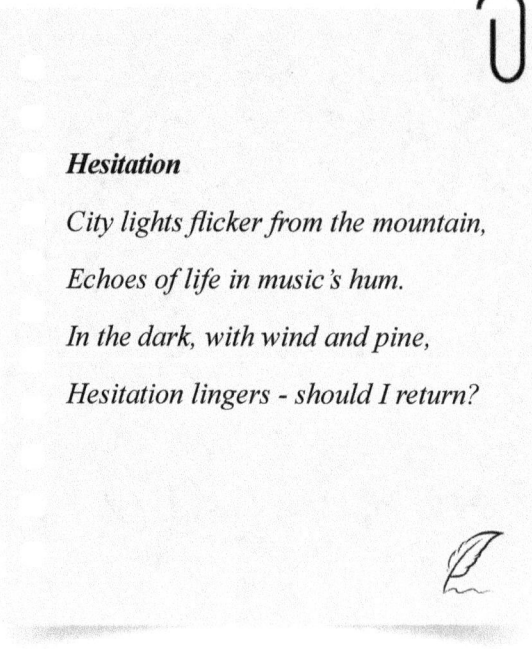

Hesitation

City lights flicker from the mountain,

Echoes of life in music's hum.

In the dark, with wind and pine,

Hesitation lingers - should I return?

8. PEACEFUL WORLD

The world speaks often of precious peace,

From ancient days to now, and on to tomorrow.

But those are just sparkling words,

Dissolving in the crowd of unfulfilled desires.

Some chase wealth and fleeting fame,

While others wander lost in the haze.

Be they fat or thin, ugly or fair,

Weak or strong, bad or lucky

Each will find what they seek,

In this life or the next.

But in this very moment,

Humanity battles its incomplete desires,

Making peace feel ever so distant.

9. WONDERFUL TIMES

The truly wonderful times in life sneak up on us, like when I was sick, and no one was home. My daughter was out all night with her friends. Daddy missed her terribly but didn't want to admit it. Late in the morning, she returned, hugged Daddy to apologize, and massaged my legs as a peace offering. Then there's the youngest son, who disappeared for a week only to reappear, hugging Daddy like a baby and expressing love by devouring all the leftovers - especially the vegetables he usually avoids - then proudly announcing his team made it to the finals, hoping Daddy would be there to watch.

There's nothing quite like resting on the couch, listening to music, with the kids nearby, engrossed in their games. The eldest calls, filling Daddy in on a trip to a music festival with old friends. What did they eat? Yesterday, the eldest daughter, who's far away, texted Daddy, dreaming of a trip through Vietnam with all four siblings and Daddy, just like old times. Of course, Daddy's just waiting for you to come back.

In the smooth flow of music and memories, I wish you all were close by, even if just for a moment. It brings back the memory of hugging my own mother when she was sick.

Recall

Years of illness can wear down your body. Difficulties at work can drain your mind. And one day, when you glance in the mirror or catch yourself in the surprised eyes of others, you might suddenly see that you've become as frail as a withered tree in autumn, its leaves yellowing and falling.

Loneliness intensifies the longing for the past. We all face that moment, just as we all have faced winters in our lives.

10. BREATHE RIGHT

"You can't interact with the outside world properly if you're not breathing right." After inhaling, compress the breath below the dantian (about a knuckle below the navel) and let the abdominal wall expand fully. Hold it for a moment. Then, exhale as slowly and evenly as possible, and pause briefly before inhaling again, quickly but smoothly. Breathe like this consistently, and you will find a rhythm after some time. If you do it right, you'll notice that people like singers, carpenters, surgeons, swordsmen, and writers, when they reach a certain skill level, also follow a particular rhythm in their work. By breathing this way, you will not only discover the source of all spiritual strength but also understand that this source flows more abundantly and easily penetrates your entire being when you relax.

11. SAD DIARY

Reading an old diary,
You find yourself small and lost.
You wished for so much,
Believing you could achieve it all
Love, victory, and glory.

You've seen rivers, mountains, and deserts,
Oceans, storms, and abysses.
You loved your homeland, the blue sea and sky,
And felt deep pity for its sorrows.
You once craved civilization and beautiful words,
Sought out cities and bright souls.

But after so many years, what remains?
A sad diary,
Carrying the essence of a human life.
The vestiges, wild souls, and ruins of time,
Now captured in a few lines of poetry,
Strange marks etched on moonstone.

And now you see,
Why old dreams never came true.
You were too small, too ordinary,
Surrounded by pale desires,
Your heart swayed by easy words,
Following a coward's path.

But there's one more thing you realize.
Maybe one day, your people will stand proud,
Honored among all nations.
But time will still take them away,
Until the wind blows and the hills grow wild.
In the end, what remains if there is no love?

12. ALTERNATIVE SOLUTION

Life changes daily, whether hard, fortunate, or easy - you must accept these changes and find a wise, skillful response to the flow.

Don't give up, turn back, or let go. Instead, actively embrace life, finding contentment in everything that happens as a natural course.

Each problem offers different solutions, just as there are many paths to a mountain's peak. Focusing solely on one path limits your potential and creates imbalance.

Obstacles challenge both mind and body, but they also train us, pushing us to new heights and beyond our limits.

When faced with an obstruction, seek new solutions. Don't insist or struggle - relax, be natural, and find a new, brighter, and better path.

13. UNTIE

I had a non-stop creative day at the monastery, juggling meetings about future product lines, planning a country's spiritual area atop the Nine Falls Mountain, and outlining a 20-year strategy to blanket the country with smart products. Then I dashed to the car just in time for dinner with the kids, followed by a late-night call with a foreign partner. Tomorrow, it's off to HB province for a ceremony honoring the Mother Goddesses.

"Slowly, I walk like an old habit,

Heavy - hearted, burdened by years of sorrow.

No longer able to take long strides,

I untie my soul, discovering new horizons."

14. DIFFICULTIES

Early in the morning, he went to the Endocrine Hospital for a check-up. The doctor recommended immediate surgery, suggesting it would be simple now but could become more complicated if delayed. He was perplexed. Just yesterday, his traditional medicine doctor had a different opinion - bad cells, like bad children, should be taught and educated gradually… but who kills the child?

He hurried home to send his daughter off to school far away. Nostalgia washed over him as he sat in the car with his family, watching the trees blur by through the glass, thinking about how quickly time flies…

Before he could even say goodbye, a message came from the General Manager of the Sales Division, tendering his resignation because he couldn't meet the job's demands. Last year alone, the division had spent lavishly - high salaries, big talk, but no real results.

What should he do? Life is no fairy tale.

"When anxiety becomes habit

It's a sign of great altering.

Maybe depression leads to a burst,

But it ends, and you rise again."

15. LEARN TO REPAY

I've come to realize that life is a debt. You can't let it pile up forever; you should find ways to pay it down whenever possible, in whatever ways you can.

Think of it like this: after a flourishing spring and a summer of struggle, autumn comes to harvest the fruits of your labor. But then autumn fades, leaving behind nostalgia and regret, leading to a cold winter - lonely, sick, gloomy, and harsh.

If you find success, you must be brave. But courage isn't just about fighting; it's also about knowing when to be silent, discreet, and humble. Avoid arrogance.

In your youth, ambition and enthusiasm drive you to seize many things. But as life goes on, you may start to feel a pang of shame for things done or left undone. That's the conscience calling for repayment, urging you to set things right.

To keep a family peaceful through the years, you repay your debts with patience, commitment, endurance, silence, tolerance, and sometimes, loneliness.

When you have an interesting, attractive, and compatible lover, you must offer attention, care, and dedication. And yes, don't forget the thoughtful gifts.

As you settle down, life's blessings come as favors from above. Along with paying respect to gods and saints, don't forget to repay life itself. Remember, human nature is wild at heart, needing hours of exploration and communion with the natural world. Whether it's breathing in the scent of a field, picking wildflowers, drinking cool spring water, or simply cherishing what the earth gives us - this is how you repay life.

You understand now that life is finite, fleeting, and brief. You've gained much, spent much. But you begin to recognize those rare, shining moments that illuminate your path.

It's the simple joys - like a flower blooming in the early morning, birds chirping, an approaching rain, a sweet sunny afternoon, or a magical moonlit night in a vast forest.

And sometimes, the light of ancient wisdom suddenly shines in your mind. You grasp the hidden languages of nature, the true rules of life.

By day, you must be competitive, creative, and fierce. But by night, it's time to hide, be cautious, and wait for the right moment.

Then there are those twilight hours, shrouded in fog, when you tell yourself to act discreetly yet boldly, compete in moderation, create in secret, and bide your time for a breakthrough.

You're beginning to write the epic of your life.

You are the hero Odysseus in your own story - sometimes known as Ulysses by your foes - and you'll pen your own epic, without needing the blind poet Homer to do it for you.

16. A STRICT TEACHER

No one likes to talk about their own death. If the subject arises, it's usually about someone else's. Yet, deep down, we all know that our time will come.

We brush this truth aside, chasing the currents of life, navigating its dangers - even storms and lightning can't stop us. But when something hits close to home, like a family member's illness or death, or when we fall ill ourselves, it jolts us into reflection and regret. Yet, as time passes, we forget once more.

It's peculiar. We witness the seasons, flowers blooming and wilting, but rarely do we consider our own mortality. Even the elderly, who are closer to the earth than the sky, often avoid thoughts of death and make no preparations for it. They simply live each day as it comes, as they always have.

But when you do contemplate death, you realize there will come a day when all that has passed, all that's unfinished, and all that follows after death will continue without you - whether you're buried in the earth or become a beam of light soaring into the void.

And if you're ever faced with a serious illness or danger, it's frightening to feel the silent gaze of the God of Death, patiently waiting…

Yet, this fear has a way of waking you up.

So, give thanks to sickness and the God of Death - they are strict teachers, guiding us to live more consciously.

17. BREATH OF LIFE

You practice new breathing techniques until you master them. The initial alienation and discomfort will soon dissipate. In Zen practice, it is important to breathe out slowly, gently, and steadily. Only when the exhale is complete can you inhale. It can be said that the inhale breath has the function of forming life, the period of silence and holding the breath is when things align and become righteous, and the exhale breath is the completion and cessation, in which all obstacles have been resolved.

18. KNOWLEDGE

Craving, like a long day's thirst, leaves you uneasy, anxious, and longing. If you find water, you'll rush to it, drink deeply, laugh, and feel satisfied.

In life, you often face uncertainty, anxiety, and insecurity. You immerse yourself in these feelings, searching for the reason behind them. But when you finally uncover the cause, you realize you've already crossed over - you've journeyed through fear and arrived on a new shore.

As Buddha once said, true knowledge - wisdom - is the journey beyond, to the shore of enlightenment.

Sex

Love is enormous, vague, confusing, and nearly impossible to define. But sex? Well, that's as straightforward as a chemical reaction. It needs the right elements, catalysts, and just the right mix of temperature, light, and humidity.

It's an interactive process - molecules and components can smolder, sizzle, cool off, dry out, tingle, or suddenly spark into action. It can be vibrant, melting, explosive, or even a slow simmer that eventually evaporates into thin air. Sometimes it's electric, other times it's quiet, peaceful, maybe even a bit boring. Or it can be risky, dangerous, and downright dramatic.

It all depends on the dose. So, just be careful!

19. DEEP CONNECTION

In a rice or maize field, all the crops look the same, hard to tell apart. The poultry are similar too - just different sizes and colors. But when you venture into the forest or climb a mountain, nature reveals itself in countless shapes and forms, even the wild chickens come in all kinds.

Society can be like that forest. If you're not different, not profound, your connections will be as superficial and unmarked as the crops in a field. You can't go deep with everyone you meet. Real, deep relationships are rare and happen not because you plan them but because you're genuinely sincere, unique, and mean what you say.

With those you cross paths with in life, remember: each encounter should be a deep, gentle touch, as if it were the last time you'd meet. It's not easy to live this way, but it's worth it. Cherish every moment of life that you have.

So, maybe it's better to meet fewer people and focus more on yourself, for yourself.

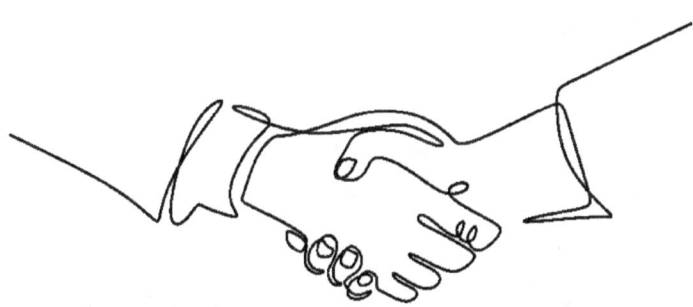

20. BALANCE

You've spent a lot of time pondering success and failure, reflecting on how you once thrived as a bold pioneer in a fledgling business environment, only to find yourself eventually outpaced by younger, more relentless waves of entrepreneurs.

To succeed in any field, you've realized that it takes more than just skills and smarts; it requires mastering the art of balance. Whether in business, politics, or even the arts - be it dance, music, painting, or even flower arranging - a sharp mind and steadfast personality can lead to extraordinary results. But here's where it gets tricky: temperament, not just personality, plays a key role.

Personality is the whole package - how you think, feel, and behave. Temperament, on the other hand, is more like your default setting - how you naturally react to the world around you. Think of temperament as the Five Elements - Metal, Wood, Water, Fire, Earth - while personality is the ever-changing Bagua, shaping your responses to life's ups and downs.

Let's not dive too deep into philosophy, but know this: temperament drives personality. It's the foundation that shapes your reactions, both psychologically and spiritually, to external challenges.

In business, the most successful entrepreneurs may not always be the sharpest or the toughest. Instead, they excel at balancing a flexible mind with an adaptable temperament, especially when navigating the tightrope of uncertainty and risk. You've heard the tale of the fox and the hedgehog - the fox is clever and quick, constantly adapting, but it's the hedgehog's simple, consistent approach that ultimately wins the day. In business, though, you need a bit of both - a balance between the fox's flexibility and the hedgehog's steady persistence.

Looking back, you see that you stumbled when you relied too heavily on intellect, becoming too subjective, and not balancing it with a simple, consistent approach when faced with narrow, difficult paths.

So, you remind yourself: there's still time, still a journey ahead. It's about correcting course, keeping things simple, focusing on what truly matters, and being persistent with what resonates deeply in your heart and mind.

Stay balanced to keep moving forward - for the best possible outcome.

You've spent a lot of time pondering success and failure, reflecting on how you once thrived as a bold pioneer in a fledgling business environment, only to find yourself eventually outpaced by younger, more relentless waves of entrepreneurs.

To succeed in any field, you've realized that it takes more than just skills and smarts; it requires mastering the art of balance. Whether in business, politics, or even the arts - be it dance, music, painting, or even flower arranging - a sharp mind and steadfast personality can lead to extraordinary results. But here's where it gets tricky: temperament, not just personality, plays a key role.

Personality is the whole package - how you think, feel, and behave. Temperament, on the other hand, is more like your default setting - how you naturally react to the world around you. Think of temperament as the Five Elements - Metal, Wood, Water, Fire, Earth - while personality is the ever-changing Bagua, shaping your responses to life's ups and downs.

Let's not dive too deep into philosophy, but know this: temperament drives personality. It's the foundation that shapes your reactions, both psychologically and spiritually, to external challenges.

In business, the most successful entrepreneurs may not always be the sharpest or the toughest. Instead, they excel at balancing a flexible mind with an adaptable temperament, especially when navigating the tightrope of uncertainty and risk. You've heard the tale of the fox and the hedgehog - the fox is clever and quick, constantly adapting, but it's the hedgehog's simple, consistent approach that ultimately wins the day. In business, though, you need a bit of both - a balance between the fox's flexibility and the hedgehog's steady persistence.

Looking back, you see that you stumbled when you relied too heavily on intellect, becoming too subjective, and not balancing it with a simple, consistent approach when faced with narrow, difficult paths.

So, you remind yourself: there's still time, still a journey ahead. It's about correcting course, keeping things simple, focusing on what truly matters, and being persistent with what resonates deeply in your heart and mind.

Stay balanced to keep moving forward - for the best possible outcome.

21. ASHAMED

Comparing the 2020 business results with other organizations, he felt like a terrible student who just flunked his finals. The thought of attending the industry meeting made him cringe - he didn't dare show his face.

At the meeting, he got mocked for his weaknesses and found himself awkwardly explaining away the difficulties. What a mortifying experience.

He reminded himself, even Odysseus had to endure ridicule and setbacks on his journey, and Hercules faced his trials with perseverance. No one achieves greatness without stumbling through a few challenges.

Waking up early this morning, troubled by the past and anxious about the future, he wrote down a few lines to remind and admonish himself. He decided to tread as carefully as walking on thin ice and let the strong lead.

Self defense

He knows when he lets things slide, he can become weak, small, and vulnerable to the situation. He also understands that knowledge and connections are never enough to combat the dangerous, formidable, and lurking forces around him.

At those times, experience, silence, patience, endurance, humility, and acceptance, combined with a heart full of tolerance, sharing, and giving, are the best protective shields.

22. FEELING

Instead of endlessly thinking, analyzing, or explaining, learn the art of feeling and allow others to feel your presence.

You connect with the world not just through thoughts, but through colors, scents, sounds, and touch - by direct contact with life. Calm your mind, and let your body fully immerse in nature. When you become one with the universe, you'll find yourself in harmony with the sound of waves and birds, the scent of earth and sea, the colors of clouds and flowers, the taste of trees and fruit. Your heart will slowly open, blossoming with emotion and poetry.

Similarly, when you do something for someone, it's not the expensive gifts or eloquent words that matter most. True meaning is often found in the quiet actions, the silent efforts that speak louder than words ever could.

23. GET DOWN – GET UP

At the annual industrial meeting, he attended reluctantly - there was a new leader, and rumors had painted him as arrogant. But arrogance wasn't the issue; it was his illness, his solitary nature. Years of struggling without support had taken a toll, leaving his organization in a weaker position. Fewer relationships, fewer connections... the perception of arrogance grew.

While other business units thrived, the lag in his own made him more self-conscious, guilty, even frustrated. To pull himself up, he dove into self-help books, studying ways to conquer fear, and learning from history how to succeed in adverse circumstances.

Let's enjoy life
Spring arrives with a warm drizzle,
After nights of restlessness,
And sighs of troubles.
See the wind kiss the colorful roses.

Though no one waits,
It still blooms.
Small and fragile,
Knowing it will bloom and fade,
The flower still gives its all.

So let's enjoy life and every moment,
And fight as long as you can.
Life is like that.
Get the fullest of your life.
Even in the face of challenges, embrace life with all
its colors, and push forward with determination.

24. NARROW DOOR

Life isn't a straight highway where you can speed ahead without obstacles. Instead, it's filled with twists, turns, and narrow paths that often feel like a tight squeeze.

There are moments when you find yourself on that narrow road, burdened with responsibilities, feeling like a stubborn mule trying to push through a narrow door. You might even feel like crying out for someone to open that door a little wider.

But at such times, patience is your only friend. And perhaps, the wisdom to step back and look for a different, more open door.

Let it be

He has weathered ups and downs, holding onto a belief. Though it may flicker like a candle in the night, it remains a pillar, a support, an anchor. It keeps his thoughts and feelings steady, propelling him forward. Sometimes he rushes ahead, even when there's no clear destination or task at hand, just the need to keep moving.

Even when he's tired and longs for a break, he knows that life flows onward, and he must flow with it.

25. SYNCHRONIZED MOVEMENT

The journey of an enlightened action unfolds in distinct stages: preparation, the initiation of movement, deep bodily focus, and finally, the completion of the act. Each stage begins with an inhalation, moves through a controlled pause, and concludes with an exhalation. This sequence occurs naturally, with the breath guiding and harmonizing every movement.

Breath is not just a rhythm for the body; it is a rhythm of life itself, unique to each individual based on their mastery of it. Though the process is segmented into stages, they are all synchronized, flowing seamlessly from within. Unlike other forms of physical exercise, this process offers the freedom to adapt - adding or subtracting stages - without losing its essence or purpose.

26. ENCOUNTER

He had days that felt like they would never end. One endless loop of travel - bouncing from meeting to meeting, city to city, airport to airport.

After spending a few weeks in the serene mountains of Bhutan, quietly practicing from morning till afternoon, listening to lectures, visiting monks, performing ceremonies, and praying, he returned to his office. But the meetings resumed, relentless, from morning till afternoon.

Then yesterday, he went for a health check. The results? Confusing, to say the least. The tumor had shrunk, but more lymph nodes were involved. The only advice: surgery.

What to do?

Another day dawns. He continues to ponder, with countless unfinished tasks looming, worries and pains as vast as the ocean ahead. Where can he find a place to stop and rest?

"Keep fear at a distance,

Live in quiet patience."

27. SILENCE

It's hard to find a moment of true silence. Even when meditating early in the morning or late in the afternoon, the mind remains busy, always active. Yet, in those rare moments when silence does descend - when the mind is truly empty, free of thoughts - a sweet, peaceful sensation begins to spread through the body and mind. Such moments are both wonderful and rare.

In truth, you're often too caught up in the busyness of life, too preoccupied with yourself. Your ego demands all sorts of things: honor, money, emotions, status, knowledge, lust… You find yourself constantly arguing - sometimes with real or imagined opponents, sometimes even with yourself.

But do you really know who you are? Are you the one who thinks endlessly, who is driven by desires, who is emotionally turbulent? Or is there another side to you - a wiser, more mindful self that occasionally surfaces, yet remains silent?

It's difficult to say.

28. TIME CHANGES

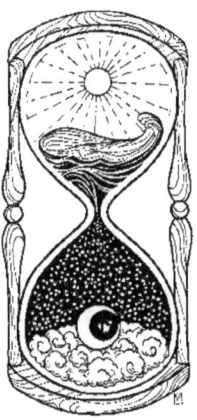

In 30 years of working, he rarely felt so uninspired. But this morning, after finishing his detox routine, grabbing a quick breakfast, and rushing to the car, he walked past the serene, green garden and suddenly wished he didn't have to go to work.

Reminder

No matter who you are,

Life is valuable only when lived fully.

No matter what you do,

It's meaningful only if you love it.

Whether you are happy or lonely,

Always keep the flame of passion alive.

Whether you face glory or hardship,

You are composing the melody of your life.

29. WISH

You don't want a lover; you crave adventure. You prefer to possess, conquer, be challenged, and embrace the new, the unexpected, the thrilling. You're not interested in playing games, pretending, or sulking. Instead, you long for harmony, to give freely, and to find satisfaction in the exchange.

He feels strong, firm,

Alive like a serpent,

Twisting and coiling,

Moving with intensity,

Deep, slippery, hot, and controlled.

She remains silent,

Her breath heavy and her skin damp.

She wishes to curl up,

To dissolve into him,

She feels exposed,

Open, trembling, and yearning,

While she holds, grips, demands,

And rushes to meet him.

30. DAY OF TERROR

It started like any other day, but by the end, he knew it was one for the books.

He woke up early, as usual, running through his morning routine - stretching, breathing, a few push-ups, a quick prayer. The fresh air gave him a fleeting sense of peace, as if the day held promise. But that promise quickly went south.

First stop: his father's house. The old man, freshly out of the hospital, looked thinner than ever. "Thin is good," he lied, trying to sound upbeat. "It means the body's getting rid of toxins." But as he massaged his father's swollen leg, the frailty of life hit him like a ton of bricks.

He left for the office, already feeling drained. Traffic was a nightmare, and he fought to stay awake as the car crawled along. At the office, the bad news started rolling in. A key manager was quitting over some ridiculous reason. Then, the spiritual charlatan who had scammed the company months ago reappeared, all smiles and empty promises, acting like he was their savior.

By lunchtime, he was running on fumes. He barely tasted his food, just eating so he could take his medication. But there was no time to rest; the day wasn't over yet. Meetings blurred together - more problems, more people to appease, and his patience wearing thinner than his father's legs.

When he finally got home, he collapsed into bed without even taking his meds. His phone buzzed with messages from his family - pictures of mountain views, words of encouragement from his kids. It warmed him for a moment, reminding him of why he kept going.

And then it hit him: despite the chaos, he was still here. Still breathing, still fighting, still alive. The world might be full of crap, but it was also full of beauty, love, and the quiet moments that made it all worthwhile.

"Due to darkness, we can see light.

Due to hollow, full is noticed."

With that thought, he finally let go. The tension melted away, and for the first time all day, he felt at peace. Tomorrow would bring new challenges, but for now, he was content to just be, knowing that even on the worst days, there was always light at the end of the tunnel.

31. INHIBITION

When you're misunderstood, misjudged, or even disparaged by others - when they twist the truth about you, dismiss your explanations, or refuse to give you a chance to clarify - you feel the heat rise. Resentment, fury, and frustration bubble up, and all you can think is, "This is drama."

But then, there are those other moments. When you desire someone intensely - wanting to make love, possess, even devour them - but instead, you keep quiet. You maintain a calm gaze, wear a polite smile, and pretend you're above it all. Inside, though, you might feel a twinge of shame, cowardice, maybe even a touch of self-deception. "This," you think, "is pain."

Drama is the inhibition brought on by others. Pain is the inhibition you impose on yourself.

And both, in their own ways, make life just a bit more... interesting.

32. RELAX

You may think you're breathing properly when you focus on one part of your body, preparing it to interact. But instead of relaxing the rest of your body, you unintentionally make it tense. You also become overly concerned with maintaining a steady position when you're meant to be at ease. This happens because you're thinking too much about it. In truth, all you need to do is focus on your breath, as if there's nothing else in the world but that breath. Let go of control, and allow relaxation to flow naturally, for sometimes the effort to control creates the very tension we seek to avoid. True ease comes not from forcing relaxation, but from letting go and trusting the process.

33. FATE

It was one of those trips that seemed destined for chaos. Finally settling into my plane seat, I let out a sigh of relief.

The day before, at the airport, I had a spur-of-the-moment idea: why not change my flight home? Instead of a boring transit in Guangzhou, I'd swing by New York. After all, my visa was still valid for a few days. So, I switched my flight, and the adventure began.

Hours passed in the airport: buying tickets, exchanging money, wandering aimlessly, eating apples, drinking juice, and visiting the Tibetan Buddhist shop more times than I care to admit. The plane was delayed, so I tried to catch some sleep, but the waiting area was a cacophony of noise. Just when I thought it couldn't get worse, I woke up to find everyone else had been sent back to a hotel. I was left standing on the street in the middle of the night, waiting over 30 minutes for a ride. When I finally got to the hotel, I realized no one spoke English. Lovely.

The next morning, after setting two alarms (just to be safe), I found out my flight was delayed again. So, I went through the process of getting a refund and buying a new ticket. More hours of waiting, more fruit, and a disappointing bag of nut candies that were actually just sugar bombs. Feeling desperate, I caved and bought some fried chicken. But, of course, they didn't understand that I just wanted bread to go with it. So, I ended up with a full meal, and a stomachache to boot.

Finally, I made it to the boarding gate, only to be rejected because someone had forgotten to stamp my boarding pass. Another delay. Back to the Tibetan shop, where I decided, on a whim, to buy a Buddha statue after all. The shopkeeper's enthusiasm was hard to resist. I rushed to the counter, swiped my card, and finally made it onto the plane - barely.

As the wheels rolled down the runway, I breathed a sigh of relief. I had been going back and forth between those Tibetan shops for two days, staring at Buddha statues, snapping pictures, and feeling like something was keeping me there. Maybe it was fate. I had promised to return to Chengdu to see the Buddha, but my kids missed me, so I changed my plans. Yet, somehow, Buddha made sure I stayed.

34. PONDERING

He was deeply concerned about his organization's situation, even though he'd recovered from a severe mental breakdown six months prior. Now, with a clearer mind, he assessed the challenges ahead. Calmer, yes, but the reality remained daunting. Difficulties arrived one after another, like an endless wave.

Internal weaknesses made it tough to stick to the plan. The pandemic and economic downturn only added to the pressure - finding foreign investors was nearly impossible, and even when found, meeting them or traveling was out of the question.

He pushed himself daily, overcoming illness and adversity. Always encouraging his staff, standing by their side, even when it felt like they were all hanging on the edge of a cliff. He turned to books about great leaders, political intrigues, and historic wars, hoping to glean some wisdom to navigate these treacherous times.

The offers for mergers and acquisitions flooded in, each accompanied by advice, criticism, and consultations. There were so many voices, he could no longer tell friend from foe. In the end, he decided to trust his instincts and keep moving forward.

"Despite fear and danger, if you learn to accept your situation, and let go of petty and trivial desires, you'll find the path to peace."

35. LET IT GO

He remembers clearly who he was and where he stood, surrounded by beautiful, fresh young girls and captivating, alluring women. He saw himself as a thirsty man, diving into a river of lust, floating endlessly without reaching the shore. From dawn until nightfall, he was fully engaged, sometimes hurriedly, sometimes indifferently, trying to swim to the other side.

Then he realized he had to let go. To avoid drowning in that stream of desire, he knew he must release it. He had to repress his cravings, withdraw, endure, and tensely strain toward the finish line. Inevitably, he choked a couple of times, swallowing mouthfuls of water.

Hunch

Like a bird soaring in the vast blue sky,

He senses the storm of change approaching,

Threatening to drown him in life's darkness,

Reminding himself to hold back and hold on.

Struggling to glide through the treacherous calm,

As lightning flashes and winds howl,

The clouds darken, and the rain is relentless,

Cold stars drench his body until it turns blue.

In solitude, he flies toward the light,

At the farthest end of the sky.

36. SINCERITY

Sincerity is always likable.

The older we get, the more masks we've put on that are different from our original innocence.

Despite the years, the smile and eyes of a child still make us flutter tenderly because the child is sincere and innocent and radiates a positive charismatic energy.

Concealment is darkness. Innocence is light.

The mind is dark because it has been painted with the colors of the years of life. The mind is clear when we know how to settle, rinse, and let go of impurities.

Hence true maturity is when one can find his childhood smile, return to the original innocence, unite with the pure child with the understanding of an adult, using both the conscious and the unconscious as well as love and wisdom. We call it sophistication.

It requires a life-long process of perseverance, patience, experience, anger, and especially suffering. Just like when we exercise, our body sometimes reacts negatively with pain, begging us to give up. And when we overcome and manage that discomfort, we find ourselves stronger and more positive than before.

It is the obstacles and sufferings of life that bring us love, training and teaching us to be accepting, to be generous, to share, to be grateful for obstacles that helped us understand the meaning of everything.

Therefore, we should remind ourselves to go back to our true selves, nurture our positive energy, keep an innocent smile on our lips, and walk step by step toward the wise shore of love.

37. STRETCHING ARMS

After the premiere of "The Memory Show," the first week was a blur of sparkling eyes and glowing smiles, with praise pouring in from the press and media. But as the second week rolled in, the criticisms began to creep up, slowly at first, then in a deluge. By the third week, I was stuck in a cycle of explaining, defending, and pleading for support until everything seemed to settle. Just when the storm appeared to pass, I boarded a plane to Thailand for a much-needed break with a few friends who were already waiting for me there.

As the plane touched down and rolled along the runway, I shook myself awake and grabbed a few newspapers to catch up on the latest. Flipping quickly to the last page - the most critical one, of course - I was greeted with a long article, complete with pictures of "The Memory Show." I rubbed my eyes in disbelief. Surely, I was seeing things. But no, there it was - a full spread of articles. I reached for another newspaper, hoping for better news, only to find another review riddled with questions and doubts.

Panic gripped me. I rushed to the hotel where my friends were eagerly waiting, hoping to relax on a river cruise in Bangkok at sunset. But I waved them off, insisting I needed a moment alone. As soon as they left, I collapsed on the bed, fully clothed, arms stretched out wide. The sheets were still crisp, smelling faintly of jasmine and cinnamon, offering a small comfort as I stared up at the ceiling, frustration gnawing at me.

The floral scent and pristine white linens began to calm my nerves. The next morning, after a night of restless sleep, I joined my friends for breakfast, where we chatted, laughed, and I even had my fortune told by a local Thai master. He predicted nothing but good news ahead, a relief that encouraged me to book an early flight home the next afternoon.

Back on a Vietnam Airlines flight, I drifted off again, waking only as the plane landed. I grabbed the fresh newspapers on board, skimming through the pages filled with joyful news about a football match, flags waving triumphantly. But as I turned to the last page, my heart sank. There it was again - an image of the construction site and stage of "The Memory Show," accompanied by another scathing article lamenting the loss of a once-beautiful deserted island, now marred by our project. I froze. Was this the same article from yesterday? No, it was fresh off the press.

I arrived home, utterly drained, skipping dinner and heading straight to my room. I lay down, arms outstretched, staring blankly at the ceiling, feeling utterly defeated. But then, out of nowhere, a poem popped into my mind: *"I want to stretch my arms in the air and scream!"* But why not rewrite it? How about: *"I want to stretch my arms in the air and sing?"*

With a sudden burst of inspiration, I sat up and put on some meditation music. The gentle sound of running water and the soft notes of a flute began to soothe my frayed nerves. My mind expanded, reaching out like the wings of a bird soaring between heaven and earth, and my heart began to hum along with the melody.

In that moment, I realized something profound: whether in joy or despair, when emotions run high, there's nothing better than stretching out your arms and releasing it all - whether in a shout or a song. After all, it's only when we're buried deep in the earth, a few inches under, that we can't stretch our arms anymore. But then again, perhaps our souls will have already sprouted wings, ready to soar freely, traveling anywhere they please.

38. LISTENING TO ADVICE

When his work turned into a mess, a miserable stalemate with internal threats and external hostility, and even strife with relatives, he sought advice. He met with the people involved, asked for their input, and desperately looked for a way out.

But after gathering all the advice, he could only see gray. The advice seemed to boil down to this: Do nothing. The more you do, the more mistakes you make. But if you don't do anything, you're doomed anyway. It felt like being trapped in an ambiguous regulation where any action would result in a mistake. And as if that weren't enough, the law itself was, well, moronic. Their only advice? Follow the laws, even if they make no sense.

They compared it to a rampant epidemic, where the main disease was unknown. Those with weak resistance would die on their own. Trying to help them was futile, they said. And if you couldn't cure them, they might just spread their misery to others.

The situation was indeed desperate, yet in his heart, he still believed in the goodness of people.

Early one morning, a leader who worried about him went away to pray for his peace. This leader asked for orders from the Holy Saint, calling him to come and receive the blessing of the Holy Spirit. It was a soothing gesture. Other leaders he had met with recently showed him sympathy. His employees were especially devoted during those tough days, standing by him.

Making friends with bad people is like walking on thin ice,

Not knowing when you will fall into the water.

Making friends with a gentleman is like drinking from a summer spring.

The more you drink, the sweeter it becomes.

Despite the mess, the advice, and the confusing regulations, he found solace in the sincerity of a few good souls around him. In the end, it was the sweetness of genuine connections that kept him going.

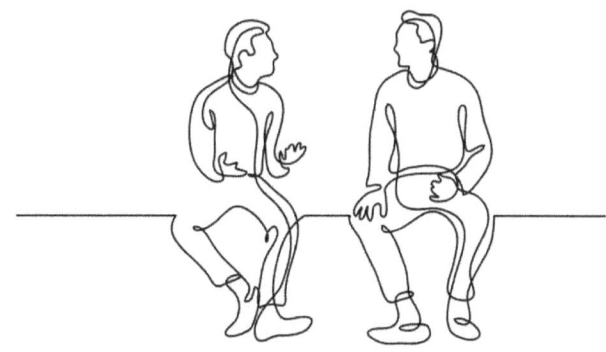

39. BREAKTHROUGH LEAP

Whether it's religion, spirituality, or science, they all acknowledge one profound truth: everything begins from nothing.

Modern physics tells us that the universe itself began with a big bang - an explosion from nothing. It may seem paradoxical, but within that void lies limitless potential.

You are no different. While your body is a gift from your parents, your spirit is a fragment of the universe, imbued with Love, Spirit, and Soul. This means your potential is boundless.

The key is learning to tap into and release this inner energy, much like harnessing the power of a nuclear reaction. To achieve this, you must embrace persistence, believe in your potential, and move forward without fear, even when faced with obstacles.

Trust in your journey, strengthen your inner reserves, and when the time is right, make that breakthrough leap.

40. SPIRITUAL ACTION

You should learn to let go of your breath until you feel as if you can't breathe on your own, yet still find yourself breathing. You were taught this, even though it seemed strange. You've pondered it for hours, recognizing that your mind resists this unfamiliar concept. Sometimes, you must acknowledge that the breath sustains itself, just as the Zen master said.

Over time, with each session growing longer, one part of your body becomes active while the rest remains completely relaxed. You will maintain a firm balance throughout the action, even if you can't explain why. The difference becomes clear and convincing. Between successful efforts and failed attempts, you finally understand that this 'enlightened' act refers to the 'mental power' of action. From now on, you will simply call it a 'spiritual' action.

41. TRUTH AND FEAR

He clearly understood that his organization's weaknesses stemmed from:

- **A lack of creativity**, which stifled innovation and left them trailing behind competitors.

- **A lack of discipline**, which allowed disorder and inefficiency to creep in.

- **A lack of talent**, which restricted their potential and made growth seem distant.

These realizations fed his fears, both personal and professional:

- The fear that gripped him when traveling by motorbike across high mountain passes, with deep abysses below, especially during treacherous rainstorms.

- The constant anxiety that the organization he had painstakingly built might crumble under pressure.

- The dread of monotonous tasks that lacked creativity, draining his spirit and dampening his drive.

In moments of reflection, he found himself contemplating the five fingers of his right hand, each a symbol of life's essential values:

- **Health**: The bedrock of all pursuits, without which nothing else is possible.

- **Love**: The bond that connects us, gives us purpose, and enriches our existence.

- **Wisdom**: The insight that guides us through life's challenges, helping us navigate with clarity.

- **Spirit**: The inner strength that fuels resilience, enabling us to rise above difficulties.

- **Belonging to the collective**: The recognition that we are part of a larger whole, interconnected and interdependent.

But life also brought its challenges, which he saw as symbolized by the five fingers of his left hand:

- **Illness**: The inevitable tests of health that remind us of our fragility.

- **Hatred**: The poison that corrodes relationships and breeds conflict.

- **Ineptitude**: The lack of skill that hinders progress and invites failure.

- **Ignorance**: The darkness that blinds us to truth and limits our potential.

- **Loneliness**: The void that isolates us, creating a sense of disconnection and vulnerability.

He realized that life is a delicate balance between these dual aspects. True peace comes not from denying the existence of challenges but from accepting them as part of the human experience. It's in the interplay between these forces that one finds the wisdom to live a fulfilled life.

A Life :

We are a universe full of telepathy,

Both hunter and wild animal.

Sometimes we are brave, sometimes we are afraid,

With heroic and cowardly experiences

Threaded throughout a lifetime.

Life's journey is a continuous balancing act between strength and vulnerability, light and darkness. By acknowledging both the gifts and the challenges we face, we cultivate a deeper understanding of ourselves and the world around us. In this balance lies the true essence of wisdom and peace.

42. A SEASON OF DISEASE

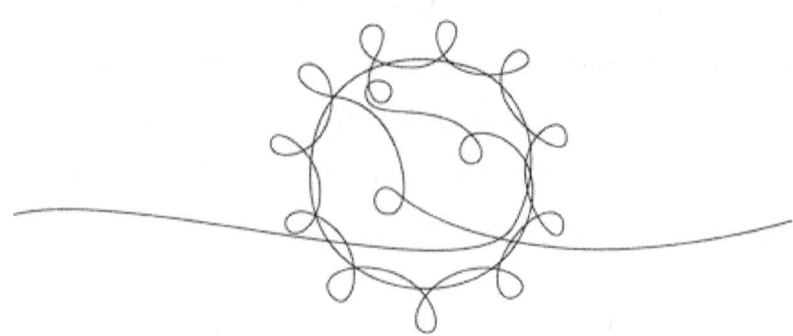

The disease raged on for another year, not diminishing but instead mutating into new and more dangerous variants.

He saw the world change - vehicles carrying bodies, hastily erected cremation grounds, overcrowded hospitals filled with muffled cries, frightened and panicked faces. Streets lay empty, fences stood tall, and the eerie cleanliness of dawn and dusk lingered like a ghost.

The disease had reached the big cities in his homeland, spreading through industrial parks and crowded markets. Each day, the number of infected grew with no sign of decline. People began to speak of hoarding medical supplies and food.

Every day, he met with colleagues online, sharing words of encouragement. Afterward, he would sit down and write continuously from morning to night. The promises made over the years gradually piled up, turning into a vast store of memories stained with the dust of time.

Death and the fleeting nature of life had awakened him.

He recalled the joys and pleasures, the trips and encounters, the victories and mistakes, the people and the animosities of the past - all now seemed like a distant dream.

There was nothing left.

43. THE REAL SELF

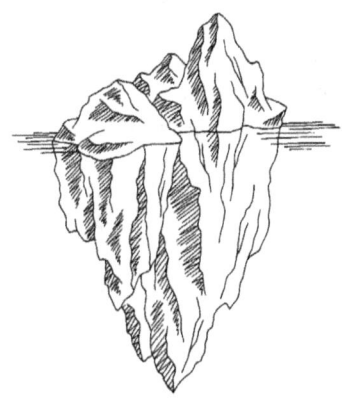

It's odd, isn't it? When we judge someone, we tend to rely on what we see - their outward expressions - and we proudly call that objectivity. But, let's be honest, this so-called objectivity is merely the surface of things, a peek into their subjectivity. The real understanding lies beneath the surface, in the sinking part of the iceberg.

Simply put, if we were to evaluate ourselves honestly, we'd quickly realize that our bad habits outnumber the good ones by a wide margin. Remember those school days when we tried to list our virtues and vices? After hours of soul-searching, we might have come up with a few lines of goodness and ability - but we could fill pages with flaws and weaknesses.

Now, fast forward almost 40 years, and I bet the proportions haven't improved much. Sure, we might have added a few more good lines, but let's face it, the list of flaws has probably grown longer too.

We like to present ourselves as strong, intelligent, elegant, kind, chivalrous, brave, subtle, tolerant, forgiving, generous, and faithful. But our real selves? Well, they're often weak, ignorant, vulgar, greedy, stingy, petty, competitive, obstinate, lethargic, dominating, and betraying.

Don't believe it? Go ahead, give yourself another honest look.

The silver lining? Despite being well-acquainted with these shortcomings, we also understand what is good, and we keep learning, striving, and rising - doing our best to stay afloat, like the tip of an iceberg.

44. THE GENTLE WAY

Mastery of the breath, as previously discussed, leads to obvious success. In time, you will find yourself able to engage with any task or subject in a state of complete relaxation.

After about 20 years of practice, you will discover how to act in a 'spiritual' way - effortlessly. This realization may seem subtle, but it brings a quiet joy and a deeper understanding of why people refer to this approach to life as 'the gentle way.'

As Lao Tzu wisely said, living rightly is like flowing water - adapting and harmonizing with the world around you.

45. AWESOME

I once watched a scene from Pink Floyd's "The Wall." A lifeless line of children marched into a factory, only to emerge as soulless sausages at the other end. It's a disturbing image, but it made me think - time isn't much different.

Time is like a cold, mechanical beast, a giant machine of gleaming gears. It grinds together the threads of love and hatred, weaving history, culture, traditions, and races into the tapestry of civilizations, nations, dynasties, and all the grand feats and follies of humanity.

But here's the kicker - the same mindless machine that creates all these wonders also devours them, crushing everything in its path, endlessly. Almost nothing is truly new. What seems different is just the current moment, ticking along to the relentless rhythm of time's wheel.

It's a bit terrifying, really! So, go ahead, give time a respectful bow - stand in awe of its power, but don't forget to laugh at the absurdity of it all!

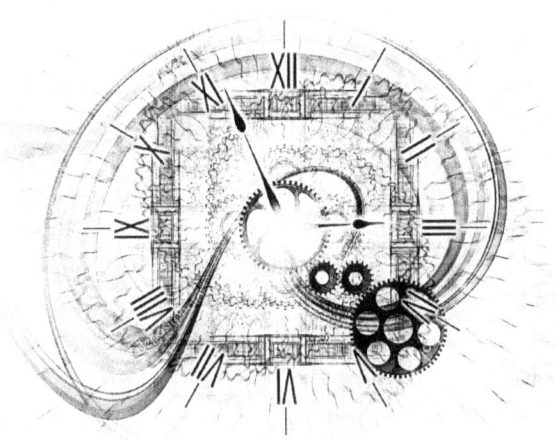

46. ILLNESS

It's time to think about his illness. The first time he heard the word was when the doctor called just after his plane touched down in Hanoi. The biopsy results were in, but he felt oddly normal. He went home, not giving it much thought.

But then he forgot about it entirely. From the airport, he headed straight to the office, diving into a marathon of meetings. Yesterday was no different - more meetings, project deadlines, and dealing with troublemakers trying to scam money.

When he finally got home, his children asked if it was cancer. He downplayed it, saying it was nothing serious, not wanting them to worry. They talked about fun things instead, though a bit of sadness lingered because his wife had told them the truth.

This morning, the first thing that crossed his mind was… cancer. *Haizzz... what to do?* A quick Google search, of course.

"If I had only five years left, how would it be?" he wondered.

He picked up a book, "Untie the Soul," and read a few pages. The wisdom within hit him: Death is the greatest teacher. You must come to terms with the Death God's arrival - whether it's a few years or just a few months away.

So, what to do now? Focus on what truly matters.

You're swimming in an ocean of raging sounds,

Inside and outside of your mind.

These are the calls to wake you up.

But you must stay still to be aware.

All renunciation is salvation.

So rinse it all away - desire, lust, fame.

47. TOUGH TIME

This year he faced the daunting task of restructuring his organization, but the pandemic struck, and the strict demands from upper management made the mission feel nearly impossible.

He scribbled down his options:

1. Move forward with its risks.

2. Fail to progress, with its own set of risks.

3. Consider a Merger and Acquisition, and then tackle the risks that follow.

Was stoic acceptance his only way out?

Acceptance?

• Don't demand or be greedy.

• Don't chase what you can't control.

• It's unsettling but clear.

And then, a familiar thought surfaced - *Cause and Effect.*

Cause and Effect

Hey man, the arrogant,

Why do you turn a blind eye

To what you must do?

As a righteous person, do you dare to accept?

Be careful, for the day karma comes back to you.

***

"You, like me, just came out of mud and clay."

He chuckled at the last line, realizing the truth in it. No matter how high he aimed, or how complicated the challenges seemed, the simplicity of cause and effect grounded him. After all, even in the mess of restructuring and looming risks, he was just another soul, molded by the same forces of life, trying to find his way.

With a sigh and a smile, he decided to take the day one step at a time, not demanding too much, and not fearing what he couldn't control. Because in the end, he, like everyone else, was just trying to navigate the tough times - mud, clay, and all.

48. THE MEANING OF LIFE

You've spent years searching for the meaning of life, haven't you? Along the way, you've hit milestones, gained new insights, and edged closer to understanding both yourself and the grand puzzle of existence.

The meaning of life, it turns out, is a bit like fashion - it changes with the seasons, depending on what you're after at the moment. But, despite the shifting trends, there are five timeless truths that remain constant:

- You want to do what you love.

- You want to do what you're good at.

- You want to do something that pays the bills.

- You want to contribute to society and your community.

- You want to live in harmony with your sacred beliefs.

Throughout your journey, you've found ways to tick off a few of these boxes. But something always felt a little… off, like a cake missing its icing. Half-meaning happiness, if you will.

Now, the light bulb goes on. Life becomes wonderfully simple when you find work and a way of living that satisfies all five of these conditions at once. That's the moment when life is truly meaningful, a time to savor every bite of this rich, full cake we call existence.

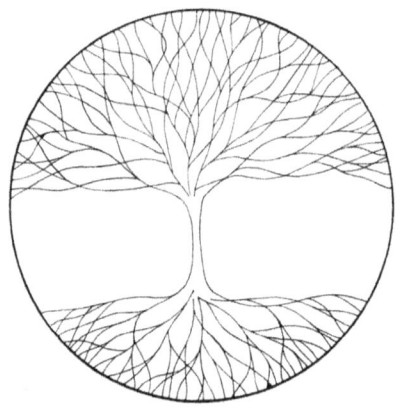

49. EFFECTIVE INTERACTION

When is the right time to truly understand the effectiveness of your interactions? Up until now, you've been focused on using tools to interact with the world around you, but without fully grasping the impact of those actions. Directly acting on an object, even as part of your practice, only touches its surface, leaving you unable to accurately gauge the results. Sometimes it works well, other times not at all, and often it falls somewhere in between. Why? You find yourself unable to fully grasp the essence of the interaction.

50. HUMANITY

The ancient Chinese once said, *"Human nature is good,"* and if you strive to cultivate yourself, you can become wise, even noble. Meanwhile, another ancient sage countered, *"Human nature is evil."* Yet with education, humans can become better - more or less, depending on the individual.

So, the advice often given is: it's better to lean toward good than to drift toward evil. From a personal perspective, both views can be right, which is why they say personality is a work in progress. After all, the definitions of Good vs. Evil or More vs. Less are all a bit... relative.

Buddha had his take too: *"All sentient beings without exception have a Buddha nature and can practice to become enlightened like Buddha."*

He explained that the mind is like the ground - everything sprouts from it, whether Good or Bad, True or False, Pure or Evil. The key is to cultivate the mind, to purify the body, and reveal the bright nature within.

So, perhaps the goal isn't the most important thing; it's the process. The journey from suffering to happiness, from delusion to clarity, from evil to good, and from failure to success. Whether your aim is internal or external, every step marks the progress of your inner growth.

When you focus on the process, you start to see the unity of Evil and Good. You begin to realize that everything is interconnected - nothing should be sharply divided. The world is full of possibilities, yes, and a bit of a mess too. But when you learn to purify your mind, you start revealing the good nature within.

The process is like a lotus growing from the mud, reaching out of the water to catch the light and bloom. Mud, water, light, and air - all are essential for the lotus to grow.

Now, picture two people on opposite sides of a battle line, confronting each other. Both understand the truth of good and evil, both have a Buddha nature, yet they still clash. If you think, *"Well, they're only human,"* you might find it in you to sympathize.

And if one of those adversaries happens to be you, you might become even more compassionate and just. This is especially true when you reach a point where you can feel grateful for those who have treated you badly.

You've reached the time when you no longer harbor resentment in your heart.

51. FLUENTLY

Speech is the verbal expression of thought, and writing is its non-verbal sibling. It's why, as children, we first learn to speak and then tackle the art of writing.

But in today's world, flooded with information from both the virtual and real realms, many of us read and write less, opting instead to watch and absorb. The habits of reading, jotting down notes, and crafting sentences are slowly fading into oblivion.

As a result, people often stumble over their words when speaking, and their writing? Well, it's often a tangled mess. Ideas, sentences, and words overlap, repeat, and intertwine like a ball of yarn in a cat's paws, leaving the meaning vague and ambiguous.

So, to untangle this mess and make your thoughts coherent, it's time to pick up a book again. Cultivate the habit of writing. And if you can, persistently record those memorable events that dot your life.

And here's a tip: writing by hand with a pen and notebook often yields more thoughtful results than tapping away on some mechanical device.

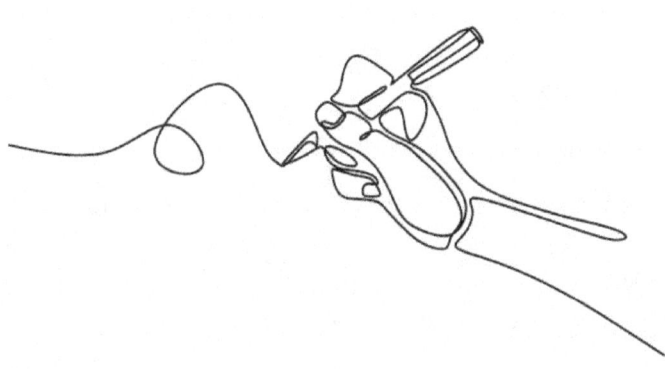

52. THE PRESENT MOMENT

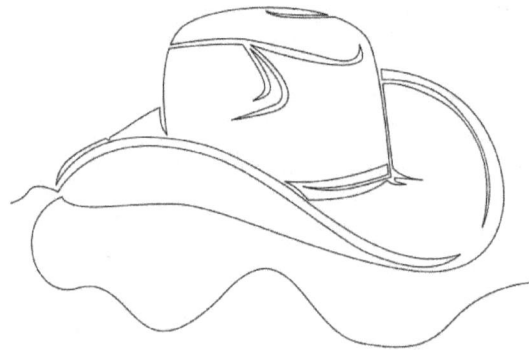

You've long understood that the present moment is all that truly matters. The past and future are mere wisps of thought, elusive and intangible. Yet, embracing the present fully can be challenging.

Daily thoughts and worries weave a dense fog around your mind. The more you dwell on them, the more entangled you become, which does little to bring clarity.

Let Me Offer You

My lady, with a cup of sweet wine,

There's not much left of our thirty-six thousand days.

I offer you this calyx, without a hint of regret,

On bended knee, let me present it to you.

53. SHAKING

Over the years, you've put in relentless effort, constantly adjusting, correcting, and pushing yourself forward. When you faltered, you regained your will, sought help, and tried your best. Yet, the line between success and failure often remains elusive. Some endeavors, despite immense effort, still ended in failure, while others, seemingly unplanned and effortless, brought unexpected success. It's difficult to pinpoint why - perhaps a mix of luck, hard work, and skill honed over time.

There were moments when you could have acted swiftly, while others hesitated. But in the end, you found yourself moving slowly, finishing last, outpaced by those who once seemed far behind. In this way, both you and your career have been shaking, struggling to find a steady rhythm.

54. A GAME

Life is like the ebb and flow of nature - one moment fresh and blooming, the next withered and fading. It's a cycle of seasons, where sunshine and rain play their unpredictable game. Sometimes, it feels like we're merely players in the Creator's grand game. That's why we often say, *'Life is a Game.'*

Passion

Passion is a wild and unpredictable dance.

It's the bittersweet taste that lingers on your lips.

Yet, it's passion that colors the canvas of life,

Turning the ordinary into something unforgettable.

55. SYMPATHY

The night before, I was flooded with touching birthday wishes and heartfelt clips. Early the next morning, I joined a group of employees on a visit to the Zen Monastery in Squirrel Mountain. We spent the day cleaning the garden, sharing a frugal lunch, and practicing meditation. The atmosphere was filled with joy and tranquility.

I couldn't quite tell what they thought as they saw me - thinner, frailer - but their eyes were full of sympathy and sincere promises.

On the eve of our gratitude day for customers and the community, a monk, a close friend, reminded me that only optimism and love can conquer both disease and hardship.

I realized I need strength and energy to heal both my body and mind.

"You must find the wellspring of your soul,

Write the song of your life,

And play that melody yourself,

For your body to resonate like a lute."

56. DRAMA – UNJUST

After much effort, his friend finally met with the boss. That afternoon, his friend called him in a panic, asking for an urgent meeting.

Upon entering his room, after respectfully acknowledging the Buddha statues on the wall, his friend sat down, looking both sad and out of breath. He then recounted the meeting with the boss.

What was supposed to be a brief 10-minute discussion turned into almost an hour-long session, mostly filled with the boss's complaints about his organization's weaknesses, his management team's flaws, and even several unflattering comments about his character - arrogant, ignorant, deceitful, a breaker of promises, and someone who never bothers to meet with customers or responsible parties.

His friend was visibly shaken, mentally disturbed, and deeply disappointed.

He knew his organization inside out. It was a place where thousands of people had been giving their all for the past 6-7 years. Sure, there were shortcomings, but those people had been working diligently, despite receiving little to no significant support. The only advice they'd ever received was to "be patient." They had self-advocated with a shared spirit of compliance with the law. And as for himself, he'd been sick, even shaved his head at times, yet still managed to care for the organization. When did he ever go out (except to see investors) and act arrogantly toward anyone?

Flipping through the pages of Buddha's teachings in weariness, he stumbled upon a passage that suggested being unjust in this life could be the result of having scolded many in a past life...

"Well, it's karma," he mused. *"I suppose we have ourselves to blame."*

> ***Accept***
>
> *People say that I'm ignorant and arrogant*
>
> *While they hold positions, talent, and virtue*
>
> *What's wrong if I fall in love with flowers and books*
>
> *With being alone and away from the noise?*

57. LETTER TO MY SON

To my beloved son,

Daddy hopes you're feeling better and happier now that your friends and sister have visited. At home, Mommy is very worried about you. She's ready to fly out to see you as soon as she can.

Daddy misses you a lot too, but I'm not overly worried. I believe in your strength, and I know you'll get well soon. Everyone goes through tough moments like this when they're young. It's like a tree growing from the ground - it has to face all four seasons: the chilly Spring with fresh flowers and singing birds, the hot Summer with stormy winds and sudden rain, the gloomy Autumn with falling leaves and long showers, and the cold Winter with dark clouds. But the tree keeps growing steadily, getting stronger through it all.

When Daddy went to school far from home, I had my own crises and worries. Back then, I worried about a long-distance relationship with a girlfriend who might no longer love or miss me. I also worried about studying, what if I couldn't pass those tough exams? I didn't have many friends, so I was often alone, sometimes going a whole week without talking to anyone. The mood could get heavy, but gradually, every worry passed away, just like a tree growing through the seasons.

Daddy was in love with a smart and beautiful girl, but she was stubborn, and we often argued. Even though we lived in different cities and barely saw each other, every time we met, we argued... It was exhausting. Traveling back and forth to see her often left me sick and broke. I only had a scholarship, and the train ticket cost a week's worth of food... Those were hard times, but looking back, I see how those difficulties, along with her stubbornness, helped me grow up.

Eventually, she broke up with Daddy. At first, I was very angry, but after a few years, I realized I needed to thank her. She helped me mature, and I'm not mad at her anymore. In fact, we became close friends after that. I share this story with you because I believe you'll understand.

Daddy sees you practicing at the gym with great discipline, and I know you'll be stronger than I ever was. It's late now, nearly midnight here in Vietnam. I'm staying at a hotel in Saigon after a long day of endless meetings, so I'll stop here. The doctor says I should sleep eight hours a night, starting at 9 p.m., but I usually only get five hours... so busy.

I hope you stay healthy, study well for your exams, and come home with me in the summer. Then, let's go on a road trip across the country, and I'll share more stories about my school days and my funny experiences.

Remember to stay strong and come back to help me out... I'm over 50 now and getting older...

Daddy's off to bed now. Kissing you.

Solitary

Lonely in the high garden, under the moonlight shining,

Far away from the chaos, beside the flower trembling.

An empty quiet place, in a bright cold house,

It is the mind, busy thinking about life.

58. SMOOTH COMBINATION

"All that you have learned so far has merely prepared you for the spiritual journey. Now, we face a new and more challenging task that demands a higher level of professional artistry," the Zen master would say.

At this moment, the Zen master within you might take out a special instrument, performing a flawless act that connects your entire body with the object in front of you. The movement flows seamlessly, from beginning to end - fierce and decisive, yet gentle and soft, as if it took no effort at all. This Zen master could be anyone and may appear when you least expect it. It could be a professional in the field, or just the voice in your mind, emerging when you learn to pay attention, observe, listen, and seek understanding after months of diligent training, getting bruised, and maturing in relation to the object.

From this moment, you begin to comprehend and perceive the continuous process of interaction with the object - a series of movements and states that smoothly combine together. It is as if your body and mind, the entirety of your being, and the object become a unified whole. You realize that from here on, all your interactions are a journey through the object, characterized by flexibility, harmony, and unity.

Your level of interaction with the object has become reasonable, natural, smooth, and most effective, aligning perfectly with the desires of your mind. According to the spiritual teacher, interacting with objects, whether in work or play, is very simple and requires no effort because, in essence, it is all just play.

59. TOUGH RELATION

He's got a knack for making friends, even with people he's just met. With those caring eyes, thoughtful words, and warm hugs, he has a way of moving others. He never forgets the small details - the little things most people overlook but that leave a lasting impact.

*

Every morning, I feed the pets and watch them gather around. In the afternoon, I play with them, seeing them happy, mischievous, and close-knit. But once, I was away for a week. When I returned, I rushed to see them. Epi, the cat-fox, ran to me immediately, curled up on my lap, begging for attention. But the others - Rosette, Purple Brown, Grey, and Snowy, who usually scratch, bite, and tumble around me - gave me the cold shoulder.

*

From the balcony, I can see the sprawling city, with its undulating buildings and winding streets, but they leave me indifferent. It's only the potted green plants swaying in the breeze that stir something in me, reminding me of a small stream murmuring through the forest, purple flowers lining a path, or a cluster of white-capped mushrooms on a rotting tree - memories that stay with you long after you've left the jungle or the mountains.

*

I've come to realize that building a good relationship requires a keen eye for detail and genuine care for the little things. Grand gestures often go unnoticed. It's exhausting! If you don't want to bother, then maybe it's best not to do anything at all. Don't rely on anyone, don't ask for anything, and don't make friends.

Wait a minute... Are we humans or pets? Or maybe we're humans who want to be pets? Or perhaps we're pets trying to be humans?

Who knows? Maybe we're just a bit of both.

60. BEING HAPPY WHEN BEING SAD

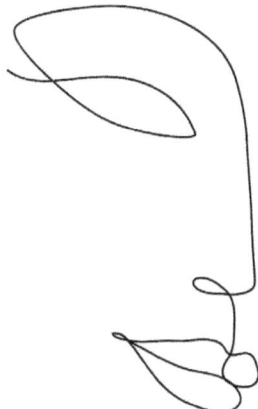

After being discharged from the hospital, he found himself thrust back into a whirlwind of meetings. With crutches under his arms, every step was a struggle. His experienced employees were either on sick leave or off on business trips, while his family and relatives were miles away. The new employee, eager but inexperienced, had made a mess of things. Lying in bed, staring at a full schedule, he felt the weight of it all press down on him, sinking into a pool of gloom.

He couldn't shake the feeling of incompleteness. He had ventured into trading early but had been late to manufacturing. He had delved into real estate in leading provinces but still lagged behind. He had been a pioneer in finance, yet somehow ended up the smallest player. Thoughts of unshared feelings for those who had passed - his teachers, his mother - haunted him. The sadness pulled him deeper into a spiral of regret.

But then, memories of happier times began to surface. He thought of traveling around the country with his teacher, of being wrapped in his mother's warm embrace. Yes, the work hadn't always gone as planned, but he had still accomplished some meaningful things - the first new urban area in certain provinces, a memorable art show called "Memory," and the journey through thick and thin with his colleagues. He had done some good for life, for people, and for himself.

So, he realized, he did have reasons to smile.

Let's forget the current worries - it's just life, after all. Why not enjoy it? Smile at the difficulties and find the positives.

> *"Mistakes are fertilizer for good things to come;*
>
> *Use them to nurture the good fruits..."*

61. LIGHT UP

It's only when you're sick, lying in a hospital bed, that you realize no one can be sick for you, no matter how close they are. Especially when they're far away. In that solitude, you understand - you have to light the fire in your heart yourself.

*

I am joy,

I am sadness,

I crave pleasure,

I thirst for sweetness.

I am a flowing stream,

Driven by strong desires,

Knowing the road ahead is long.

But after the cold winter,

Cozy warmth will return,

As spring shines bright tomorrow.

*

Light that fire, let it burn with passion, and carry you through the darkest nights. For in your heart, you hold the power to bring warmth, even when the world feels cold.

62. THE FULLEST

As time passes and after years of chasing our desires, you gradually come to understand that nothing lasts forever. In the end, all you can carry with you is a faint memory of the things that happened. The images, silhouettes, smiles, bracelets, sayings, the moments of sadness and happiness - they all fade away.

So, you're told to live in the present.

But how can that be, when your mind and body are constantly worrying, acting unconsciously for the future? Even when you meditate in silence, the mind keeps wandering.

Yet, in those rare moments when you're passionately in love, lost in desire, longing to possess, or deep in disappointment and endless silence - that's when you realize that the present is the only beautiful and pure eternity that truly exists.

And that's what it means to live fully in the present, what Zen masters call *Mindfulness*.

Dust

The sun shines bright on every day of toil,

The full moon's joy, a silent, monthly spoil.

The fountain of love and comfort guards your trust,

Embrace it all, for in the end, we all return to dust.

63. THE LIFE CYCLE

Last night, colors sparkled bright,

Dreamy music and dancing light,

With passion, the wine flowed free.

Tonight, far from the festive tree,

Shadows linger under the streetlight's glow,

Lonely steps in places unknown.

Years have wandered in melancholy's embrace,

Pilgrimage to life's rhythm,

A cycle of time, a journey full of grace.

Yet I wake at dawn, heart beating strong,

Eager to embrace the day's new song.

Out there, life's bitter and sweet tides sweep the past away,

I take and give it all, with love that lasts.

I know life is worth every breath,

Though moments of hardship may come,

Be strong, wait for danger to pass,

Forget hatred, let forgiveness become.

Generosity heals the heart's deepest scars,

In winter's chill, life's tree begins anew,

As spring's warmth whispers, "Hope is true."

64. SUDDEN

Let go of thoughts about what needs to be done and how to do it. True actions flow effortlessly when the moment arises unexpectedly. It happens naturally when you strike the right chord at the right time. No need to exert force or apply pressure deliberately. Simply allow the moment to unfold, and the right action will arise on its own."

PART 3: PURSUIT

A Moment of Emptiness

Whenever I feel empty, I often dive into various thoughts about life - the things I'm involved in, their purposes, for whom and for what they are meant, and where they might lead. Sometimes, life seems to stand still, and I struggle to find a way out. All paths seem narrow and tangled, and I'm never sure if the one I've taken is the right one.

At such times, I often try to separate myself, going somewhere empty and quiet to meditate. That time, I went to Bhutan - a happy and peaceful country I had long heard about - to admire the natural beauty of the mountains and hills, and to learn more about Tantra, a somewhat mysterious practice derived from Buddhism, intertwined with Tantric Yoga. Both have their origins in India but found their true flourishing in Tibet - the land of snow - before spreading to the lands around the Himalayas. Bhutan is one of those countries that still retains the purity of this mystical branch of Tantra.

Today, I gather notes from the journey, recalling past experiences - moments that flash in my mind. Simple, close things I thought about all the time but never truly grasped. I may not have found all the answers to my questions, but I've come to know myself better, getting closer to the root of my life's troubles. This has brought me a lot of inner peace to move forward.

The Winding Path

I arrived in Bhutan in the early afternoon, my mind already racing with thoughts about what I might discover. The car wound its way around hills and narrow roads. On one side, high mountains and lush green forests stretched out; on the other, a deep, winding river hugged the mountainside, with scattered houses perched along the banks. The fresh colors of the houses shone in the sunset, with distant mountains wrapped in white clouds.

We stopped by the roadside, and I stepped out into the vast space, taking in the endless sky, inhaling the fresh breeze. The houses seemed familiar, as if I had seen them before in a dream. Suddenly, I heard a soft song, and a bird spread its wings, flying across the trees and disappearing. I couldn't help but wonder, where was it headed in such a hurry?

"On the mountainside stands a house.

In the sky, a bird spreads its wings.

Where are you heading?"

The River's Whisper

The house I rented leaned against the mountain, facing the river. All night, I heard the sound of rushing water, a natural lullaby. At dawn, I followed the stone steps to the water's edge. Waves crashed on the shore, water overflowed with white foam, murmuring sounds of endless happiness. The morning sun rose, shining brightly on the far side of the hill. I suddenly felt that the busy days were gone, like they belonged to another lifetime…

"With worries about fame,

Wandering for years,

For miles, then here.

The water keeps flowing."

The Master's Invitation

I made an appointment to visit a Zen master's house in the mountains. A few weeks earlier, he had come down from his retreat to teach me some practices. His retreat usually lasts seven years, but he had entered his eighth year and planned to remain in seclusion for eleven years, only coming out when absolutely necessary. Because he knew I had come from afar, he politely broke his rule and opened the door for me. At the end of the course, he returned to his retreat but invited me to visit his monastery.

The path followed the mountainside through the forest. Scattered pagoda roofs peeked through the trees and cliffs. Groups of people went up and down, with a few monks in red robes walking slowly, smiling, and mumbling mantras.

This country is full of dogs - everywhere. With friendly faces, they lie around, lounging or playing. And, of course, they are never heard barking. Dogs and humans live in harmony, each enjoying peace in their own way. But the sleeping dogs are the most peaceful sight - happy, content. Perhaps happiness really is just getting plenty of sleep. Busy walking, my hand brushed against the forest leaves as I pondered what happiness truly is. Suddenly, I saw a long wooden bench under the eaves, submerged in the green canopy, in the sunlight with a few forest flowers scattered about. A dog was stretching its limbs, sleeping soundly.

"Oh, the old bench on the roadside.

A good dog in its sound sleep.

People's voices heard."

The Monks' Retreat

I followed the seemingly endless stone steps, through the forest and mountains, under the shining sun and windy clouds. On a hidden path, a few houses appeared behind the groves. There were no longer paved roads, just a few dirt paths covered in weeds and vines. Passing a few huts with brown corrugated iron roofs exposed to the sun, with sketchy fences slanting with the trees and entrance gates locked from the outside, the guide explained that these were occupied by monks in retreat. The doors were locked to warn tourists not to enter. The scene was lonely, but strangely, wildflowers bloomed everywhere, and a few scattered wild orchids hung from the roofs. My heart felt lightened, relieved.

"Monastery locked.

Weeds everywhere.

Purple flowers welcome."

The Bridge of Silence

One day, I visited an ancient monastery, a former rock-walled fortress high in the mountains. It was surrounded by a small, fast-flowing river. We needed to cross a wooden bridge with long eaves over the river. The silver wooden boards bore footprints from countless pilgrims. The blowing wind made the colorful Buddhist flags flutter on the ropes. The sound of the flowing river mixed with the sound of the flags. There was no one around, just a yellow and wooden puppy sleeping in the middle of the bridge.

"Trodden path.

Flowing river.

Blowing wind,

Fluttering flag.

Sleeping dog,

On the bridge."

The Rooster's Domain

The monastery was bathed in sunshine, devoid of people. White stone walls, intertwined square and round wooden doorways, and sharp rising peaks on the roofs of the golden towers. I wandered, admiring the altars with majestic Buddha statues. It was sunny outside, but here, rows of candles flickered at the feet of the Buddha. I walked slowly along the stones lining the yard. Along the corridor, a big rooster walked as if he owned the place. Then suddenly, he stopped and puffed out his chest. In that moment of silence came the deep voice of prayer.

"Empty monastery.

Sunny yard.

White rooster spreads its wings.

Distant prayers."

The Pine's Bloom

Once, I busily walked through the overgrown forest, eyes glued to my feet due to the steep climb. Sparse sunlight shone through the thick foliage. Then we reached a place where the wind blew, trees stood behind us, and mountains lay ahead. The vast sky was embraced by bright white clouds. A large pine tree with a rough trunk, covered in green moss, rose from the mountainside. A deep hollow in the tree revealed a small flower. I didn't know its name, but in the midst of the vast sky, it bloomed fully. The old pine seemed to share in its happiness.

"A few branches,

Smiling,

A yellow bloom."

The Old Wooden Door

In the courtyard of the monastery, dogs lay or sat everywhere - white, black, yellow, brown - each with a different look, but all seemingly well-fed. Passing through the thick wooden gate, I saw a fierce, yellow-faced dog squinting as if just woken up. As I walked over, he peeked but didn't move. One door was closed, the other open, with the dog lying right at the sill, his knee resting on it. Behind him were stone and brick steps with some grass poking through. The door was small, but the wooden frame was thick, painted black and yellow, stained by years of time. Tiny white dots dotted the stains of time. We, the dog and I, might not see each other again. "Keep sleeping," I thought.

"Lazy dog awoke.

Under the frame,

Tinged with time,

Piled stones,

A few weeds."

The Monkeys' Cliff

On the way to the nearby city, I stopped on a pass. High mountains stretched far. The cliff close to the road was steep, with a few small rocks on which sat two monkeys, one old and one young, side by side, both looking in one direction. Following their gaze, I saw a few warm green-roofed houses nestled on the mountainside, with smoke rising from the chimneys. In the canyon below, a rolling river flowed.

"Afar mountains,

Houses with smoke.

Cool river,

Lonesome cliff and monkeys."

The Tower's View

I finally climbed to the top of the monastery's tallest tower, located at the top of the hill. From here, the view of the city was spectacular. Everything below seemed small and bright. All peaks were craggy. But the most interesting thing was that this was where we all come from.

"High sky, rolling clouds,

Winding river flows.

Oh, from a small window, I watch life."

Sunset Hurry

Now, I come back from the mountain, the old road curving through many forests. Quick footsteps, no one seen. The afternoon was approaching, the forest dyed with golden light, the air cool. Only mountains and forests. My mind just wandered.

"Time for sunset,

Forest moving,

No one to be seen.

Why in a hurry?"

The Sacred Path

After a period of quiet cultivation, my son came to join us from the United States. We spent happy days together, peacefully in an empty inn far from the city. Early that morning, we departed to visit the most famous temple in the country. The road was difficult, but horses leisurely carried us along, and the tiredness melted away. Only the last part of the journey, when we had to dismount and climb the mountain, was arduous. Along the way, the scenery was full of life, and I met a few travelers. We walked and talked all the way, so the journey didn't feel long.

The roof of the pagoda soon appeared, nestled on the other side of the mountain. The high mountain stood tall, the famous temple looked humble from afar. Surely, thanks to much human effort, the monastery was built here. Then, I suddenly saw before my eyes a small tree stretching out two branches with flowers - one white, one pink - radiant in the morning sun. The swaying green leaves still held a few drops of dew. The sacred ancient pagoda with old legends rose majestically in the sky.

Humans are great, but nature is magical. There is something secret, deeper than what we utter.

"The pagoda on the mountainside,

Quiet with time,

Little rose rising proud."

Yellow Flowers in the Wind

After contemplating the sacred and listening to the legends of the Buddha Padmasambhava - the heroic miracle who attained the union of Compassion and Wisdom - we returned along the old path. A little nostalgic, mourning the distant history mixed with the near miracle. The horse kept passing through the forests. Something was left behind with regret and longing. Then I saw on the roadside fallen leaves, new green grass groves, and yellow flowers emerging, smiling and swaying in the wind.

"Walking on an empty canyon,

My heart feels so happy.

Just met a few yellow flower buds to say hello."

The Dog's Watch

At one rest area, there was a small shrine with a prayer wheel containing Buddhist scriptures. Pilgrims passing by often spin the wheel many times, praying for good things, hoping to accumulate good karma and purify the body and mind. I, too, came there and spun the wheel a few times. Walking away, I looked back and saw, right in front of the shrine, a smooth, shiny black-haired dog with four yellow legs and a yellow tummy. He sat with his back to the shrine, looking at the visitors. Perhaps he had accumulated merits by guarding the Buddhist scriptures.

"The prayer wheel in an empty shrine

Waiting for pilgrims to turn.

Why does the dog look away?"

A Shared Path

I went ahead, my son followed, and the horse walked rhythmically. The mountains and forests receded. I thought about how I should live in this life, what I should do to accumulate merits for future generations. Returning to the city, with all its calculations, intents, and considerations, it would be difficult to keep peace of mind. The street was empty of people; everything was bright and strange. Only flags with colorful sutras stretched across the way. I brought back a little echo of the Buddha.

"Father and son from different places

Rarely spend time together.

Finding peace, walking the same path."

Homeward Reflection

Coming back to my country, I returned to daily life - the familiar rhythm of nearly 30 years. Time faded away more or less the things learned, filling me with numerous daily worries. The vortex of work sweeps us along, and sometimes we think we'll wait until retirement to live more fully. In fact, for many years, my relatives have been away. I only come home to see a few security drivers, clean up, and enjoy familiar dishes. In the past three years, most of the food has been vegetables and seeds. So, working continuously seems to be the optimal alternative.

However, with longing for the peaceful moments I had in that happy country and the demands of my body, I took up the habit of leaving the office before dark. I gradually resumed my old passions - writing books and poems, reading stories, watching movies, listening to music, practicing meditation, yoga… Quite exciting, but anyway, living alone requires a strong will. So, you need to practice a lot.

One day, I came home earlier than usual. Maybe there were still a few rays of sunset through the lush trees in the garden. Entering the courtyard through a familiar alley, I was stunned to see my daughter's dog, Haichi, standing pensively by the Bodhi tree. He seemed to be contemplating or waiting for someone in peace. He has aged with the years since my daughter went away for her studies. Like me, he has gradually gotten used to the solitude of the house. Who was he waiting for? Or was he also meditating, as he used to when his mistress sat here? I did not know. From whom do we learn? Why do we search so far for peace? Then I felt Tagore's words deeply:

"I have spent a fortune

traveling to distant shores

and looked at lofty mountains

and boundless oceans,

And yet I haven't found

time to take a few steps

from my house to look at

a single dew drop on

a single blade of grass."

1. GOING AROUND

On the way to the airport, I noticed a gray-haired man squatting on a bench at an empty bus stop, his austere face bent over a food box. Beside him, a red hand-drawn suitcase stood alone, looking as out of place as the overcast sky. Very few travelers were around.

Well, it's just a meal, after all. Everyone's got to eat, even monks need to go for alms. But what's life really for? Is all this hard struggle worth it?

Forward, backward - where are we all heading? For a woman, for convenience, for wealth, for fame, or just for the sake of competition... Everyone's going somewhere, planning something, eating, meeting, resting... only to set off again early tomorrow. We could be eating while walking, worrying while acting, sleeping while seething with anger...

Everything's constantly on the move.

"When someone offers you a helping hand with money, fame, or affection,

Don't look at the hand or what's being offered, but at the person."

2. LEARNING TO KEEP BALANCE

Changing a way of life? It's no small feat. Caught between the comfort of the old and the desire to change today. Between the demands of the present and the expectations of the future. Balancing this delicate dance is nothing short of an art form. But still, you've got to try. One must be able to do it.

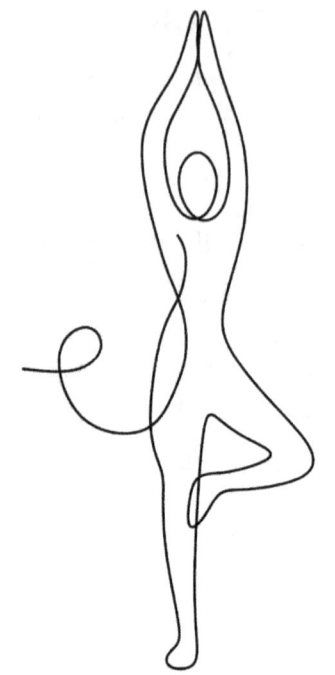

Sure, if you could just drop everything, retreat to the mountains, leave behind the noisy city, and live in silence... that would be fantastic! You'd live the life you've always wanted. But let's face it, that's not happening - at least not anytime soon.

And you can't just wait until it's possible. You've got to start balancing things right now. Every single day. It takes a lot of energy and courage. "Determination" and "Persistence" will be your best friends.

"Open your heart and open more,

Open wide the circle of existence.

Learn to unite all within.

You will find the way of clarity."

3. WEB OF LIFE

Buddha warns us to steer clear of greed, hatred, and ignorance. Why? Probably because they're so darn tempting and hard to avoid. If it were easy, Buddha wouldn't need to remind us.

He also teaches us to embrace love, compassion, joy, and equanimity, not just for ourselves but for everyone around us. Sounds simple enough, right? But the truth is, it's anything but easy.

And here's the twist: If you've never played the game of life with all its greed, hate, and ignorance, how would you know their pitfalls? How can you truly appreciate the value of love and compassion if you haven't grappled with suffering or the impermanence of the world?

At the start, we're all like pristine white silk threads. Life, with all its experiences, dyes and weaves us into something unique - a fabric of patterns and shapes. We're like worms spinning our own cocoons, patiently weaving, growing, and eventually breaking free to become butterflies.

So, when you're tangled up in greed, hatred, and ignorance, you're that worm in a cocoon. But when you embrace love, compassion, joy, and equanimity, you emerge as a butterfly, fluttering freely in the vastness of life.

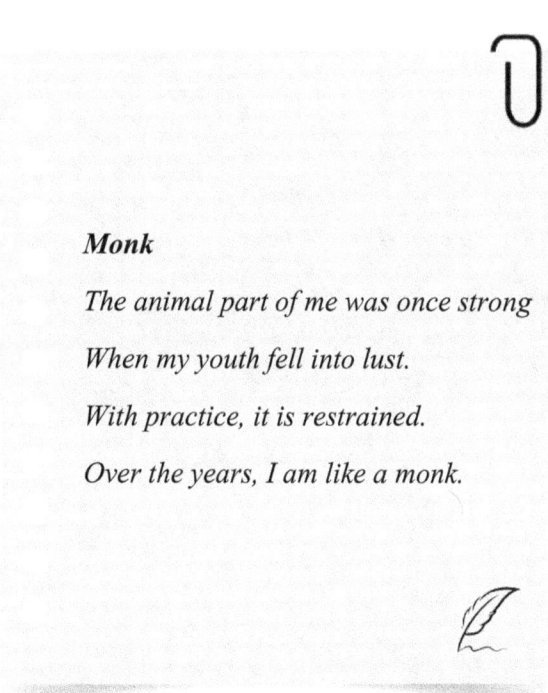

Monk

The animal part of me was once strong

When my youth fell into lust.

With practice, it is restrained.

Over the years, I am like a monk.

4. SOULLESS

After weeks, months, and even years of intense practice, you begin to develop your own yardstick to measure the true essence of professional interaction with honesty. But success doesn't always come easily. Sometimes, despite your best efforts, the interaction misses the mark, and the results fall short of expectations.

When you try to force things, you find the outcome even worse, disappointing both you and those around you. If you push too hard on your colleagues, the pressure only reflects back on you, creating constant stress that affects everyone. The result is often a resounding zero, and you find yourself slowly unraveling, both physically and mentally.

You stand there, motionless, your limbs stiff with the weight of your own strain. The sense of ease you once had is gone, and your spiritual master laughs gently, seeing you as if you were a lifeless stone statue.

5. LIFE PRINCIPLE

This morning, my son shared his worries with me - his concerns about his studies, the sadness over his recent breakup, missing school friends, and the anxiety about finding a place to rent in the near future.

As we chatted by the waterfall in the garden, memories came flooding back. I told him about my first love and the ups and downs of my own life. With a few words, I boiled down three key principles:

· **Rely on yourself.** No one can walk your path for you.

· **Live in harmony.** Life's rhythm is easier to dance to when you're in sync with it.

· **Awaken to the present.** Mindfulness leads to fulfillment, and fulfillment resides in the now.

Digging a well

"You must make earnest efforts

To dig deep the well of life,

Until you find the underground spring

That nourishes your soul."

6. RECITING THE BUDDHIST SUTRAS

When chanting Buddhist sutras, whether in Vietnamese, Thai, Burmese, or Sanskrit… whether you understand the words or not, you can sense the letting go, the journey into solitude, the embrace of emptiness, and the quiet acceptance of life's impermanence. You feel the echoes of grief, farewell, and the silent promise of enlightenment.

The verses in Buddhism are like a warm embrace - calm, loving, and gentle. They comfort, fill, and cleanse the spirit. They remind you of the adventure of life, encouraging you to keep moving forward, even when the path is uncertain. They flow like a peaceful stream, endlessly fresh, absorbing your worries and replacing them with serenity.

Sincerely

"Praying silently at the feet of the Buddha,

Praying to Him for the way to peace.

Yet the debt of the world still clings,

The mind still seeks the tranquil place."

7. THE SECOND LIFE

Today, he sits down to write a plan for the next thirty years - the rest of his life. Thirty years have already passed since he entered the world, and in the grand scheme of things, it's just a brief moment. There have been many ups and downs, but they're just the currents of life, drifting along with desires that once seemed so personal, but were really about observing social prejudices and conventions. These desires - money, wealth, fame, power, sex, love, and enjoyment - often bring along their companions: anger, hatred, jealousy, and ignorance.

With just a glance at the future, perhaps there are only thirty years left. But realistically, maybe only twenty of those years will be spent in good health, enough to truly do something meaningful for himself.

And so, he commits to:

1. Individually:

- Purification (body and mind)

- Gratitude (appreciation)

- Forgiveness (kindness)

- Giving (sharing)

2. Socially:

- Create a manufacturing industry

- Create and cultivate traditional culture through artistic activities

- Build a national spirituality through spiritual activities

- Support talents and serve the community

3. Life purpose:

- Devotion

- Happiness

- Carefree living

- Overcoming obstacles

A small sip

Gone are the days of joyous parties with wine and girls.

Now are rare full glasses of wine.

Only quiet friends and long-lasting love.

8. NO CACULATIONS

You realize that when you try too hard, the interaction becomes forced and unnatural. Yet, when you loosen up too much and appear indifferent, the result is almost nothing. Stuck between these extremes, you find yourself groping for a solution with no clear answer.

The spiritual master chuckles and says, "Hold your means like a small child holds an adult's finger. The child grasps the finger so tightly that you're amazed at the strength of such a tiny hand. But when the child lets go, there's no force, no vibration, not even the slightest tension. Do you know why? Because the child doesn't think about holding or letting go. There's no calculation, no strategy. He just darts from one thing to another, fully engaged in the moment, as if he's playing with life, not being played by it."

9. START A NEW THING

Last night, I had a dream where the Goddess whispered:

"Quicker steps are not to overtake, but to continue. Slower steps are not out of weakness, but for reflection."

•

"If you can't find a reason to continue the old, perhaps it's time to find a reason to start something new."

What do you seek, what do you gain?

Looking back at the well-trodden path,

The youthful cup of hot wine has now been drained.

Those wonderful years in the sunset's light,

What is there to find, to gain, and for whom?

10. ROLE PLAY

Society is a grand stage, complete with its structure, system, regulations, conventions, and methods. You must learn to play your part well, to dance in sync with the rhythm of the scenes, and to adapt to the ever-changing situations. Accept that what happens onstage, behind the curtains, and in real life are often worlds apart.

You need to rehearse your roles, memorize the lines, rhythms, and emotional cues. Master the art of self-control, skepticism, repression, and attraction. And yes, even the nuances of daydreaming, suffering, indulgence, perversion, nervousness, and anxiety. These are the costs you pay for the success of your performance.

Society is also a wild, mysterious jungle with its own hidden rules. You must sharpen your skills in dodging, faking, fooling, defending, hiding, and even attacking when necessary. It's a place where illusion and vanity reign, where dangers lurk behind every corner. Don't waste your energy criticizing or blaming society. Instead, adapt, compromise, and play your role.

You can criticize others, but remember, they are always right - at least in their own eyes. It's you who must perfect your act.

Play

Human life is but a play with many acts

Some short, some long,

Some joyous, some sad.

People laugh, people cry,

In moments that quickly pass.

Reincarnation, the endless cycle,

Coming and going, non-stop.

So why think you are forever?

11. CONSCIENCE-STRICKEN

In her final days, he longed to visit his mother. He woke early, eager to see her, but when he arrived, his family had already gone in. He waited outside the door, hoping for his turn, only to be told he couldn't enter. The next time he was granted permission to see her, a nurse intervened, ushering him away because his mother had just been taken for dialysis.

It felt as though some invisible force was keeping them apart.

Two days later, his phone rang early in the morning. The moment he saw his brother's number, his heart sank - he knew what had happened. Their mother had been battling illness for more than half a year, in and out of the hospital. Whenever he could, he would rush to her side, holding her hand, hugging her, trying to comfort her…

He had clung to the hope that she would live for another ten years, so he never fully allowed himself to consider the worst. But now it was too late. The weight of reality pressed down on him, leaving him feeling utterly lost and depressed.

No one had the courage to break the news to their father. When he came to visit, their father still asked after her, unaware of the truth.

The family was busy preparing for his eldest brother's son's wedding. He suggested postponing it, but the wedding proceeded as planned, adding to the ache in his heart.

Each day, morning and evening, he would turn on the Amitabha Sutra, praying silently for his mother to find peace in the Pure Land. In the afternoons, he would visit his father, who would show him old photographs of his mother, her smiling face captured in better times. This deepened his sorrow, reminding him of the fleeting nature of life, love, and human connection.

What remains after all is said and done? What legacy does one leave behind? Are these remnants meaningful, or do they, too, fade away with time? The brevity of life, the inevitability of loss, and the harsh truth of impermanence were now painfully clear to him.

Cancer, work troubles, the death of his mother, the quiet solitude - they all weighed heavily on him, plunging him further into despair. The thought of retreating to the mountains to find solace and peace haunted him.

But amidst the darkness, a stream of positive thoughts crept in. He had accomplished a few things in his life, for himself and for others. His children were growing up, and some things were improving, continuing. Life was continuing. He was a part of his mother, and his children were a part of him. This continuity offered some comfort.

Yet the truth remained: loss, separation, and the cessation of existence were inevitable. He knew that life was finite, and the time he had left was limited. Ten, twenty years - just fleeting moments in the grand scheme of things. So he resolved to live meaningfully in the time he had left. He would focus on doing well in one or two significant areas, living not just for himself but for those he loved. He would take care of his health, practice mindfulness, stay close to his relatives, share his experiences, and train the next generation.

This was his path forward, his way of honoring his mother's memory while embracing the life that remained.

12. CHANGE

Last night, his close friend called. They talked for an hour, sharing thoughts, worries, and a bit of laughter. His friend jokingly called himself a charlatan, dispensing life advice with the ease of someone who's seen it all.

Personal theory: *Work hard, more sex, less food*. The brain is the boss, the body, the worker. Stress is a stubborn guest - it needs to be shown the door right away. Movement meditation is the way to go, he insisted.

"And don't buy into that nonsense about a low sex drive being a sign of poor health," his friend added with a chuckle.

To truly heal, one must change their lifestyle. Fight the good fight, but don't forget to keep your mind balanced. Worry less, and savor the relaxing moments life offers.

"Snow drifts to ice, the world grows still,

But ice melts down to feed the hill.

From cold and white to dark and wet,

Life cycles on, no need to fret.

Ice holds firm, yet water flows,

Both are needed, each one knows.

A snowflake's dance beneath the sun,

Signals change, a new day begun."

13. BREAKDOWN

"When you focus all your energy on interacting with the object, there will come a moment when it feels as though, if this immense effort doesn't yield results soon, the pressure will become unbearable. And what happens then? You find yourself suffocating, stressed, and perhaps even on the verge of a breakdown.

In such moments, it's essential to recognize the signs and begin to gently release the pressure. You cannot afford to wait any longer."

14. OBSESSION AND ENLIGHTENMENT

He was always haunted by three relentless forces:

- **Instinctive Lust**: An unyielding desire that clouded his mind and kept him tethered to earthly pleasures.

- **Unusual Anger**: A fire that flared up, especially with his subordinates, leaving scars on relationships and himself.

- **Anxiety**: A constant companion, gnawing at him, reminding him of his imperfections and unmet expectations.

Despite years of dedicated practice, countless hours spent in repentance, and diligent study, these three poisons - greed, hatred, and ignorance - remained deeply rooted within him. He knew they made him weak, foolish, and led him astray. Yet, their grip was strong, and he struggled to break free. It was akin to a monk who, despite his vows, still craves recognition, chastises fellow monks and nuns, and feels a deep sadness for not having reached true wisdom and peace.

One morning, sitting quietly before a statue of the Buddha, he found himself deep in thought. As he watched the incense stick burn slowly, a metaphor for life unfolded before him:

- **Impermanence**: Like the incense, life burns away, leaving only the memory of its fragrance.

- **Suffering**: The incense shortens with each passing moment, a reminder that time is slipping away.

- **Selflessness**: Once the incense is fully burned, only ashes remain. The form is gone, its essence dispersed.

As he pondered this, he realized that if incense were a person, it might discover these truths:

- The faster it burns, the sooner it is consumed.

- The heat it generates can harm those who come too close.

- The scent it releases, though sweet, also carries the soot of sorrow.

But if the incense were enlightened, it would recognize:

- **Patience**: Burning slowly allows it to give more of itself.

- **Warmth**: Its light provides comfort to those around it.

- **Guidance**: Its fragrance soothes the mind and spirit.

In this realization, he saw the life of the incense as a parallel to human existence. When it is lit, it serves its purpose by guiding the spirits of those who seek solace. In doing so, it fulfills its entire life, even as it turns to ashes.

He knew that to live a life of true meaning, he must train himself to embody:

- **Devotion**

- **Love**

- **Peace**

He recognized that, like the incense, his body would one day be reduced to ashes, returning to the earth, preparing for the cycle of rebirth shaped by the karma of his actions.

Thus, he resolved to rid himself *of greed, hatred, and ignorance*, and instead, to fill his life with devotion, love, and peace. He recalled the Buddha's methods for practice:

- **Precepts**

- **Patience**

- **Generosity**

- **Diligence**

- **Meditation**

- **Wisdom**

He understood that while he knew these teachings, following them was a lifelong journey, one that required unwavering commitment and the grace to continue, even when the path was steep.

15. CONSIDERATION

This is the third time he has found himself at a crossroads, facing immense troubles.

The first time was in the late 1990s. Under pressure from an opponent and the indifference of a leader who overlooked the interests of others, he made the difficult decision to leave. He walked away to start over from nothing. At that time, the company was on the brink of bankruptcy, and leaving felt like a final blow. But he carried the weight of that decision, knowing it was the only way to preserve his integrity.

The second time, in the early 2000s, he faced overwhelming pressure from too many opponents - people who had once invited him to join them, only to show their true colors later. The shrewdness and cunning of many others left him with no choice but to voluntarily withdraw. It was a bitter pill to swallow, but he believed it was better to walk away with his dignity intact than to stay and be crushed by forces beyond his control.

Now, for the third time, he stands at the precipice of uncertainty. Accumulated difficulties within the organization, unreasonable pressure from the top, his deteriorating health, and family worries weigh heavily on his mind. The burden feels almost too much to bear.

Persevere in the fight, or retreat once more? The question lingers, haunting his every thought.

Will his dream of many years finally come true, or will it remain forever out of reach? Will he see the organization he built become an industrial pillar of the country, providing affordable products to everyone? Or could it evolve into a spiritual center, a beacon of national cultural pride?

To realize these dreams, he knows it will take immense dedication and effort, requiring him to overcome countless difficulties and obstacles. But does he still have the strength to continue?

He reflects on his journey, the battles fought, and the lessons learned. In the quiet of the night, a realization dawns on him.

" Respect the hard life, a strict teacher,

The one who forges us on the way to adulthood.

Stay away from the sweet guys.

Those make us lazy and complacent, because

Then the thing that follows us will be a bag

Full of lamentations and regrets. "

He knows now that the hardships, the struggles, and the suffering have been his greatest teachers. They have shaped him, refined him, and made him resilient. The sweet temptations of an easy life would only lead to complacency and regrets. The path ahead may be arduous, but it is the only path that leads to true fulfillment.

With renewed determination, he decides to press on, knowing that every challenge he faces brings him closer to his dreams. And in this moment of consideration, he finds peace.

16. MEANS

For many years, he lived in the shadow of anxiety, fear, and insecurity, grappling with the towering barriers of life and work. But now, he begins to understand that there are three ways to confront these challenges:

• **Hold fast to purpose:** Maintain a sense of meaning in life, dedicating oneself to the pursuit of hidden greatness, serving others with humility.

• **Embrace forgiveness**: Purify oneself through love and kindness, turning enemies into partners and friends, spreading compassion where there was once animosity.

• **Adapt and endure**: Accept life's circumstances, reflect on them, and flexibly adapt to changing situations with patience and creativity, staying present and righteous in all actions.

Perhaps all three of these approaches are necessary, and he constantly reminds himself to live in the moment and uphold what is right.

People often believe that freedom comes from the ability to do what they desire, granted by external circumstances or the influence of others. But when they fail, they feel their freedom slipping away, leaving them feeling constrained, powerless, and defeated. This is passive freedom.

He realizes he needs to change his perspective and approach. He must actively solve his problems in his own way, embracing a freedom that is not given by others but earned through righteous and deliberate action.

> **_Live well_**
>
> _Disease teaches us to avoid indulging too much._
>
> _A lot of vegetables, little meat and no wine._
>
> _Life then is so dull._
>
> _I would rather have a little wine and fun than die in boredom._

17. SELF MAKING

Throughout life, a person carries many burdens: earning a living, chasing fame, fulfilling responsibilities… He often imagines that one day, when all the work is done, he will finally find peace. Yesterday, he sent his second son off to school, then dove straight into back-to-back meetings, assigning tasks to his staff. But today, he has decided to start a new chapter, practicing patience, hoping to heal both his body and mind. The journey continues, but he now sees the mistakes of the past:

- An unhealthy diet, leaving his body burdened with toxins.

- A life lived in extremes, unbalanced and constantly stressed.

- A mind too occupied with thoughts of the past and future.

From now on, he resolves to live in the present, seeking happiness and freedom. He must learn to let go, to savor life, and to secure peace of mind. It's time to take care of himself, to nurture the tree of his life, and to find joy in the simple moments.

Self-Reminder

You are both prey and hunter,

Caught in the snare of your own ambitions.

Beware, for when you lose yourself,

You tread the path that leads to hell.

18. FAILURE

Do you know why you cannot wait, why your breath is blocked before the results come to fruition? It's because you hold too tightly to the outcome, never leaving space for the right result to emerge in its own time. You constantly strain yourself toward the goal, but deep in your heart, you are always anticipating failure. As long as that is the case, you will only meet the defeat that you have unconsciously invited. Your body and mind are out of sync, not aligned with the flow of life.

Let go, and learn to move with the ease of a child holding hands, trusting in the journey rather than fixating on the destination."

19. MIND WANDERING

Dad paid a visit today.

It was a day when I felt weary, battling a cold. My body ached, so I decided to play a CD of Pham Duy's music - "Returning Day." The disc was unopened, a relic from 15-16 years ago. Dad sat quietly, his gaze far away, lost in thought. The romantic music stirred up old memories, a bittersweet reflection of the past.

As the melodies played, I remembered years ago when my parents would visit, often when I was unwell. My mother would sit beside me, gently rubbing my shoulders, while Dad would hesitantly inquire about my health.

Today, it was just my father, dreamy and deep in thought, immersed in the flow of time, feeling the lyrics as they weaved through the air. It all seemed so recent, yet it was now a distant, vague past.

Dad asked if I had any old music. I rummaged through a drawer filled with forgotten discs and found *"Prewar Autumn,"* untouched for over twenty years, covered in a layer of dust tinged with the passage of time.

As the music filled the room, emotions welled up from deep within.

"You promised to come with me to the riverside...

Then the two directions, which one to take?

In the dark, the stream of dreams is quiet. ...

Oh man, remember the heart song that night?

Thousands of years resounding by the moon stream...

Remember the people far away in the smoke?

People are parting because of the war. ...

A day of absence fades memories. ...

Now being far from each other,

Do you still remember or forget,

The old days when the moon was waiting for you?"

– Le Mong Nguyen

As my father mumbled and softly sang these love songs, a sense of magnanimity enveloped him. For a long time, he had only listened to modern music filled with memories. Was this more suitable for his lonely, romantic heart?

Oh, time.

Time of memories.

Time of changes.

Time of oblivion.

Time of ambiguity.

Time of longing.

Time of sweetness.

Time of boundlessness.

Time of sorrows.

Time of parting.

Time of separation.

Time of loss.

20. INNER MATURITY

Humans are indeed small in the face of nature. We are nurtured and sustained by it, yet we also endure its fury and unpredictable weather. Evolution has taught us not just to reap the fruits of nature but to navigate its risks. The key lies in avoiding, supporting, practicing, adapting, hiding, preventing, and sheltering - finding ways to live in harmony and balance with nature.

In the vast society we inhabit, as if surrounded by wild animals, we face not only responsibilities and obligations but also jealousy, deceit, hatred, oppression, traps, and malice. We confront our own guilt, mistakes, shortcomings, despair, boredom, loneliness, anger, and weakness, as well as those of our loved ones.

Inside us, there are times of anger, storms, drought, frost, heat, and waves. We are, in essence, a reflection of the entire universe.

Learning to accept the erratic weather within us and living in harmony with it is what we call inner maturity.

Who eats who

We eat chickens, chickens eat worms, worms eat leaves, and leaves draw nutrients from the soil where parts of us may one day lie.

If you truly understand this, then:

- *Be humble, avoid arrogance.*

- *Respect others, for you never truly know who is greater.*

- *Never assume ownership over anything or anyone - perhaps they own us.*

From this, you can see that life and death, success and defeat, reputation and humiliation are all relative. Don't burden yourself with the past or the future. Live happily in the present, know your limits, and let go when the time comes.

21. THE ANIMAL PART IN A PERSON

Animals don't need words to express themselves - they act. Whether it's a bark, a song, or a whine, their feelings are clear. And those eyes? They say more than a thousand words ever could. As someone who prides themselves on subtle expression, there's much we can learn from our animal friends.

One day, I found myself observing a stray dog outside my window. It didn't have much, but the way it looked at people - hopeful yet cautious - said it all. There was a delicacy in how it approached, a silent request for kindness without demanding it. It struck me: in life, we need that kind of delicacy, to express ourselves without overwhelming others, and the wisdom to know when to step back, when to wait.

So, people need to train in two areas:

• **Delicacy of animals**: The ability to communicate emotions and needs with subtlety, using actions and presence rather than words, much like how a dog's wagging tail can convey joy or a cat's purr can show contentment.

• **Profundity of a wise person**: The depth of understanding that comes with experience, allowing us to navigate life's complexities with insight and patience, much like how a sage remains calm in a storm, knowing that it, too, shall pass.

Life lesson

The enthusiasm of youth has earned me scars,

Hatred as a thank you for kindness,

Coldness from those I hold dear

Now, I learn to save love wisely.

22. SOULMATE

We all crave someone to share our lives with, to care for, to be passionate about - someone we might call a soulmate. We want someone who shares our joys and burdens, who cares for us deeply, and who's just a little bit crazy about us too.

But where do we find that one perfect match? The answer might be simpler than we think: we are our own soulmates.

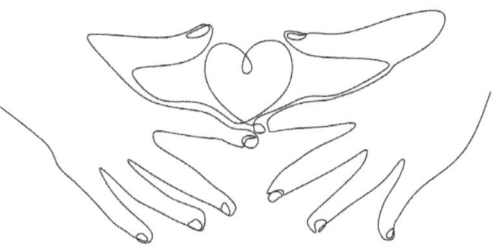

Love

Love is noble, deserving of a thousand praises.

And sex? Well, there's no shame in that.

Two sides of the same coin

For where there's love, sex naturally follows.

23. THINGS LEARNED

After fifty years of living, here's what I've picked up along the way:

I've learned that it takes years to build trust, but only seconds to shatter it - like dropping your phone after finally getting a screen protector.

I've learned that no matter how sincere you are, some people just won't reciprocate - kind of like sending out heartfelt emails that only get automated replies.

I've learned you can't make everyone like you. All you can do is be true to yourself, and let the world do what it will - like standing in a storm without an umbrella.

I've learned never to plan too far ahead or count your possessions, but rather count how many true friends you have - because in the end, friendships are the real treasure.

I've learned that sometimes you can make decisions that haunt you for the rest of your life - like ordering the wrong thing at a restaurant.

I've learned to say goodbye sweetly, because it might be the last time you see someone - life is unpredictable, so make those goodbyes count.

I've learned that if you don't control your attitude, it will control you - kind of like trying to tame a wild horse with a carrot.

I've learned that no matter how passionate a relationship starts, passion may fade, but something deeper will always take its place - like a slow-burning fire that keeps you warm.

I've learned that forgiveness is essential, even if it's not always easy - especially when you're tempted to hold a grudge like a winning lottery ticket.

I've learned that true friendship and love grow stronger over time, despite distance - because the heart knows no boundaries.

I've learned never to tell a child their dream isn't real - that's the kind of tragedy that breaks hearts before they've even started dreaming.

I've learned that if a close friend accidentally hurts you, it's worth knowing how to forgive - after all, we're all human.

I've learned that forgiving others is good, but forgiving yourself is essential - because carrying that weight is far too heavy a burden.

I've learned there are countless ways people can love each other - each as unique as a fingerprint.

I've learned that your life can change in a few hours, often by a stranger - like meeting someone on a plane who changes your entire perspective.

I've learned that those you care about most will eventually leave you - but the memories they leave behind are what shape you.

And finally, I've learned that when passion calls for courage, there's often no second chance - so seize the moment, because life doesn't always offer do-overs.

24. FRAGILE

"True art is aimless. The more tightly you cling to professional achievements in your quest to go far, the more elusive your destination becomes. What hinders you most is not the journey itself, but the driving ambition that fuels it."

A career is like a life - fragile and delicate. You may not grasp the full meaning of this yet, but consider another analogy: an occupation is like a weight suspended by a fragile thread. The upper end reaches toward the sun, while the lower end anchors to the earth. In your pursuit of goals, if you interact too forcefully, the thread may snap. For those driven by greed or violence, the thread will surely break. A career, like life itself, is fragile, suspended delicately between heaven and earth.

25. SELF HEALING

Today, he embarked on a quest to find the Medicine Buddha statues and began practicing light meditation. Along the way, he found himself tangled in a web of conflicting advice from both Eastern and Western doctors. It wasn't exactly the most reassuring experience, but his heart didn't sink - he was more puzzled than discouraged. Determined, he pushed through some lingering tasks, though his real wish was to drop everything and retreat to the mountains.

He didn't even bother to look up his friends' or girlfriend's phone numbers - what was the point? Living alone seemed like a much better deal. All he really wanted was to set up the company so it could run smoothly without him, hand over the reins to his relatives and young managers, and then disappear to his retreat with peace of mind.

Self-Help Mantra

If sharing is absent, togetherness should not be named.

When love fades, the bond may still remain - be patient.

A temporary goodbye might just ease the pain,

For who knows? Love may bloom again someday.

26. INNER FIRE

He had heard about the transformative power of qi - the breath that could awaken the "snake fire" within, clear all the meridians, and burn away the three poisons: greed, anger, and ignorance. It sounded almost too good to be true. But after years of stress and sleepless nights, he figured it was worth a shot. Why not aim for enlightenment while he was at it?

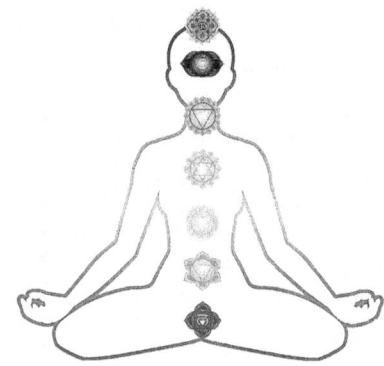

Practicing qi, he discovered, wasn't just about sitting cross-legged and breathing deeply. It required keeping the spirit in check, maintaining the precepts, and purifying the body and mind every single day. It was like running a marathon, only the finish line promised something far greater than a medal.

As he delved deeper, he realized that understanding impermanence and no-self wasn't just philosophical mumbo jumbo. It was the secret sauce to letting go of worries and reaching a state where body and mind were free from disease - a sort of DIY enlightenment. And today, for the first time, he glimpsed that truth. It felt like striking a match in a dark room, a tiny flame of clarity amidst the chaos of life.

Loving consciously

This life offers many religions,

Promising heaven after death,

But I choose half of virtue, half of passion,

For a life of conscious love here and now.

27. MOVING ON

There are moments when you find yourself stuck in the relentless spiral of growth, where the lingering troubles just won't resolve, and new problems seem to pop up like weeds.

You think you've got it all figured out, and then - bam! - another obstacle appears out of nowhere. Sometimes, you're left scratching your head, wondering what on earth to do next.

In those moments, you might find yourself reading about the rise and fall of empires, or the creators who must have faced similar roadblocks. It's comforting to think that even the greats had their moments of confusion. But then it hits you: a peaceful life is one where you do nothing at all. And that's not really living, is it? So, you take a deep breath, dust yourself off, and decide to keep moving on.

When opportunity comes

Who knows when this life will end,

Or how long high status will last?

When Death calls your name, you'll be empty-handed.

So, adore the flowers when opportunity presents itself.

28. 10 COMMANDMENTS TO SELF

First, don't reincarnate just to suffer.

Second, don't join life only to forget your home.

Third, don't fall in love just to be jealous.

Fourth, don't marry to avoid more burdens.

Fifth, don't pursue something just to dodge the stress.

Sixth, don't fight just to follow revenge.

Seventh, don't offer help just to avoid blame.

Eighth, don't depart just to escape sorrow.

Ninth, don't ask for help just to avoid debts.

Tenth, don't promise without keeping your word.

Upon birth, we enter the sea of strife,

But still, we must commit to life.

You may wish to ease the heart, let go,

But lingering love won't let you part.

29. LETTING GO

So, you must learn the art of waiting patiently.

How do you do that?

Free yourself by letting go of your ego and attachments. With nothing left, simply maintain your non-seeking concentration.

Then, you practice non-seeking intentionally. You need to wait for the right moment.

First, bring your mindful way of living into your daily life. Make your life journey a non-seeking journey.

Step by step, artfully build a mindful way of living, allowing it to become the foundation of your life.

30. TEMPORARY RESIDENCE

Houses are dear, but even the coziest can feel lonely at times. Throughout your life, you live in many different homes - some warm, some cold, some just pit stops along the way. But in truth, every house you inhabit is a temporary residence. In the end, we all return to our final destination, wherever that may be.

Distant star
Oh, faraway land,
Where vague memories dwell.
Is there soil beneath my feet,
Or just a speck of dust from a past life's shell?

Does the wind carry a voice,
A wandering soul from some dreamland?
And that twinkling star,
Could it be the home I left a million years ago,
Where warm love still lingers?

31. PURIFICATION

This morning, she came into the room, a rare visit, to say goodbye before heading to the airport, off to some distant land for charity work. As she left, I called out to remind her to close the door - the cold wind was creeping in. It was only the second lunar month, and winter still lingered like an unwelcome guest.

I searched for Kitaro's music, hoping the soft sounds would soothe my aching feet, like heaven and earth finding harmony despite the cold outside. Thankfully, many things can be controlled remotely these days.

I leisurely made the bed, fluffed the pillows, and dusted off the surfaces. I asked the maid to bring in the books I'd been reading the night before, to take away the old mugs, and to move the table a bit. I even found a switch to warm the dark corners with some light.

Then, I carefully pushed my crutches to the cupboards, gathered a few personal belongings, and made my way back to the room. Slowly, I folded the crutches around the legs of the chair, spread out some towels, and arranged a few things, including a full pot of coffee.

The daily ritual of purification, both of body and mind, began. My injured leg had kept me from getting up early to go upstairs to worship Buddha and meditate, so I used the music to cleanse my mind instead.

I opened a book to a page about Alexander preparing to face King Darius of Persia. He had been shaken by the sheer number of enemies and the fact that he was fighting on foreign soil. But thanks to his prayers to the gods, his perseverance, courage, ingenuity, and brave comrades, the Greco-Macedonian army eventually triumphed.

I told myself not to waver in times of trouble. Perhaps the enemy is more afraid than I am. Maybe they're even more confused.

The music seemed to slow down, so I switched to something new by Oliver Shanti - music I hadn't heard in ages. The familiar rhythm echoed in the room.

I opened another book, this time finding a passage about how to guess someone's personality based on their physical appearance and behavior. It reminded me of someone I knew, someone often overlooked. He spoke little, mostly kept quiet or just agreed with others, avoided eye contact, and stammered as if hiding something.

Ah, yes. I thought of others like him, some who had left me, others who returned only to cause trouble.

The ancient texts are often profound, but sometimes, they're just plain confusing.

The music continued, like a gentle reminder in the background. I turned to yet another book, landing on a poem about the author's deep feelings for his wife - or maybe his lover - their 30-year argument that never seemed to end. It spoke of fate, lifestyle, personal thoughts, and the tolerance of differences. No right or wrong, no gain or loss, no good or bad. Just the choice to live together and keep the love alive.

I chuckled to myself; it sounded familiar. Then, I got up and moved around the room on my knees. Sometimes, I even crawled on all fours. Crutches were just too cumbersome in such a small space. But it was good, moving slowly but steadily. I arranged a few things - warm water, a towel, my brush - enjoying the simple pleasure of taking care of myself.

I was careful with every little thing. The music played on, and everything seemed just fine. I added a touch of perfume; my facial skin felt cool, though my cheeks were warm.

I hopped on one leg to the door, suddenly feeling hungry and a bit worn out. Ha! It was probably from all the hopping around on one leg. It was nearly 10 o'clock.

On crutches, I made my way downstairs to find something to eat. Passing my daughter's room, I noticed the door was open, and the maid was inside. After exchanging a few words, I learned my daughter had gone out the previous night and was home alone this morning. Thank goodness I still had the maid.

As the meal was nearly ready, my daughter returned home and asked me to wait while she took a shower. Of course, I'd wait. After all, it's nice to have someone to share a meal with.

A good day, indeed.

32. PERSISTENT OVERCOMING

He closed the book and gazed out the window. The morning light had finally made its way into the house. The past few days had been nothing short of stressful. Pressure mounted from every direction - from the organization, from opponents eager to take over, and from his own failing health. It was all too much, so he retreated to the remote mountains, seeking a hideaway to recover.

This quiet time brought a sense of calm. He found solace in studying the strategies of ancient confrontations and the ways the Japanese organized production, turning creativity into a fine art.

But how could he retreat gracefully in the face of obstacles, insensitivity, and disturbances? How could survival be left in the hands of infamous mercenaries and courtesans?

He remembered Honda's words: success is made up of 99% failures. All creation, all perfection, all beauty begins with training, purification, and the relentless pursuit of simplicity.

The Buddha himself taught that enlightenment comes from the purification of mind and body.

Every day, he worked to purify his body, but his mind - oh, his mind - was infected with new toxins daily.

He studied over and over, perhaps through many lifetimes, and realized a profound truth: progress, righteousness, and happiness are persistent processes of purifying body and mind on the journey to creativity and perfection.

Perseverance

Persevere, embrace the challenge,

No matter the pain or loneliness,

For this is the path of growth,

And the quiet joy of self-made happiness.

In silence

Those in high positions are often deemed wise,

Their words carry weight,

But I, socially inferior, know my place,

And so, I choose to be silent.

33. PERSPECTIVE

There are people and situations we encounter that, in the moment, seem utterly hateful and exhausting. Yet, with time, when you look back, you realize they weren't so terrible - perhaps even a bit endearing or amusing. And sometimes, what seemed lovely from a distance loses its charm up close.

Maybe it's just the way our minds work, turning fleeting moments into lasting impressions. A graceful figure disappearing into the distance can suddenly stir up a thousand forgotten dreams.

I've spent too much time wandering in my thoughts,

Floating in unfulfilled desires.

I can't embrace a figure, but I can hold onto memories.

Sorrow is pointless - I know joy will return.

The world isn't perfect, but there's a beauty in that imperfection that I've come to love. I pass through this land, walk through someone's life, and navigate the transient eddies of the world, leaving behind betrayal, deception, and loneliness.

But still, I believe that being alive is a priceless joy, and there's so much beauty yet to come.

Reflection

Tell yourself this: don't regret what has slipped through your fingers,

Or long for what was never truly yours.

No more sadness - I know where I'm going.

34. TIME TO LET GO

Is the renunciation of self that the spiritual teacher spoke of truly the path to emptiness and solitude? Have you reached the point where the influence of Zen on the art of living has been revealed to you?

Yet, you still wonder how waiting intertwines with timely and precise action, and how genuine interaction will be achieved. But why ponder so deeply on matters that only experience can clarify? Isn't this the perfect moment to release that fruitless attachment to the desire for success or the fear of failure?

Let go, and trust in the unfolding of the path.

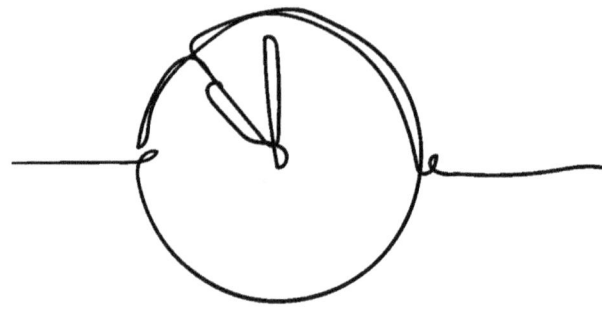

35. HAPPINESS IS SIMPLE

A writer once remarked that happiness is about solving physical problems. To clarify, our human experiences are deeply rooted in emotions. Whether we feel happy, sad, hot, cold, esteemed, kind, victorious, defeated, or well-informed, we are constantly influenced by external factors that stir our emotions and shape our feelings. Good feelings bring happiness, while discomfort brings us down.

Being human is a sum of our parts - body, feelings, intellect, interactions, and spirit. In Buddhism, this is understood as the unity of Body-Mind (Nāma-Rūpa). When one part falters, the entire system can become unbalanced. These parts interact closely, and if one develops incorrectly, the whole system can come to a standstill, halting any growth. A deadlock in the body can lead to a deadlock in the mind, and vice versa, resulting in suffering and unhappiness.

Buddha pointed to "the Middle Way," where a balanced and unified Body-Mind leads to peace and happiness. This is the path of enlightenment.

Lin Yutang, the aforementioned writer, also quoted an American scholar who humorously claimed that happiness is found in reading the Bible diligently and avoiding constipation.

You know what? I think he was onto something.

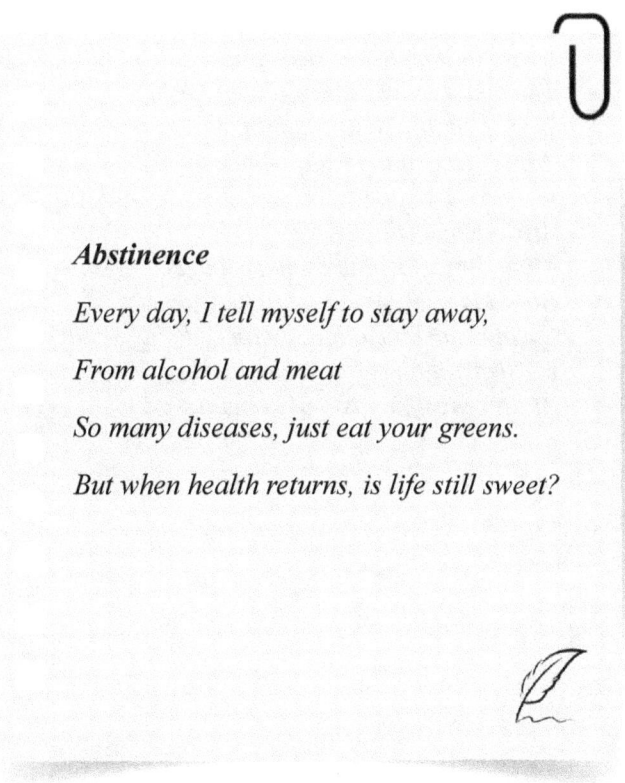

Abstinence

Every day, I tell myself to stay away,

From alcohol and meat

So many diseases, just eat your greens.

But when health returns, is life still sweet?

36. RELIVING

Over the years, the weight of life's responsibilities accumulates on your shoulders, pulling you further and further away from the passions of your youth. At some point, you realize that it's time to pause, to soberly assess where you've been, to let go of what no longer serves you, and to set new priorities. It's about rekindling that old flame, rediscovering the youthful passions of a time you are now reliving.

Because in the end, you can let go of many things with time, but you cannot part with yourself. Eventually, you return to who you truly are.

Call of the Wild
Time wears down all things,
Freezing desires in its cold grasp,
Chilling both body and mind.
But I've forgotten:
A kiss that melts all resistance,
The tender savagery of a wild beast,
A groping in the wet jungle,
A muffled groan in the swamp.

Anxiety fuels desire,
Monotony dulls the hunter's edge.
But today, it's as if I've just awakened,
Spring sunshine dances with seductive charm.
My heart ignites like a smoldering fire,
And I crave the taste of delicious prey.

37. TIME

Time is like money - sometimes wasted, sometimes saved and cherished. But the more you struggle against it, the shorter it seems. Paradoxically, when you slow down, when you become quieter, time stretches - deeper, longer, more profound.

That's life, after all - a blend of ups and downs, much like the ebb and flow of human emotions.

Life is short and fleeting. I want to savor the time I have left, to pursue the desires I've kept hidden for so long. Finding a way to leave a legacy that endures even when life does not is a journey of awareness. This journey is a winding path - sometimes obscure, sometimes clear.

Let's keep moving forward. Time is within you, it moves with you.

You are time. When you die, time stops. No before, no after.

Only the rhythm of time, in sync with the beat of our hearts -

The present moment.

38. TRANQUILITY

How does one find calm, embrace solitude, and live a quiet, peaceful life amid the chaos, disturbances, and endless tasks that surround us?

Perhaps we must journey across all the world's oceans, savor every flavor, and then - only then - can we bid farewell to the noise and realize that simplicity holds the freshest sweetness.

String of Invaluable Pearls

Along life's path, I've gathered wisdom from the ancients, crafting a bracelet of pearls to remind yourself:

1. *Know yourself.*

2. *Know enough.*

3. *Know when to stop.*

4. *Know how to compromise.*

5. *Know when to surrender.*

6. *Don't act impulsively.*

7. *Don't seek visibility.*

8. *Don't engage in unnecessary battles.*

9. *Don't chase fame.*

10. *Don't speak without reason.*

11. *Be simple.*

12. *Be patient.*

13. *Be humble.*

14. *Be kind.*

15. *Be free.*

39. WISHES

This morning, I visited the Buddha Shrine. Flowers bloomed across the yard, and the air was crisp and fresh. I couldn't help but hope that the New Year would arrive peacefully. Kneeling before the Buddha, I offered a simple prayer: for the enthusiasm to stand strong with my team, to steer the ship with unwavering resolve, navigating the ocean of fear, danger, and envy. May we persist through storms of doubt, enmity, conspiracy, and threat, and finally anchor at the harbor of success, peace, joy, love, and kindness.

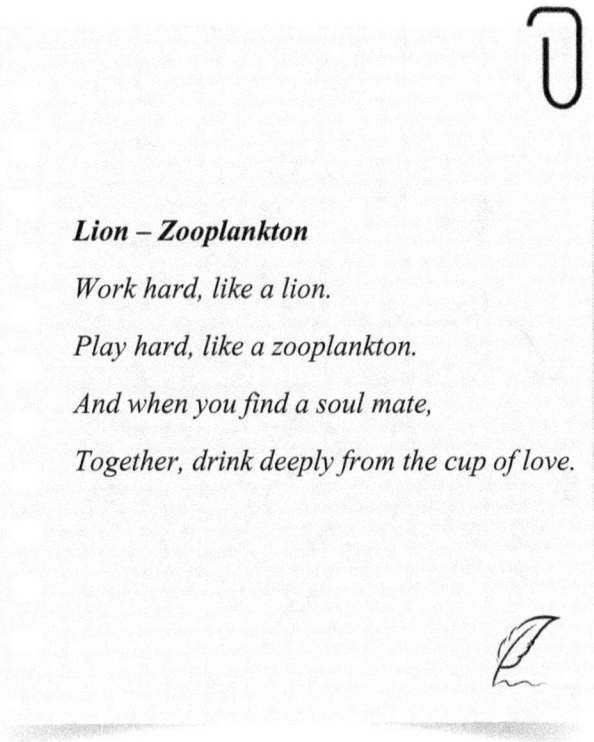

Lion – Zooplankton

Work hard, like a lion.

Play hard, like a zooplankton.

And when you find a soul mate,

Together, drink deeply from the cup of love.

40. CONCENTRATION

"From now on, as you journey to work, focus on maintaining wakefulness. See yourself meditating on your tasks. Approach each task with mindfulness, letting go of distractions, as if there is only one real and important thing in the entire world: to act rightly and with intention in your profession."

41. SELF-MADE PEACE

Today, he realized that every difficulty and suffering is a challenge, every challenge an opportunity, every opportunity a path to success, and every success a step toward satisfaction. But true satisfaction, he discovered, only comes when it brings inner peace to both mind and body. And, as always, all difficulties start from within the heart.

To be truly safe, you need a mix of love, repentance, forgiveness, purification, and spiritual tranquility. The highest form of well-being lies in peace within the non-self, the unconscious, the mindless - Emptiness - the gateway to the Formless Meditation of Loving Kindness!

All creation springs from either excitement in the unconscious or peace in the unconscious. To solve external problems, difficulties, and dilemmas, one must first heal oneself, both in body and mind. This creates unconscious peace, which then spreads love throughout the universe, sparking creativity born from tranquility.

Everything that happens around you is, in some way, your responsibility.

He learned that to heal his relationships and ease the pains caused by external factors - be it relatives, wife and children, parents, friends, partners, enemies, public authorities, women, colleagues, corporations, or organizations - he must first heal his own body and mind. This includes his internal struggles with lust, love, dreams, beliefs, passion, dedication, and health.

So, when you reach your own well-being, you've attained transcendental wisdom - purity. This is the path to the purification of both body and mind!

42. TAKING REFUGE IN THE BUDDHA

You might think that taking refuge in the Buddha comes solely through training. But if you're still attached to the physical world, or if you haven't yet experienced enough of it, that refuge is only temporary. You might still long to return to the old ways. And for those who haven't tasted the world but aren't destined to, finding true refuge can be challenging. Attaining the way isn't just about training the mind.

It's best to experience life fully. When both your mind and body grow weary of the world, the path to refuge will naturally open.

Worldly rose

The flower stands quietly beside Him,

Day after day, whispering softly.

Prayers rise with the smoke of incense,

Even as the world outside keeps spinning.

Yesterday the flower bloomed, now it fades,

Tomorrow it will bloom again - the worldly rose.

Together, the flower and I, we both wholeheartedly devote to Him.

43. GAIN – LOSS

Life is a game where sometimes we win, and sometimes we lose. A strategist once said that total victory is what truly matters, no matter how many small battles you may have lost. So, if you win a glorious battle but lose the overall war, what have you really gained?

But what is this final victory? Is it the end of life, death, or something else? Every win or loss, every gain or setback, eventually fades away, disappearing into the grave of time. When you understand the impermanence of all things, you no longer need to worry about gain and loss. You can move forward calmly, welcoming whatever comes. Perhaps the greatest victory, the ultimate success in life, is finding inner peace - both now and in the years to come.

Welcoming Autumn

Summer has passed, and the time has come,

Autumn brings cool rains,

Spreading joy across the fields and orchards,

Nurturing young rice to grow, and fruits to ripen.

Warm houses glow with the fire of togetherness,

Village streets echo with children's laughter.

The lonely return to the arms of love,

As the sky spins golden light to welcome autumn.

44. RELAXING SMILE

In the early morning, before the first light of day, he lit incense and sat down to meditate in front of the Buddha. The door was slightly ajar, letting in a bit of the morning chill. He let his sorrows sink away and smiled, just like the Buddha. The mind danced in harmony with the prayer music.

Let Your Heart Rejoice

Flowers wither, then bloom again with the seasons,

Worries and happiness take their turns.

Only those who have passed away can't return.

So why fret? Let your heart rejoice.

45. MEANING

If life is an illusion, then everything may seem meaningless. But understanding impermanence allows you to cherish the fleeting moments, to patiently engage in what brings meaning and satisfaction, so that someone else may find happiness - and you live without regret.

Leaving

He knows enough - the noise of fame, so he ceases the competition.

He has enough - the burdens of worry and hollow giving.

He's had enough - fleeting appearances and romantic farewells.

So, he sets off in formlessness, embracing quiet joy.

.

46. BODY – SPEECH – MIND

I couldn't sleep after listening to *"the ways to get rid of worries."*

In summary:

- Life is short

- Breathe in, stay present

- Smile

- Live in the moment

- Quietness brings peace

- Give love

How to do it:

- Stay whole

- Breathe gently

- Smile

- Focus the mind

- Embrace quiet

- Love

Body – Speech – Mind = Quietness – Smile – Meditation

Where is heaven, you ask?

"Live with virtues," they say - people will teach you.

Live a good life here, and in the next life, heaven awaits.

But anyone who's been there,

Could you tell me - just how much better is it?

47. SPIRITUAL FREEDOM

If you seek true interaction, physical relaxation must transform into spiritual relaxation. Go deep, allowing the mind not only to function but to be liberated and free. Function with the intention of achieving freedom. This freedom transcends physical ease - what we call spiritual freedom. It's not just about controlling the breath to rise above challenges, but about letting go of all attachments, fundamentally forgetting the self. In this way, the spirit returns to its essence, finding absolute relaxation in its own unnamed source.

48. INSTINCT – EGO – ORIGINAL

Dawn

Recently, I've realized that death is a great master, and illness is a strict yet wise teacher. They teach us the art of letting go - of fears, burdens, responsibilities, and the ego - so we can embark on a new path toward awakening and enlightenment. The trick is to let go, be brave, and keep moving forward.

Sunset

As I sat on the beach, watching the waves crash endlessly against the shore, I recalled a story about the president of Hyundai. Early one morning, in his rush to the construction site, he missed a roadblock and drove straight into the sea. As the car sank, he struggled to open the door, nearly accepting his fate. But then, a thought struck him - his unpaid debts and the creditors who would surely label his death as a desperate act over money. That jolted him awake. He broke the glass, swam to the surface, and lived to tell the tale. He was in his mid-50s then and later reflected, "Trials may come, but they don't have to end in failure."

The Dark Night

I once read about purification and self-healing. Injured animals often retreat to a secluded cave, fasting, hiding, and slowly licking their wounds until they heal.

In the midst of life's troubles, sickness can strangely be a comfort, and death offers a gentle invitation: to let go, to say goodbye. A Thai doctor once told me, "If you want to heal, go to the temple, shave your head for a month, or stay home and observe the precepts for three months."

49. A SAD DAY

He drove for what felt like an eternity. Disheveled, lost in relentless thoughts that wouldn't let him be. Last night, he'd met an old friend, a close one from nearly 20 years ago. They'd stumbled into each other's lives back then, forming a bond, only to drift apart as life took them down different paths.

He was on a trip, stopping at a coastal city that held memories of its own. The city had changed - a fresh wave of young, enthusiastic officials had swept in - but it was still as charming, dreamy, and magical as he remembered. And there, he saw that friend again.

The once sharp and lively former Provincial Party Secretary now struggled with every step, his movements burdened by age. Every gesture - a shake of the shoulders, a nod of the head - carried echoes of the old days, filled with innovation and delight. It was bittersweet, how time could be so indifferent.

As they parted, his friend mentioned that the city's liberation anniversary was in 15 days. He wanted to honor the memory of his comrades who didn't live to see that victory. Hearing this, he was moved, squeezing his friend's hand in encouragement.

Back in the party room, jubilant music filled the air. People sang with joy, but when he saw a staff member flexing to the beat, his heart sank.

How fleeting, how arduous, how short and impermanent is human life. The war was over, yet the pain, the loss, the regrets - they'd be forgotten, buried under the sands of time.

Leaving the noise and bitterness behind, he walked to the sea, feeling the fine sand beneath his feet as the waves drifted endlessly, to where, he wondered?

Discerning

Power fades, wealth is fleeting - mere vanity.

Compassion endures, love sustains - a quiet mind is the essence.

Life's wine, aged in the casks of Earth and sky,

Pours wisdom, drawn from the deep wells of heart and spirit.

50. DESIRES

You might think all desires are troublesome - whether it's the craving for fame, money, or love.

But let's be honest, desire is the spark that ignites passion. And passion, well, it's what gets us out of bed in the morning.

When you're passionate about something, you work for it, sweat for it, sometimes even lose sleep over it. And that's not all bad - it's how we create meaning in life.

The trick? It's all in the giving. Desire for fame? Use it to uplift others. Desire for money? Share it wisely. Desire for love? Pour it out with open arms.

Anger can be a teacher, happiness a gift to spread around. If you balance these with compassion and wisdom, maybe that's the real secret.

And perhaps, just perhaps, that's why some find peace in a simple life - one that harmonizes the sacred and the secular, much like the dual practice of Yab-Yum in Vajrayana, where opposites unite in perfect balance.

51. PEACE

The times of meeting and parting are uncertain,

Happiness and suffering come and go, gains and losses, unpredictable.

But after experiencing it all, looking back, we see them as fleeting moments,

How many old stories and people have faded away, never to be encountered again.

Understanding this early, we learn to live peacefully while we still walk this earth.

Life

My heart slows, my blood cools,

No passion, no lust, an emptiness fills my core.

In this life, I've missed echoes of the past,

Counting the dust, picking up pieces of nostalgia.

Life is brief, ever-changing,

Understanding feels like a misunderstanding as the body slowly wilts.

Fame is fleeting, power is like the wind,

Faith, a beautiful madness, fate, a mysterious dance.

Life, like a river, flows onward,

Away from its source, into the fog of forgetfulness.

Will we meet again, in another form,

Or rise like the mist, into the infinite unknown?

52. FOCUS ON BREATHING

The core of practice begins with closing the doors of the senses - not by forcefully shutting out the world, but by gently stepping aside, allowing external influences to pass without resistance. For this gentle disengagement to succeed, the mind needs an anchor, a steady focal point, and that is found in the breath.

This concentration is intentional and precise, each inhalation and exhalation clearly marked and fully experienced. You don't have to wait long to feel the effects. The more you focus on your breath, the quicker the noise of the outside world fades, becoming a distant hum, like the murmur of ocean waves. Eventually, those external impressions dissolve, leaving you undisturbed, as if cocooned in a shell where distractions cannot reach.

With time, you'll find that you become immune to strong impressions, gaining a quiet independence from them. The key is to always remain aware of your body - whether standing, sitting, or lying down - keeping it relaxed. When you awaken to the breath, you find yourself within a protective space, untouched by the external world.

53. BE

Some pec   ok. Their
lives are l   that quiet

Kindness

234 - Pl

Mountains stand with the grace of a sage,

Branches extend, offering shade, springs remain cool.

happiness brings.

Others, however, embrace the wild currents, riding the waves of life's ups and downs. They shape-shift with the times, standing tall in triumph and sorrow alike, always poised with a heroic grace, no matter the storm that rages around them.

Many kinds of flowers bloom, each unique, yet all undeniably beautiful.

54. PRICELESS

Everyone knows that life demands a price for everything. We constantly weigh trade-offs, always striving to be practical, effective, and valuable. But here's the twist: it's often not until the end of the search that we realize what is truly valuable. Most of the time, we're busy with things that seem meaningless - mundane, aimless, monotonous tasks that feel dull and repetitive. But, take a moment to ponder this: these seemingly trivial, boring things are our life. Perhaps Lao Tzu was onto something. Is it not the emptiness of the pot that gives it its capacity - its value? Space, after all, must be cherished. So, perhaps that which seems useless is indeed priceless.

Life's value is, after all, unfathomable.

Present

Each person born is a gift, a precious offering from their parents.

We live our lives, yet we do not truly own them. We are the result of countless others, shaped by fates and generations, molded by conditions and circumstances beyond our control.

And when we die, we return to dust and nothingness.

So, our task is to pass this gift on, to make it valuable and worthy. That is the true meaning of life.

Live a life worth living - not measured by the length of time, but by how we live it, what we create, and to whom we give it back.

55. LIFE PHILOSOPHY

There's a time in everyone's life when dreams of grandeur fill the mind, when youth brims with enthusiasm. But as the years roll by, that fiery mind gradually cools. Most people grow into adulthood - some take on great responsibilities, contributing to society, or leading industries, while others focus on building homes and nurturing families.

Looking back, many feel a sense of satisfaction, deeming themselves mature enough to impart wisdom to the younger generation. Yet, when faced with life's unexpected challenges and sorrows, even the wisest of us may want to retreat from the world, seeking solace and peace.

Is escaping to the mountains, the forest, or a temple the answer to our worries? How can we continue to live in the world, surrounded by its impurities, and still find peace?

The Buddha taught that all afflictions stem from greed, hatred, and ignorance. But perhaps we can take a cue from water.

When confronted with greed and lust, think of the bubbles in a waterfall cascading into an abyss - temporary and fleeting.

When faced with anger and hatred, think of water seeping into the ground - calm and patient.

And when dealing with ignorance and delusion, think of the water's surface reflecting clouds in the morning and at night - ever-changing, yet clear.

Like water, we must adapt to our circumstances. This is how we live a life of philosophy and spirituality, without needing to hide away from the world.

56. READING

Last night, he found himself drawn to the soft glow of a bookstore, a place he hadn't visited in a while. It was as if the shelves, stacked high with stories and wisdom, were calling out to him. Life had been busy - too busy, perhaps - and reading had become an occasional indulgence, reserved for business trips when he would pack a few thin books in his bag, hoping to find a moment to lose himself in their pages.

But standing there, surrounded by the comforting scent of paper and ink, he realized that waiting for the "right time" might be a fool's errand. The only time that truly mattered was now.

He made a quiet vow: to return to the books that once fed his soul, to explore works on spirituality, health, nourishment, and the deeper aspects of life that had always intrigued him. It was as if a spark had been rekindled within him - a passion that had lain dormant for too long.

As he left the bookstore with a bag full of new treasures, he felt a sense of calm and purpose. He decided that from now on, he would work only six or seven hours a day. The rest of the time, he would dedicate to living in the present, enjoying every moment, and finding peace in the simple pleasures of life.

"I'm back where I left off," he thought to himself, a gentle smile playing on his lips. *"Gradually loosening the cage that imprisons the being."*

And with that, he walked out into the night, a man renewed, ready to embrace the wisdom that each new day would bring.

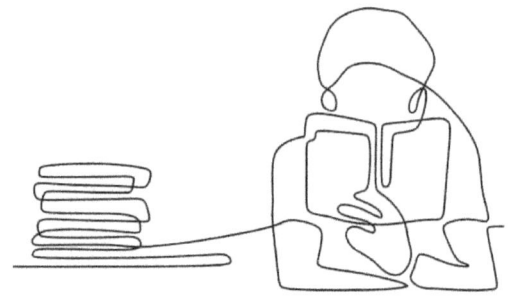

57. QUESTION

If one day I depart,

On that quiet, final journey,

Will those who walk the same path

Hold memories of me in their hearts?

The days I wandered,

Tending the life's garden where I toiled,

Who will care for the blossoms

When I no longer return?

If I leave that house behind,

Never to cross its threshold again,

And the library fills with dust,

Will someone, flipping through yellowed pages,

Catch a glimpse of my wandering eyes,

And wonder where they've gone?

58. FORBIDDEN WORLD

Enlightening:

- Don't waste your energy carelessly (Body).

- Don't twist the truth maliciously (Speech).

- Don't dwell in nostalgia (Mind).

Awakening:

- Don't take life, but embrace rebirth.

- Don't indulge in obscenity, but be devout in spirit.

- Don't get addicted, but savor life's pleasures.

- Don't speak ill, but share your wisdom.

- Don't steal, but seek knowledge.

Unity: Kindness + Intellect

Ignorance:

Ignorance tempts us with fleeting desires,

Like a fly trapped in a pot of sweet honey,

Desire swells, the body dances by the fire,

While devils and restless spirits quietly encircle.

59. NATURAL BREATHING

Only through breathing can you truly understand and connect with your surroundings.
Letting go of knowledge and sensation becomes effortless, as your breath naturally slows.
Over time, you find yourself needing it less, until the transitions blur without boundaries,
And gradually, you realize you no longer hold on to it at all.

60. PRAYERS

This morning, I carefully changed the water in the Buddhist Shrine and lit incense, watching the smoke curl upwards. From the depths of my heart, I prayed for peace - for the world, for the country, and for all my loved ones. And for myself? I asked for just a little more energy, wisdom, faith, and health to navigate the rough seas ahead, alongside my team, as we chase our dreams.

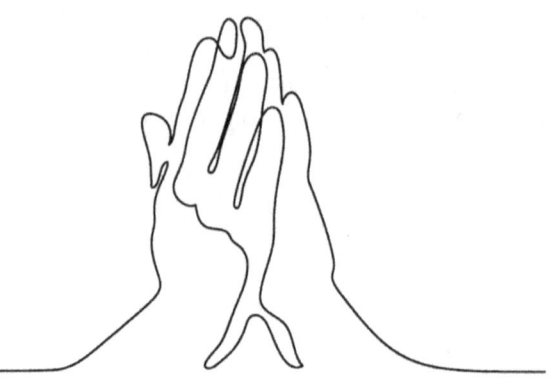

As the incense burned down, I couldn't help but think, Life is so hard. It dawned on me that these moments, right here in the quiet of the shrine, beside the serene Buddha, were the most peaceful I'd ever known.

Deep in Thoughts

Power, you've hurt me deeply,

Is this the price of a life spent chasing ambitions?

Once, I craved you, with burning passion,

Now, all I ask - leave me in peace.

61. ADAPTATION

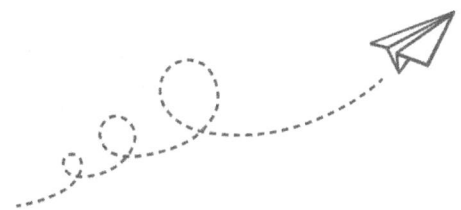

Looking back over the years, we all realize how arduous life truly is. Everything feels like the wind - fleeting, impossible to grasp. At times, we desperately try to hold on to something - people, things, emotions - but then we come to understand it's like trying to cup water in our hands; it slips away, no matter how tightly we grasp. The water of the mind gradually flows through the fingers of time. Nothing and no one remains permanent. We learn that we, too, are dissolving, and in this realization, we must adapt to the ever-changing physical world.

Giving

Gone are the childhood years,

More than half my life now lived.

Friends - some still here, some long gone,

Happy and sad stories fade with time.

Why hold on? Let them go,

Lighten the heart, let memories flow.

62. THE PAST

Reading *Les Echos* by Modiano, I found myself adrift, forgetting the childhood memories that once defined me, and the faces of those I loved. Dates and details blurred, slipping away like sand through fingers. Yet, when I paused to think of milestones, those faint threads linking one moment to another, memories began to surface, bringing back the scenes of shared laughter, tears, and whispered secrets. It was as if the events we attended together had left an indelible mark, waiting to be uncovered.

Great writers, poets, songwriters, and philosophers often find themselves trapped in the labyrinth of their own minds, haunted by the very truths they seek to understand. They grasp the impermanence, the fleeting nature of life, and yet, this understanding sometimes leads them to despair, driving them to the brink. Perhaps it is the weight of knowing too much, feeling too deeply, that makes their souls restless.

When we listen to songs and poems, the lyrics become a key, unlocking the doors to our past. Suddenly, we are transported back to those old days, where every note and word bring a rush of memories, vividly recalled, as if they happened just yesterday. The beauty of it lies in how these recollections stir the heart, adding a touch of nostalgia, a sweet sadness that lingers.

Wine of love spilled

The wine of love spills over my heart,

No need to fret over what once was.

Later, when bones and dust are one,

Where will the soul find the body?

63. THE INN AT THE EDGE OF AUTUMN

As the leaves of his life began to turn, he found himself approaching the twilight years like a weary traveler arriving at an inn after a long journey. The road behind him had been filled with many things: ambitions pursued, responsibilities carried, battles fought, and memories made. Yet now, as he stood at the threshold of this quiet place, he felt an overwhelming need to put it all down.

The inn was simple, its charm lying in its stillness. There were no grand decorations, no bustling activity, just a place to rest and reflect. As he entered, he left behind all that had weighed him down for so long: the fancy belongings that once seemed important, the obligations that had tethered him to the world, the ambitions that had driven him forward, and the stresses that had knotted his mind. Even the memories of friends and foes alike, who had once seemed so vital, were now left at the door.

Inside, he was alone with his thoughts, away from the noise of the world, as if it all belonged to someone else. The street outside buzzed with life, but it was distant, muffled. Here, he was a stranger to it, listening without really hearing. He felt himself letting go of the fatigue, the fears, and the insecurities that had followed him on his journey, as if washing away the dust of the road.

With each passing moment, he cut loose the ties that bound him to the past - nostalgia, sadness, longing. Vague emotions and fleeting desires, once so important, now seemed distant and irrelevant. Instead, he focused on the present, on the simple sensations of life: the warmth of the sun on his skin, the coolness of the breeze, the taste of a simple meal, the sound of his own breath.

He realized that this was the essence of living meditation. Peace came not from escape, but from acceptance - from being fully present in the here and now. He observed his thoughts, not as a participant in their drama, but as a witness. He listened to the quiet within, finding clarity where once there was only noise.

As night fell, he understood that his journey would soon take him elsewhere, to a place beyond this life. But there was no fear in this realization, only a deep, abiding calm. He knew what he had to do, where he would go, and how he would go. He had brought meditation into his life, and in doing so, had found peace.

And so, as he drifted into sleep, it was without dreams or nightmares, just a simple, fresh contentment that settled over him like a gentle night. The inn was quiet, the world outside continued to spin, but he was at peace, ready for whatever lay ahead.

64 – MYSTERIOUS FAME

This world is brimming with mysteries, and it takes a lifetime to grasp even a fragment of its essence. People play countless roles in the grand theater of life, each one demanding a new face, a different costume, a shift in gesture or tone. They adapt, they role-play, they become what the moment requires. But when, if ever, do they stop acting? When do they finally reveal themselves?

Maybe they never do. Perhaps the true self is as elusive as a shadow at dusk - there, yet always slipping just out of reach. And so, we wonder: are they always performing, or is this who they really are?

You might have met someone who seemed kind, with warm eyes and a gentle manner, only to discover later that behind that mask was a thief, a rogue, or worse. Life is like a novel or a play, full of characters who wear the cloak of virtue while hiding the knife of deceit. They speak of honor and kindness, but their actions betray a heart steeped in selfishness.

Yet, let's not forget the opposite. Some souls, wrapped in plain garb and unassuming words, radiate a quiet strength. They are the ones who listen more than they speak, who offer a smile rather than a boast. These are the truly generous, the ones who give without expectation, whose compassion runs deep like a hidden well.

An old man, all elegance and wit, might secretly harbor a yearning for lost youth. Two businessmen at a gala, toasting to success, could very well be scheming frauds. And that sharp-minded woman, whose beauty lies not in her face but in her spirit, has the power to ensnare even the most gallant of men.

We all carry an aura, an invisible halo that resonates - or clashes - with those around us. Perhaps we sense it without knowing, perhaps we learn to tune into it as we age. Is it a sixth sense, a spiritual attunement, or just intuition?

As we grow older, we might become better actors, slipping seamlessly between roles. The transition between the 'real' us and the roles we play blurs until it's hard to tell where one ends and the other begins. The play goes on, life goes on - until the curtain falls. Then, all roles end.

Unless, of course, one finds enlightenment, seeing life as it is - without illusions, without pretense. A life clear, simple, and utterly delightful.

Life is a play, and death is but the end of the act. To enter Nirvana might be to step into that final scene, where all the illusions fall away, and only the truth remains.

And isn't that, in its own way, a form of blissful release?

PART 4: CONTEMPLATION

Hello, to the one who walked with me through the years.

No matter the times we argued, the moments we clashed,

Mistakes and misunderstandings only strengthened our bond.

We are like the banks of a river,

Holding time's loneliness, fields of sadness, jungles of danger.

On this journey, I've seen mountains of greatness and the shadows of deceit,

Sipped the rain of grace, wandered through gardens where bees and butterflies dance.

What we have, we've earned in life's marketplace,

Bartering youth for the illusions of the world.

From the land of love, we ventured into the unknown,

Explored the vast storehouse of knowledge,

Only to part ways when dreams began to fade.

Together, we crafted moments of joy amidst the toil of long days.

I thought I was climbing toward the light,

Not realizing I was still rooted in the mud.

Today, I saw death waving

One hand pointing to the sky where saints soar,

The other to the earth beneath our feet.

And in that moment, my past crumbled to dust.

Suddenly, I understood - my time is nearing its end,

Years of twists and turns behind me,

The old companions have gone, only a few remain.

I walk alone in the wilderness,

Side by side with life's roaring waves

Here, the lure of wealth; there, the grip of power.

Enough. I am done. Worried no more.

Goodbye.

From now on, I'll let the shore evaporate into the sky,

Following the sacred wishes of the heart.

I'll blend into the earth, becoming sand and gravel,

Rolling along with the world's ephemeral currents.

But I hope to see you again in another life,

Where I'll dig a new river, wide and beautiful,

For all to bathe and revel in,

Filled with love and wisdom,

Embracing the heavens and the earth.

1. CIRCLE OF LIFE

At noon, I visited my parents for lunch. My aging mother held me close, as if trying to hold on to time itself. My parents have become like two big children - repeating questions, forgetting things, and piling rice on their plates. I often remind myself to be patient and understanding, yet sometimes, I can't help but feel a twinge of frustration. As I drove back, memories of my own infancy flashed before me - eating, grasping with tiny hands, messy and innocent. Now, my parents are like that, and I realize there's no room for complaints.

Later in the afternoon, I spent some rare, meaningful moments with my son. We talked like two friends, discussing relationships, love, women, intellect, emotions, friendship, and the confusion between love and soulmates. We touched on man's inherent loneliness and the endless search for connection.

Life is a dance of dynamic balance - there's no other way. If you stop moving, the balance breaks, and with it, you fall. Success is knowing how to maintain that balance, even when the world tilts. Until we join the majority, the dance continues.

Reincarnation

Seasons shift, heavens change,

All things reincarnate - over months or years.

Our lives, too, move in restless waves,

When we wish to pause, we enter nothingness.

2. DEALING WITH DISTURBANCES

The serene state of deep concentration is, unfortunately, fleeting. It's often disrupted from within, as if intrusions from the vastness of space suddenly descend. Emotions, fleeting joys, sorrows, desires, anxieties, and random thoughts swirl together in a chaotic mix. The more foreign they seem, the more perplexing they become. The less they relate to the focus of your consciousness, the more stubbornly they persist, as if seeking revenge for being excluded from the calm.

To navigate these disturbances successfully, maintain your breath, stay calm, and allow them to surface without resistance. Observe them with peaceful detachment, as though they were passing clouds in the sky. Eventually, the mind will tire of this dance, leading you to a state akin to the drowsy calm before sleep - a deeper layer of stillness.

3. INNERMOST FEELINGS

Oh, do you know? I just had a dream.

Could you hear my soul whispering

In the stillness of the night?

The curtains gently flutter in the dim light,

I woke, adrift in a dream, feeling empty.

Thinking of you, my soul steps softly,

On the dark road, where the insects sing.

I come to you, embracing your thick hair,

Filled with love, tender and deep.

Listen to me, though we feel alone,

We are always together, even in the solitude of night.

The flow of life carries me away,

Whether near or far, it's fleeting.

Oh, the burden of a world heavy with worries.

Let go of the dim curtain that divides us.

My heart alone weaves the delicate silk of love,

Each night, spreading a soft mattress of affection,

Cradling you in a sweet, sound sleep.

The scent of love lingers, a subtle aftertaste of life.

A damp pillow holds the stream of tender memories,

And I lull you in my arms with a love song, softly.

4. LEARN THE OLD THINGS – LEARN THE NEW THINGS

He found himself revisiting the stories he once read as a child, discovering new depths in the tales that had enchanted him years ago. What he once loved for their thrilling plots and vivid imagery, he now appreciated for their profound sayings, rich language, and deep meanings. Literature, he realized, flowed like the wind, like a waterfall, like the ocean - ever-changing yet timeless.

In his collection were numerous Russian music records from the 1980s, covering a range of genres. From guitar solos to violin sonatas, from famous symphonies to pop hits by artists like Alla Pugacheva, Sophia Rotaru, and the Beatles, these records had been his companions throughout his student years. They echoed on the streets, in the dormitories, and in the forests, marking moments of youthful exuberance and quiet introspection. But as life moved on, and new music trends emerged, those records gathered dust.

Recently, nostalgia had nudged him to play some of those old records again. The sound brought back memories, and his interest in music rekindled. An old friend, now a music professor, encouraged him to pick up an instrument again, even gifting him a few guitars and offering private lessons. "I don't know if I can study anymore," he laughed, "but I promise I'll start one day!"

His home housed a vast library, with entire rooms dedicated to different subjects. One corner, especially, was filled with books on theoretical physics - a subject that once consumed his college years. He remembered the long nights spent scribbling formulas in notebooks, though now those pages seemed like a foreign language. Despite the daunting complexity, he felt drawn to revisit these topics, perhaps as a way of reconnecting with his younger self.

He had read less than a fifth of the books he owned, yet as the years passed, he felt a growing desire to immerse himself in them. The thought of retreating to the mountains in a few years played on his mind, where he envisioned paying off life's debts and finding peace. He started writing new songs, inspired by old beats, and even contemplated a farewell concert. More and more, he found himself captivated by classical music and the idea of learning to play the violin that sat in the corner of his music room.

Most intriguingly, he returned to the study of physics, pouring over books published in the last three decades. The excitement of learning surged through him, reminiscent of his student days when he would skip meals to spend hours in libraries. The process was like climbing a mountain - arduous but exhilarating. He dreamed of finding a common voice across the universe, people, and society - a "Language of Creation," as he called it.

It was a journey filled with excitement and anxiety, a tribute to his beloved Russian teacher, and a promise to himself to finish writing the pages of his life.

5. FRAGILE NIGHT

There's nothing new under the stars.

All wars come and go, leaving scars.

The old soldier, wrapped in memories,

Longs to honor fallen comrades,

Those who gave their lives

Before the final victory.

We once danced, carefree and jubilant,

The day I met him, amidst fleeting joys.

But time, ever indifferent, marches on,

Leaving man lonely,

In life and in death, a quiet solitude.

Along the shores of his hometown,

The waves crash, relentless,

The sky stretches, blue and boundless.

Who truly gains, who truly loses?

In the silence of a fragile night.

6. LIFE FLOW

Mom was sick for a month in the hospital. I could only visit her once a day. I sat there, rubbing her hands, squeezing her biceps, hugging and patting her. Her wrinkled hands, gray hair, and labored breathing weighed heavily on me. I just looked at her, silent. What could I say? She once cared for me day and night, and now she was the one in need. The doctors and nurses did their best, and daughters-in-law came and went, every morning. But she waited for me, for the laugh, for a few funny stories from the past. Sitting there, watching her sleep, I couldn't help but wonder what I would be like when I grow old.

When I was younger, I often traveled, leaving my children in the care of others, the house filled with strangers. Perhaps, in my old age, I too will be surrounded by loneliness.

The time will come when my hair turns gray. I may be cared for by a stranger, the flow of life never stopping. I wish time would slow down so that, after all the moments of this life have passed, my children will always be by my side.

Is that possible?

Truth

What is left when we dissolve?

Death and rebirth – infinite time.

Before and after are only moments apart.

Happiness and sadness are all illusory.

7. HIGH ARC

The city stirs in the morning light,

Trembling like sands that shift beneath our feet.

Through troublesome turns and crowded streets,

The new sun's hazy smoke embraces all

The houses, the trees, the wobbling birds,

On the high arc of life where we all tread.

In a car that feels like a lonely home,

The murmuring music whispers of faraway places,

Reminding me of years now gone,

Of lyrics that linger, deep as a sigh.

No matter the paths we've crossed,

It feels like many lives we've lived,

Yet we still walk the same old road.

**

Winter days blurred by wind and snow,

Summer days brightened by birch trees.

Tall buildings stand, silent sentinels,

On either side of our journey's path.

I once lost my way on a foreign road,

In a strange city, far from home.

Oh time - time that slips away,

Separating us from youth's sweet memories.

Oh river - glittering in the afternoon light,

Reflecting silent cathedrals,

Soaring to the sky like a sad prayer,

Of souls romantic and kind,

In a land so vast and grand.

**

The music softly reminds me

Of endless vortices we've passed through,

Coming and going, meeting again,

In the hard work and monotony of life.

Sadness drifts like a distant stream,

Yet evening finds us at that arc,

Returning to the quiet red-tiled home.

Distant music seeps through the doorways,

Lights flicker with faint joy.

The puppy waits, licking my hand,

But dinner is cold, as is the whole of life.

The Paths – The Maze

He has traveled many roads. There are entirely new paths he has never walked before, and then there are roads he has crossed that now seem unfamiliar, as if seen for the first time.

For a long time, he felt as if he were on an endless journey, chasing, searching for something undefined. He encountered many fascinating wonders, experienced countless emotions, and weathered numerous ups and downs - most of which he has forgotten. But he clearly remembers the significant roads he has traversed and the unfinished ones that linger in his mind.

Now, he understands that all roads lead to a final destination - not victory, glory, or fame, but the discovery of the true self, the source of his being. If this is the truth, then is it necessary to travel so far and so often? Perhaps, just stopping and patiently walking the inner path is enough. That path alone suffices, and there is no more getting lost along the way.

8. PEACEFUL AWAKENING

Immersing oneself completely in mental melancholy is a perilous state, one that demands direct confrontation. He faces it by awakening his awareness, perhaps like a sleeper jolted by the sudden realization that his very existence hinges on that moment of awakening. If he succeeds in this awakening, it becomes a skill he can summon again and again. Through each awakening, the mind traverses a phase of pulsating calmness, rising to a state of sublimation, and ultimately reaching a peace that sometimes only dreams can offer. It's a serenity that feels weightless, accompanied by the quiet assurance of one who relaxes and wields his energy at will, no matter how intense that energy may be.

9. STAYING AWAY

He wanted to give up and go,

Looking back at a colorless show.

Just then, the racetrack began to stir,

But now, he just wants to leave it all behind.

He's like a calm soul silently screaming,

A poor life, why so wasteful?

Desire, like a jealous lover,

Pulls him in, then pushes him away.

What's left but melancholy?

Love is gone, the house stands empty.

A lonely afternoon with yellow sunlight,

Purple flowers fall from the old stem

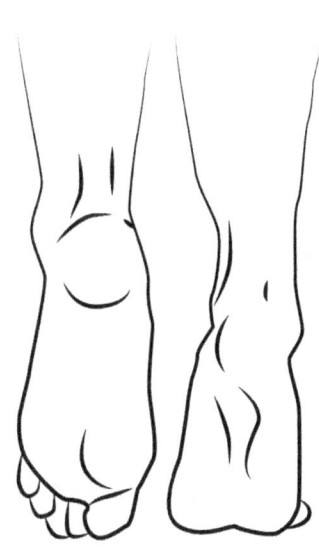

10. IMPERMANENCE

Yesterday afternoon, he visited an old acquaintance he hadn't seen in 30 years. The man, once full of life, was now serving a 30-year sentence and confined to a hospital bed. Though still agile in his movements, the medical record he showed was a stark reminder that his time was running out.

The days of glory had long faded, replaced by the simple concerns of daily life - health, children, diet, and books. That morning, as he entered his wife's room to say goodbye before work, she held out a necklace, saying it was a gift from his mother.

He froze. His mother had passed more than a year ago, yet her presence felt as near as ever. His wife explained that during a recent spiritual session, his mother had requested her cherished necklaces and bracelets be given to his brother's family and theirs.

Impermanence, he thought. All that remains is love.

Later, he visited the Buddha's shrine, his mind clouded with memories. In the office, after a whirlwind of meetings, he found a few quiet moments. Sitting alone, he was overwhelmed with tears, missing his mother dearly.

"What do you think, Mommy?" he whispered to himself. *"Your 55-year-old son, the one who never cried even when life hit hard, now sheds tears so easily."*

Ignorance

Everyone returns to dust.

How do you know it's heaven or hell?

Superiority is temporary; ignorance lasts a lifetime.

In the end, it's not worth being overbearing.

11. BY MY MOTHER'S GRAVE

It aches, Mom. It's so strange.

The earth above you, crisscrossed with roots and trees.

How sad it feels, worlds apart.

The wound in my heart won't heal,

Tears flow pure and unbidden,

An endless stream of sorrow,

A fire burns numb in the heart.

Before you, I have nothing to hide,

All my sorrows, all my sufferings,

Exposed in the loneliness and darkness.

There's something more I still don't know

When the brief light of day fades away.

I couldn't see the miracle

Far beyond, in the distant nebula, veiled in faint white smoke.

Yet after parting, there will be a reunion.

Don't forget me, dear mother.

The goodbye is merely a pause before a new hello.

In the cycle of life, we both shall return - me and her.

I'll pray for her,

So she doesn't forget the earthly way.

And I'll pray for you, dear mother,

So that you return unharmed, safe in our love.

12. LOSS

When a loved one departs, we don't just lose them; we lose a part of ourselves.

The body, a mere shadow

Of a shadow of love.

That love holds within it

The entire universe.

A bird flies by, unseen, yet still

Casts its shadow.

And where are we?

Always lingering,

In some form of love.

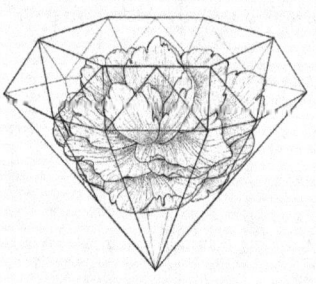

13. MEETING

(On the 25th anniversary of our company, one of my staff sent me a poem that resonated deeply. Here's how it goes:)

Meeting

In life, every encounter is destined,

Each destined meeting, a moment of joy.

But I wonder why it lingers so,

Not just in time, but deep within the heart.

If we hadn't met, we'd have gone our separate ways,

But we did, and with that, a promise was born.

When Sand Island was just a sand dune,

My memories of time were vague and fleeting.

Then I met someone who sparked inspiration,

The one I fondly called dear John.

I saw in you a burning desire,

A passion as fervent as a flame.

"Vietnamese history has many fascinating tales,

Our culture, second to none."

You wanted to share that history with the world,

And I felt proud to share in that vision.

I came to the Sand Dunes alone,

Fueled by the plans we gradually built.

The staff followed, step by step,

For a common goal centered on people.

Memories of time make a lasting difference,

Drawing visitors from all over, with melodies of pride.

That park became a place of care,

Where guests set foot and felt joy.

They left satisfied, touched by our heartfelt service.

On that journey, I faced both joy and hardship,

But I was never alone, accompanied by a determined team,

Fueled by passion and a rising will.

Together, we overcame every obstacle.

That common home, where everyone lingers,

Awaiting the moment of glory,

Where guests come to admire,

Thank you for leaving an imprint on our country!

Thanks for creating "Memories of Time."

(I don't know your name, and I'm not searching for it.

But your words are always with me,

A reminder of the journey we've shared.)

14. THE NEW LIFE

In the early morning, the cold wind came, the garden leaves rustled, and the wind chimes danced with the breeze. I entered the music room, turned on the player, and randomly chose a CD. Spreading the mattress, I laid down on my side and drifted into the smooth, soft music. My soul soared, carried away through mountains and hills, green forests, long rivers, lakes, streets, people, and roads. The stream of memories from past years rushed back.

Oh, time! That is all that is left.

Learn to let go.

Live fully.

Open your heart.

Meditate and heal yourself.

It's time to live a new life,

With a new awareness…

On the way to Death.

Slogan for Life: L2L

Life to Live

Life to Love

Life to Learn

Life to Lead

Life to Legend

15. ACHIEVING MINDFULNESS

In a state of no thinking, the mind is free from plans, desires, and needs, with no aim in sight. Yet, this is a state where energy remains undispersed, allowing the mind to discern what is possible and what is not. This state arises from a lack of desire, a dissolution of self, embodying what the Zen master calls 'spiritual.' This is the essence of 'mindfulness' - a mind that is present everywhere because it clings to nothing. It can be present in all things because, even as it attends here and there, it remains unentangled, maintaining its original utility without limitation.

It is like water filling a lake, ever ready to flow. Such a mind holds undiminished power because it is empty. This emptiness returns it to its original form, symbolized by an empty circle, encompassing all within it.

16. THINKING

In the fervor of youth,

We nurtured grand ambitions,

Believing we'd achieve something extraordinary.

But life, in its quiet way,

Pulled us through countless trials,

Through the bitter taste of relentless competition.

I've risen many times,

Amidst the tumult of life's ocean,

Gasping for fresh air,

Yearning for new shores,

Where battles are unfamiliar,

Like a lone warrior facing the windmills of fate.

Even as I stumble and ache,

Surrounded by rivals full of disdain,

Knowing well that change is elusive,

Time's rhythm and the Creator's dance,

Spin the world in its eternal cycle,

Turning the seasons, without sadness or regret,

Without the weight of right or wrong.

I see now how small I am,

In the vast expanse of humanity,

Amidst the living and the dead,

Each writhing in their own breath.

Yet, I press on, patiently,

Moving toward the threshold of Hell and Heaven,

Glancing around, searching,

For a sympathetic gaze,

In this lonely journey.

17. CONTEMPLATION

ILife is full of mysteries, some of which I've glimpsed through my own experiences and others through Deepak Chopra's "The Book of Secrets." As I reflect on these secrets, I realize they aren't just abstract ideas; they are lessons life has taught me, often in unexpected ways.

1. The Unseen Connections: Have you ever picked up the phone to call someone, only for them to say they were just thinking of you? It's as if there's an invisible thread connecting us, binding our thoughts and emotions across space.

2. Déjà Vu and Familiar Places: Sometimes I arrive in a new place but feel like I've been there before. It's a sense of familiarity that transcends logic, as though my soul remembers paths my body hasn't walked.

3. The Power of Qi: As a child, I thought qigong was something out of an adventure movie. But when illness forced me to turn to Eastern medicine, I discovered the reality of qi. I felt it coursing through me, even saw needles move as the energy flowed. It's a reminder that there's more to life than what we can see.

4. Karma and the Law of Cause and Effect: I've witnessed those with malicious intentions face consequences. It's not just a matter of legal justice; it's the universe balancing itself. What we put out into the world inevitably returns to us.

5. Spiritual Growth: Life is an inner journey, a process of spiritual growth. We all carry secrets within, dreams that seem as real as the waking world. These experiences remind me that there's a higher power at work, whether we call it God, the Creator, or the Great Self.

God – The Creator

In Indian philosophy, there are four paths to meeting God. These paths are not just theoretical; they are living experiences that shape our journey:

• **Devotion**: Through deep, sacred reverence, we draw closer to God.

• **Service**: By living a life of sacrifice and dedication, we find ourselves on the path to God.

• **Intellect**: A profound inquiry into the nature of the universe can lead us to the divine.

• **Meditation and Solitude**: The purpose of a solitary life, of meditation and visualization, is to unite with the Great Self.

The Little Self

I am just one of countless "little selves," journeying through life after life, walking these paths repeatedly, seeking union with the Great Self. It's a humbling realization. I am no different from any other creature. There is no room for arrogance, only for tolerance, love, and patience.

• For years, I sought knowledge, love, money, fame, and spirituality, chasing them like shadows. But now I realize that the real journey is within.

• When asked to define myself in one word, I responded: "a seeker." Perhaps, more accurately, "a pathfinder." I navigate life with spontaneity, allowing destinations to change with time.

• My strength to fight may have waned, but in its place, I've learned to accept what comes my way, to embrace the lessons hidden in adversity.

• My spiritual journey has led me through various teachings - Mahayana Buddhism, Hinayana, Tantra - each offering a different map for the soul. But in the end, I decided to draw my own map, one that aligns with my experiences and understanding.

Suffering and Awakening

Suffering has been a harsh but necessary teacher. It has shown me:

• The fear of losing what I have.

• The pain of comparing my failures to others' successes.

• The anxiety of losing honor and name.

• The struggle of feeling trapped with no way out.

But through suffering, I've also learned to let go, to understand that everything is impermanent. The Buddha's teachings on suffering and selflessness have become more than words; they've become lived truths.

The Path to Enlightenment

Meditation has become my refuge. It quiets my mind, allowing me to live more spiritually, more connected to the universe and the Creator.

• **Spiritual Practices**: I focus on purification - of body, mind, and soul - believing that this will bring me closer to God.

• **Positive Transformation**: I've learned to transform negative emotions into positive energy, turning anxiety into enthusiasm, anger into comfort, and distance into peace.

• **Acceptance and Letting Go**: I've come to accept that life is fleeting, that the past and future are illusions. Only the present moment is real, meaningful, and valuable.

Awakening to Freedom

Death, illness, and suffering have awakened me to the true value of life. They've shown me the importance of living fully in the present moment, of letting go of what no longer serves me.

• **Freedom in Acceptance**: I've experienced a freedom I'd never known before - a freedom that comes from realizing that I am not bound by the past or future. I am part of the universe, a vessel of love that flows through every cell, every breath.

• **The Simple Truth**: The meaning of life is not found in grand achievements but in dedicating every moment to the service of others, to doing good, and to honoring the divine within and around me.

This is the wisdom I've gathered from life's journey, from the teachings of great minds, and from the quiet moments of contemplation. It's a path of humility, of patience, and of deep, abiding love for the mystery of existence.

18. THE VU LAN FESTIVAL – THE FILIAL PIETY FESTIVAL

Missing Mom

Yesterday, as I traveled from the plateau to the sea, winding through mountains, hills, green forests, and cascading waterfalls, I found myself listening to the music of a now-departed musician. My thoughts drifted along with the song "The Rose," which adorned my shirt. As I returned home, memories of my mother filled my mind. In every step of my life journey, I think of her.

Mom is gone, yet it feels as though she's still here, just like yesterday. I can almost see her in the corner of the old house, sitting on her chair, walking with her gentle, hunched-back gait, her smile as warm as her loving eyes. Early this morning, while waiting for the dawn, the distant sea whispered lyrics about a mother. I wished, more than anything, to hold her in my arms again.

•

When the sun rose, I spread a long towel on the balcony, leaned back, and gazed at the sky and clouds while listening to the sea's waves. I sank into the nostalgia of songs about mothers, emotions rising like the tide. I couldn't hold back the tears. Could it be that these words were meant just for me?

"...The ocean waves howl one day, remembering her mother, the waves surge far away. The sky, the wind, the clouds one day cry for their mother, the moon fades and the stars fall.

Mother! The world is immense,

But not as vast as my home.

Childhood is like a soft pillow

For old people to rest upon.

Mom, I'm old now,

Crying like a child, I sit and miss you."

•

In the evening, I sat with old photos, feeling the sadness of her absence. But in those photos, she felt so close, as if she, too, missed me.

Repentance – Crying for the One Who Has Gone Far Away

Once I called for mom and dad - now we are apart.

Once husband and wife - now the moon is not full.

Once grandchildren were near - now we are distant.

*(Excerpt from the **Repentance Sutra**)*

Confession

This worldly life now blooms then fades.

Love is only a fleeting mist.

Emptiness is the faithful realm

Impermanence unites agglomeration.

Love is like a falling drop of water.

Reputation is just a show.

Keeping a low profile to let wisdom light the way,

She sought out the Dharma King to practice meditation.

Nurturing the mind and cultivating determination,

Persevering the will,

To earn results lasting into the far future.

(According to the Sutra of Confession)

Pray

Now I am on my knees, praying to the Buddha.

    · I repent of the unfulfilled past.

    · I vow to show filial piety from now on.

    · I pray for my mother to reach the Pure Land.

    · I wish my father a happy, peaceful old age.

19. REGRETS

Mom loved colorful stones. Every time I returned from a trip, I would bring her beautiful pearl necklaces. She would light up with joy, carefully examining each one, cherishing them as if they were treasures. But she always put them away, saving them for special occasions that rarely came.

These days, I find myself often exhausted, weighed down by the constant worries of life. Today, in search of something to soothe my weary soul, I sought out chakra-colored stones, hoping they might restore some lost energy. As I gazed at the beautiful rings and sparkling gems, my thoughts turned to my mother. I now understand the importance of taking care of myself, something she always knew. I wanted to find a gem ring she would have loved, to bring it back as a gift. But it was too late. She was gone.

Regret washed over me, a heavy tide pulling at my heart. I wish I had visited her more, spent more time with her, shared more moments.

Mom, please forgive me.

Empty Handed

What we have from God.

It is impossible to have less than, and

difficult to have more.

When we return to the soil, we all will be

empty handed.

We will not carry any more burdens.

20. FADING

Everything beautiful eventually fades. A figure, a smile, the light in someone's eyes, a familiar fragrance - though fleeting, these can linger with us forever. Yet, we forget that we are merely a shadow in someone else's memory.

And even that memory is fading.

Previous Life

My heart beats slow, my blood runs cold,

No love, no lust, my heart is light.

A missed appointment from a life untold,

Recounting memories, fading from sight.

21. MY DEAR

Dear Brother,

I find myself searching for the right words to address you because, for me, you embody respect, love, and a significant part of my belief. Please allow me this moment of sincerity.

Another year has passed. You, along with many brothers, friends, and dedicated souls, now stand with pride as you celebrate another birthday of the corporation - filled with enthusiasm and spirit. I imagine you must be reminiscing about the early days, when this corporation was but a dream. Those were the days when your passion and vision ignited the path we walk today. Because of those beginnings, we now have pride and trust.

Through many ups and downs, your organization has matured, achieving milestones that were once just aspirations. I remember your passionate and heartfelt words on the occasion of the company's 25th anniversary. This year, I am certain that same spirit, generosity, and pride still burn brightly within you. It is that enduring flame that will inspire future generations to carry forward the successes we witness every day.

With the most sincere affection, I, along with many other brothers and sisters, dedicate ourselves to the organization. Through every action, activity, drop of sweat, and smile, we believe that our collective dreams will soon be realized.

I have no doubt that all your hard work and dedication will be rewarded. The company will continue to thrive and grow sustainably.

Happy 26 years of brilliant flowers and fruitful endeavors.

Let us wish the organization all the best!

With deepest respect and warmest regards,

Your Younger Brother

Reading these words from a dear colleague, I am deeply touched. The journey we began together is not just a professional endeavor but a shared mission filled with purpose and heart. The respect and love reflected in this letter remind me of the importance of every step we've taken, and the people who have walked beside me. It's these bonds and this shared belief that fuel our ongoing success. The pride I feel today is not just for what we've built, but for the people who have made it all possible. May we continue this journey with the same spirit, together, as one.

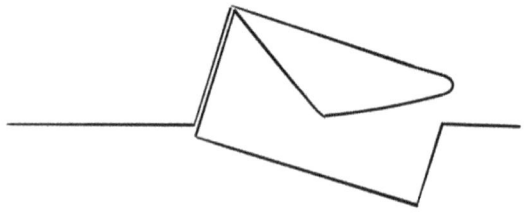

22. INTEGRATING INTO A RELIGION.

In the realm of true spiritual awareness, a mind free from all pursuits and attachments stands as the highest form of spiritual mastery. Yet, for this mastery to manifest in the world, it requires a channel - a form that opens, guides, and rehearses the spirit within. The mind, even when deeply immersed in meditation, cannot spontaneously connect with the physical world. It must first return to its original state of consciousness, then re-engage with the connections it had set aside, much like someone waking from a deep sleep and slowly recalling the tasks of the day.

He is not yet an enlightened being, one who lives in his original form and seamlessly acts from that state. He does not experience his actions as being guided by a divine force, nor does he feel himself as a mere vibration of some greater cosmic event. Instead, everything he does is conscious, deliberate, and known to him before it is done. This is why self-release and ego-liberation are essential - why introspection and the gathering of one's entire life into a single point of mindfulness are not left to chance. The more one awakens, the less room there is for randomness and luck. Determination, coupled with intense attention, builds naturally within.

In the face of every action, creation, and moment of self-sacrificing dedication, true awakening is not an accident; it is the result of a long and arduous process of training. From this point forward, he no longer gropes in the dark. Instead, in each moment of awakening, spiritual awareness is present in every interaction, profession, art, or game.

Every practice begins with a mindful breath. The gentle movements of a master express the sacredness of preparation. His bodily interaction with the world starts the moment he approaches with great concentration, respectfully acknowledging the sacredness of what lies before him. With each right action, his body and mind unite, resting in spiritual awareness. After the brief interaction, tension dissipates. He stands still, regaining his breath after a deep exhale, only moving forward once he is ready.

Thus, professional skills become a ritual - an expression of what can be called a "religion." This religion is not confined to a temple or a specific faith, but is the living practice of integrating the sacred into every moment, where every action is both a spiritual discipline and an art form, blending the divine with the mundane, the eternal with the ephemeral.

23. LIVING ZEN

A Zen master once said, the higher one climbs in meditation, the more tempting the mental traps become. The allure of success or the fear of failure can easily lead the mind astray, pulling one back into darkness.

Life, it seems, is no different. The more you stand out, the more you attract risks. But retreating too far brings its own dangers, just as living too fast invites sudden consequences.

Buddha's "Middle Way" offers a guide:

- Avoid extremes of asceticism and luxury.

- Let go of excessive desire, but don't fall into laziness.

- Don't compete aggressively, yet don't shy away.

- Be neither too high nor too low.

- Neither too bright nor too dark.

This is "*Living Zen*" - the art of *Wu Wei*, or "*Doing Nothing*." But "doing nothing" doesn't mean inactivity. It means acting in harmony with the natural flow of life, without forcing or resisting. It's about finding the balance between effort and ease, like a leaf floating effortlessly on the stream.

24. ANOTHER WORLD

You've heard tales of Heaven, Hell, and Nirvana,

Of miraculous wonders,

Glittering, beyond the grasp of human understanding.

Ultimate Enlightenment, they say,

While shadows of evil lurk in the unseen depths.

You've walked through a land like a dream,

A paradise in full bloom.

You've traversed civilized continents,

Witnessed ideologies and movements,

Fluttering like flags in the wind,

Rich with pride, love, struggle, and loss,

Only to end in ruin and betrayal.

Yet, you know no one who has returned from another world,

No one with strange dreams to share,

No miracles in hand,

No clear answers about the beyond.

Only the ancient, dogmatic scriptures speak of it.

Still, you feel it in your bones

Another world, close by,

Where strange souls wander,

Carrying promises or harboring malice.

Their nature depends on the desires within our hearts,

Whether noble or tainted by worldly greed,

Caught in the fierce currents of temptation.

You dive deep into this boundless sea of birth and death,

Tasting every flavor life offers:

Bitter, sweet, and everything in between.

You've known loss, gain, and the surging tides of emotion.

You wish for good things, for ideals that seem so distant.

But as you gaze into the deep blue sky,

Where spirits shine like stars in the night,

You find guidance in their quiet light,

In the midst of fear and confusion.

With so many lost souls adrift,

You yearn for a world of better dreams,

And so you pray:

For divine moments in this human life,

For dreams to take form and blossom.

Let yourself believe that God, or Nirvana, awaits.

Let there be a light to guide you forward.

25. BEAUTIFUL MEMORIES

In the recesses of my mind, Hanoi stands as a city of grace and charm. There are brick walls, red-tiled roofs, and streets infused with the scent of blooming flowers. Green trees line the roads, offering shade and shelter to girls gliding by in their graceful 'ao dai.' I remember foggy days that draped the narrow alleys, drizzling rain mixing with the soft rise of kitchen smoke along the riverbanks. Winters, chilly yet warm with the glow of yellow blossoms, gave way to springs filled with a riot of colors. Summers were chaotic with monsoon flashes, while autumns lingered with a bittersweet aftertaste of time. These memories tremble on the edge of the present, yet they bring joy.

What has passed is gone forever, blurring into indistinction. Only a few moments remain vivid in the mind. We pluck these beautiful flowers from our memories and place them in the vase of a quiet heart. But like all things, even these memories will wither in time. The vase, too, will be forgotten, though a faint scent may linger on the breeze of the past.

Goodbye Song

The day I say goodbye to this world,

The dawn will be shining,

The sky rejoicing,

Flowers will brim with dew,

And bees will seek their nectar.

Streets will bustle with people,

Workshops aglow with fire,

Fields dancing in the wind.

Restaurants will open their doors,

People moving in and out,

Classrooms filled with eager students.

A new day will start, with so much to be done.

When I return to my memories,

Perhaps the sunset will still linger,

Casting a golden veil over the forest.

Homes will glitter with evening light,

Dinners prepared with care.

Men lost in calculations,

Women attending to their tasks,

Old folks sharing their wisdom,

Children lost in their games.

Waves will calm as ships anchor,

Birds will either soar or rest,

And a soft melody will float through the village.

Nothing will be new,

Yet everything will be as ancient as the hills.

Streams will murmur,

Heading endlessly to the ocean.

My life, just a sound,

Echoing briefly before fading away.

I'll gather a few words,

Leaving behind whispers of my feelings,

In thin books with my shadow lurking,

All fading, all fading.

26. SUNDAY

After a long day of visiting the project site and finding little to spark his interest, he decided to break away and head to the beach for lunch. The idea of spending the day by the sea seemed like the perfect antidote to his mundane morning. Luckily, he had a few friends who were always up for an adventure and exceptionally well-organized. Among them were a few beautiful ladies who had graciously taken it upon themselves to host him for the day, adding a touch of elegance and charm to the outing.

The day unfolded with a series of spontaneous activities: surfing, swimming, singing on a yacht, and capturing fun moments with the lovely hosts in the sparkling sea. As the afternoon sun began to dip, they all relaxed on the sand, soaking up the last rays of the day. The sunset cast a golden hue over the waves, and he found himself sunbathing in the glow, completely at peace, with the sound of laughter and the sight of the waves making everything feel perfect.

But as they packed up and headed home, reality began to creep back in. He decided to check his emails, just to stay ahead of the upcoming week. Scrolling through, he suddenly came across a resignation letter from a senior manager. The very same manager who had just been appointed to a new position but apparently found it less than satisfying. The unexpected resignation hit him like a wave, jolting him out of his relaxed state.

That night, he tossed and turned, unable to shake the situation from his mind.

Reflection:

The petty man craves power,

But power shuns the petty.

The two are forever linked,

Like the left hand to the right.

27. HUMAN LIFE

Overcast winter day

    Only you and me

        Fearless, the Buddha smiles

           Do not worry about things

             Quiet night

               Music

                 Soul

                     Stream of sounds

                       Nostalgia

                         Sad

                           Vague...

Quietness

Rockies, flowing water,

Slanting sunlight, only me with a heavy heart

Bodhi tree with leaves gently hanging,

Deer forest echoes flutes in the stillness.

28. GLOOMY MOMENT

You can't deny the dark days when doubt creeps in, making you question whether refining your skills is still worth it. The effort seems disproportionate to the rewards, and now everything feels stuck, with no clear path forward.

But in this stillness, there's wisdom. Like a tree dormant in winter, gathering strength for spring, this pause isn't failure - it's a natural part of the journey. In meditation, we learn to embrace quiet moments, letting the mind settle and trusting that the path will reveal itself, not through force, but through gentle realignment.

Breathe, reflect, and trust that even in these dark moments, transformation is quietly taking root, preparing to emerge when the time is right.

29. EMOTIONAL STRING

He returned to the old city where his student days were spent, arriving on a rainy afternoon at the end of summer. The airport, voices, roads, and forests - all familiar, yet touched by the passage of time.

The next morning, the sun was warm, illuminating the streets where vehicles flowed gently and people moved leisurely. Green trees cast their shade, and colorful flowers lined both sides of the road, bringing back memories of youthful days.

He visited his teacher's grave, sitting down and whispering to the spirit, gently rubbing the fine sand on the grave as he gazed at the familiar image on the stone. The sun filtered through the branches, casting a soft glow that made the image seem as though it had come from a distant realm.

As the sunset broke, he wandered through the old streets, passing familiar houses, shops, and bookstores. The river still flowed, but his heart, once filled with excitement, now felt indifferent and cold. The place had lost its spark, and he didn't know when he would return.

Is love a fragile string?

The Old Land

First love lingers in the mind, perhaps because of its beauty,

perhaps because of its inevitable separation.

Russia, with its poetry, dreams, and mystique,

remains in my memory, tied to the beautiful ambitions of youth.

Songs, articles, and poems - quintessentially Russian, pure, and magical

- always touch me, stirring time and memories.

For me, that country has become the old land,

my soul forever tinged with a bit of Russian spirit.

30. COMFORTING MEMORIES

Last night, I stumbled upon the song "The Times They Are A-Changin'," an old American tune from the 1960s. Nostalgic, poignant, yet wandering and fading... as I looked back on the things that have passed, all that remained were memories, soft echoes of a time long gone.

When I woke the next morning, the lyrics still danced in my mind, leaving a bittersweet aftertaste. The sun shone brightly over the Buddha's shrine, and I burned incense, sincerely praying for peace amidst the hardships of life. The path remains as challenging as it was in my younger days - filled with cold winds, ringing bells, and rolling leaves.

Feeling a twinge of anxiety, I reached for an old fortune teller's book, which offered a simple wisdom: "Winter comes, the water freezes into ice, wait for time." Patience, it reminded me. The ice will eventually melt, the fish will swim again. Endurance will bring its own rewards.

I found some relief in my heart, a quiet comfort in the certainty that everything moves in its own time.

> ### *Distant Wishes*
>
> *Life is a book to which every day we add,*
>
> *Sorrows mingled with distant desires.*
>
> *This morning, I woke to an empty bed,*
>
> *In a cold room, craving a warm embrace.*
>
>

31. REALITY – ILLUSION

He's an honest man, with deep reverence for the divine. But let's face it, sometimes he lets slip a few indecent words without a second thought, and when alone, he finds himself indulging in the simpler, more earthly pleasures. The wisdom of the ancients has been with him since his student days, yet there's undeniable joy when he can let out a good, hearty laugh over something a bit vulgar.

He often meditates, contemplates the beauty of life, and has grand aspirations, but more than once, he's found himself swept up in the hustle and bustle of life's more sensual distractions. He thinks he understands people, the meaning of life, but still, he wrestles with suffering, sadness, and the worries that are handed to him each day like unwanted gifts.

He cherishes the humble beauty of both body and mind, but can't quite resist the urge to reach out and pluck the wildflowers, inhaling their untamed scent, savoring the moment. Yet, through it all, he believes in his sincerity.

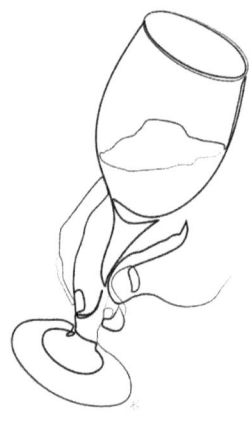

Awakening

Woke up in the quiet of night

With worries swirling tight.

What will I leave behind

When dawn calls me to earth's embrace?

Just a few dreams to fulfill

To bring my life some grace.

What's the meaning if they stay unfinished,

In this fleeting life's race?

32. SINGING FOR MY MOTHER

I spent the whole afternoon immersed in songs about mothers, letting each melody carry me deeper into memories. Song after song played, and as dusk gave way to the soft glow of evening, I found myself in tears. Lately, emotions have surfaced easily, and today was no exception.

I listened to:

- *My Mother*

- *The Rose Pinned to the Shirt*

- *Mom!*

- *My Beloved Mom!*

- *Loving Mom for Thousands of Lives*

- *Mom's Diary*

- *Shouldering Mom*

- *Seeing Mother in a Dream*

- *My Feelings*

- *I Owe You*

- *Mother's Light*

- *My Beloved Mom!*

As the evening settled in, it dawned on me that nearly 100 days had passed since my mother left this world. Time had slipped by while I had been away, caught up in the demands of life far from home. The songs must have been her way of reminding me, calling out to me through the music, a gentle nudge from the beyond.

The tears flowed not just for the loss but for the realization that in all the busyness, I had almost let the days pass without marking this moment. I whispered a promise to her, a vow to keep her memory close, to sing these songs in her honor, letting the music keep her spirit alive in my heart.

In that quiet moment, I knew she was with me, listening, just as she had always been, her love as steadfast as ever, even from afar.

33. URGE

During the annual workshop at his organization, he remained silent from morning until afternoon, listening intently to everyone before being the last to speak. What he shared reflected his sincere desire for the job, the organization, and the managers, and it resonated deeply with those present.

The remaining time was just one year ahead. It was arduous and challenging. *"Let's try to get through it together,"* he urged, emotionally overcome by the weight of his words.

At the gala dinner, emotions ran high as people expressed many valuable and secret thoughts to him. Those who had been praised were happy. Those who had been criticized quietly withdrew. Those who had not been praised complained and promised to be more determined.

He hoped they would live their lives to the fullest during their years together. And he decided he would write a song: *"Together"* – to remember these days.

The one that brings fear is in fear.

The one that brings love is in love.

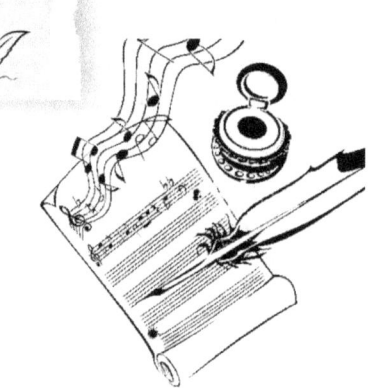

34. PATIENTLY WAITING

He sat in silence, his body and mind taut with tension. The Zen master's voice echoed in his thoughts, "You see what happens. If you are in the highest tension, you cannot wander aimlessly. Even in meditation, doubt will pull you away."

He felt the weight of his own expectations, the pressure to achieve something, anything. The master's voice continued, "Wait patiently. Don't chase after what will come or how it will come. Let go of the need to control."

He breathed deeply, releasing his grip on the need for answers. The tension began to fade, replaced by a quiet acceptance. In that stillness, he understood: patience wasn't about waiting for something to happen; it was about being present, allowing whatever comes to simply be.

35. MEMORIES

Something stirred in his mind, a fleeting presence that followed him through the streets, into the office, and back to the empty house. It was there, lurking in the shadows, flickering when cars passed by, smudged on the rain-soaked glass. It followed him into the garden as he walked late in the afternoon, where the lights were dim, and the gravel crunched underfoot. Somewhere, a voice whispered - clear, startling, then gone - shattering like glass in the silence. The echoes of a hoarse voice from the past tugged at his heart, leaving behind a tumultuous, choking sensation.

Old objects resurfaced from the past, a vivid photo fell from an ancient document, a New Year's postcard with friendly words from almost 30 years ago appeared, triggering memories. The sights blended with the surroundings, like dew on a decaying wall, like petals falling in the rain, swaying with the wind. The curtains, discreet and mysterious, swayed gently, making him sigh softly. Branches trembled in the pale moonlight, and small fruits fell from above, landing softly on the roof, only to slide down to the ground - fragile and alone.

In those quiet moments, the dust of memories returned, gently settling around him.

Moon Night

A small pagoda nestled deep in the forest,

The Mountain King's throne under a full moon's light.

He meditates to the music of all beings,

Yet sees a lovely woman, lifting clouds with all her might.

36. SEA OF LIFE

Clouds are chasing above Hai Van Pass.

High mountains. High pass follows high pass.

Today I visited the old place,

The former frontier post is now a ruin.

A picture of the teacher and me is here.

But the person is absent.

Friends running around

Taking pictures with the mountains,

Until that scene will be seen again.

Hidden behind some groves

Two monks in brown robes sat,

Leaning back against the mountains,

Contemplating the sea of life.

37. RHYTHM

Every day, your body takes in what it needs - food, air, experiences - and then, in its own rhythm, lets go of the excess. You eat, you breathe, you live in a cycle as old as time itself.

You're part of the earth, intricately connected to nature in a seamless, organic dance. You receive and release, give and take, in a rhythm that mirrors the heartbeat of the world.

You take in nourishing foods, and your body discards the waste. You absorb positive emotions, and let go of the sad ones. You gain clarity from experiences, sweeping away dark delusions. You find divine faith, and fear loses its grip. You foster friendships, dissolving old animosities.

Everything in life has a rhythm - long, short, shallow, or deep - depending on how you view the world and how you act within it.

Just as your breath has a rhythm, so does your mind. Breathing is a rhythm - beautiful when it's steady, soft, and harmonious. The mind, too, is a sound without words. When it flows smoothly, without jarring notes, it becomes a beautiful melody. A beautiful mind, then, is one that beats in tune with a harmonious rhythm, moving effortlessly with the pulse of life.

38. THE STAR OF HOPE

When I was a child, I lived in a little house that stood three stories tall, towering over the surrounding homes. On hot summer afternoons, my siblings and I would climb up to the terrace. The small yard up there was home to a few potted plants, their leaves shriveled from the relentless summer heat. The cement floor was scorching, but we'd splash it with buckets of water to cool it down. Despite the heat, it was far more comfortable to enjoy the breeze up there than to stay in the stuffy house below, especially during power outages.

Sometimes, I'd spread out a sedge mat and stay on the terrace until late at night. From that vantage point, the terrace offered a view of the sky that seemed endless. Our house was the tallest on the street, with branches of Indian almond trees stretching across the yard. On summer nights, the sky was a canvas of stars - some sparkling brightly, others dim and distant. There were clusters of tiny light spots, all scattered across the sky like a painter's masterpiece.

One star in particular caught my eye. It wasn't the brightest, nor the most dazzling, but it was unique in its own way, standing out just enough in the vast night sky. I liked to think of it as the star of my life. On some nights, caught up in the thrill of childhood, I'd strip off my clothes and spread my arms wide under the Indian almond tree, orienting myself toward my star. But sometimes, the swaying branches and leaves would obscure it, leaving me searching again. The real danger, however, wasn't losing sight of the star but the possibility of a hairy caterpillar falling from the tree - especially when I was wearing nothing at all!

After many nights spent struggling to find the star, I finally discovered a more accurate way of navigating. I had an old, glimmering blue compass, a relic from an American soldier, which helped me locate my star every time. Our house faced west, and the star was always 15 degrees to the right. This number stuck with me because I was born on the full moon of December. On full moon nights, the moon bathed the entire sky in light, and when the moon was slightly to the left, my star would emerge, shining quietly. Even though the moon was brilliant and other stars sparkled around, my star seemed lonely under that luminous sky. And so, I called it the lonely star on a full moon night - like me.

As the years passed, I left home to study, and the old house was eventually sold. Busy with the demands of life, I no longer climbed up to that small corner of the yard. My pilgrimages took me far from home, and I lost the chance to search for that lonely star from the terrace. Yet, deep within me, I never stopped thinking about it.

Throughout my life, I've often found myself metaphorically standing under the night sky, naked with arms outstretched, searching for that star. Sometimes I've found it, and sometimes I've lost it among countless others. Life, too, has presented me with its share of caterpillars - unexpected, often unpleasant, but unavoidable.

On many uncertain nights, I think back to that star, still shining in the lonely moonlight. And though I can no longer see it, I know it still humbly glitters in the sky.

I call it *the star of hope.*

39. FEARS

You have many fears in life - mainly the fear of losing what you have, like property, position, and love. But there's one thing you often overlook, something you don't fear much and spend freely: your lifetime.

You spend a little of it each day, treating it like a small expense that doesn't matter much. But time is obviously limited. Reason tells you that everything else outside of you, unrelated to you, once lost, will either be gone forever or will still be there after you're gone.

The real concern should be the gradual loss of your lifetime. If you don't spend it mindfully every day, then you're not truly alive. You've already died in spirit. So, the only true fear should be the fear of not living life to the fullest every day.

Living, therefore, is an act of adventure - full of risks, excitement, and surprises. And always remember - take it easy. Enjoy your life and fill each day with priceless moments.

Full

This life is illusory; everything will disappear.

Moreover, if you're always chasing after distant things,

you'll never find satisfaction in the present.

True happiness comes in the moments when you're content with what surrounds you.

A happy life is one that's fully enjoyed - fully in every present moment.

40. MORE PRACTICE

The Zen master looked at his student and spoke calmly, "You must start again, from the very beginning. Everything you've learned until now is of no use. The paths you sought for refuge have failed you, leaving only a shadow behind. Your desires are still clinging to you, deeply rooted, and cannot be simply shaken off. So, practice again, with fresh eyes and a clear heart."

41. WHISPERS

At noon, I returned to the empty room. After the bustle of meetings, I found myself alone with a prepared meal, just like every other day. Time moved slowly in the quiet solitude.

Mixed vegetables, stir-fried greens, and vegetable soup. The same as always, yet now touched by the passage of time. I reached for a piece of meat, soaked in orange sauce, and the sweet taste brought back memories that choked me with emotion.

These memories took me back to the days when my mother was in the hospital. I would sit by her side, gently rubbing her hand, letting her sleep peacefully. She was too ill to return home, and I was constantly traveling for work. The nurse would tell me that each time she woke, she asked if I was there. The day she opened her eyes and saw me beside her, her face lit up with joy. She hugged me tightly, asking if I was well, if my cough had gone, if I was eating enough. She promised we would have a big meal together, and she would make me duck with orange sauce.

Now, my mother is gone. Sometimes, the ache of missing her is so strong that it brings tears to my eyes. Since she passed, I visit my father more often. After a few questions, he tells me how much he misses me. I remind him to exercise, to stay healthy and happy, so that my mother can be at peace wherever she is. But the truth is, I miss her too.

My mother would often hold my hand, reminding me to keep my neck warm to avoid coughing. She would ask why I was so thin, urging me to be strong - really strong - because I am the one who carries the family. I know this well, so I try every day. I strive to lead, to stay strong, tough, and to keep a cheerful spirit.

But deep down, I know I am soft and very lonely. If I could turn back time, I would wish only to return to my childhood, to be held and protected by her, to be fed, clothed, and bathed in her loving gaze.

Every morning at the Buddha's shrine, I pray for my mother to find peace in the Pure Land. Looking at her picture, my heart whispers, as if she is already there.

42. SELF PITY

After several days of indecision, he finally decided to go to the hospital in Tokyo for a checkup. Thanks to two old Japanese friends who were familiar with the staff and had some connections, he was able to see a doctor quickly.

The doctor began asking all sorts of questions - how it had been before, where he had undergone previous examinations, what medications he had taken, and whether he had results from any blood tests, biopsies, or CT scans. As the barrage of questions continued, he felt an overwhelming urge to just get up and leave.

Then came the bombshell: if he needed treatment, a relative would have to accompany him to sign some papers. He looked around - who would do that? His children were far away, busy with their own lives. There was no one he could rely on. Reluctantly, he asked his Japanese friend, who had been sitting nearby, to act as his temporary guardian. From that moment on, he tuned out the doctor's words, lost in his own thoughts.

A wave of self-pity washed over him. Everyone had their own life, their own responsibilities. His children were far away, pursuing their own futures. Who was there for him? Who could he count on? Just himself. The thought was almost unbearable. What was the point of living? For whom was he struggling?

The idea of retreating to the mountains, living alone by a temple, by a stream, away from the hustle and bustle of life, reading books in the afternoon - this idea kept creeping into his mind, offering a bittersweet comfort.

But then, a wry smile crossed his face. Perhaps this was just another phase, another challenge to overcome. He could almost hear the echo of a Zen master's voice in his mind, reminding him:

"Whoever brings me, will bring me back.

So now it's only me.

When words are uttered,

I am silent and speechless."

Maybe, he thought, there was a kind of quiet wisdom in embracing this solitude, in finding peace in the stillness. And perhaps, just perhaps, that wasn't such a bad place to be after all.

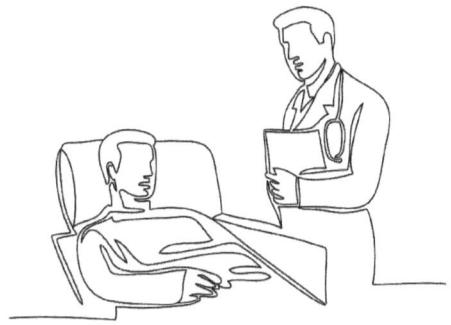

43. ECHOES IN THE DUST

We have walked the boulevards and passed through many triumphal gates,

From the continent of civilization to the new world.

At times, we attended festivals, victory days,

Remnants of great wars.

Memorials, certificates of merit,

Names etched on roads,

Yet the fanfare of banners cannot quench the thirst of the past.

The wars are now far away,

Leaving only a few lines on inanimate statues,

Amid motionless forms carved in stone,

In the wilderness, where dust and weeds spread,

Like the ruins of an ancient city wall.

Throughout life, we have savored many drinks and foods,

Loved and hated many people.

But it all comes, and it all goes, leaving nothing but a body with wrinkled skin,

And cloudy eyes, staring at an empty history.

We have passed through many cities, mountains, and forests,

Traveled along gravel roads,

Or asphalt paths that glisten in the sun, with dust

Sweeping along the endless stream of people.

But all was profoundly silent.

Only the voice in the mind keeps echoing.

Is it a faint shadow behind us?

Or is it just the dust chasing after us?

44. A DOG'S EYES

As the children grew older, they became more independent, each busy with their own world. My work kept me away most of the day, and even when I returned home, it was often late. So, whenever I got home, I made it a point to visit my children's rooms to greet and hug them. But their responses were usually more out of formality than warmth. My son, after some persistence, began to hug me a bit more warmly, but my youngest daughter remained distant. She rarely left her place to hug me; a nod or a casual *"I'm busy"* was all I got.

But she loved the dog. She hugged it often, and the dog, with its wet eyes and wagging tail, was always thrilled to see its young mistress.

As time passed, I started noticing a change. Now, when I came home, my daughter would stand up, run to the door, greet me with a light hug, and ask me a few questions. It warmed my heart, even if it felt a little scripted.

One morning, as I was getting ready for work, I caught a glimpse of myself in the bathroom mirror. I paused, startled. My eyes looked different - strange yet familiar.

What kind of eyes are these? I thought, puzzled, before the thought slipped away.

On my way out, I noticed Haichi, our dog, lying quietly by the door of my daughter's room. He lifted his head and looked at me with those big, soulful eyes, his tail wagging slowly.

I took a few steps, then stopped and turned back. The realization hit me like a soft, unexpected laugh: My gaze in the mirror had been just like Haichi's - sad, loving, and full of expression.

"So, I have a dog's eyes now," I mused. *"No wonder my daughter's greeting has changed."*

With a chuckle, I thought to myself, *"Well, okay. Better than nothing."*

45. THE SCENT OF CHANGE

He walked along the familiar red brick corridor, his footsteps echoing softly in the quiet space. As he passed by the calendar hanging on the wall, it caught his eye, staring back at him with a quiet indifference. He stopped, tearing off the old pages one by one, revealing the fresh, untouched date beneath. It struck him how the calendar still looked so new, yet the days it marked had come and gone, just like the vibrant blooms in the garden that once heralded the arrival of spring. A few more seasons had passed.

He paused, taking in the scene around him. The garden, green and leafy as ever, remained unchanged. The pine branches reached out as if to catch the sun, their needles casting gentle shadows on the ground. The fish swam lazily in the pond, oblivious to the passing time. Nothing seemed different, yet there was a subtle shift in the air, a hesitancy in the sunlight as it filtered through the familiar space.

Then, something caught his attention - a faint scent, carried on a breeze from the end of the fence. Bunches of flowers, in white, pink, and crimson, cascaded over the wall, their colors reflected in the shimmering lake below. The flowers hung from the brown doorways, intertwined with pergolas, swaying gently in the morning light that danced through the green leaves and rippled into the cool water.

For the first time in a while, he felt a quiet delight in seeing the new date on the calendar. There was something different in the air, a change that wasn't marked by excitement or the urge for grand new adventures, nor by the indifference and boredom that had colored so many days before. It was a light scent, a whisper of change that signaled a shift in both the world and his heart. He stood there, quietly thanking the presence of something greater, something that had brought this subtle, but welcome, change into his life.

46. CONTINUE TO PRACTICE

"Don't ask, just practice!" Those were the words that echoed in his mind. So, he stopped asking, accepting the urge to abandon the practice altogether. It would have been so easy to walk away, if not for the spiritual teacher who held him steadfast, offering guidance with unwavering patience.

He moved through each day, fulfilling his duties, relearning the craft he once approached with passion. Now, he noticed a growing detachment from the very things he had once poured his heart into. The fire had dimmed, and the work felt cold.

Yet, in the quiet of his mind, he realized that the practice itself held value beyond the fleeting warmth of enthusiasm. It was in the daily repetition, the disciplined return to the work, that deeper understanding emerged. Not every step needed to be filled with fervor; some steps were simply about moving forward.

And so, he continued to practice, not for the love of the task, but for the wisdom that whispered through the monotony: perseverance, patience, and the quiet strength of enduring effort.

47. MINDFUL MEDITATION

Perhaps I have not fully understood meditation. I've only dabbled, trying to experience it through brief moments and the pages of meditation books. I've never truly immersed myself in the presence of a monk or a Zen master.

Since the day Mom passed away, I've realized that human life is finite, but the mind is infinite, like the vast spectrum of colors in the world. Life and death are but two sides of the same coin, and the world constantly shifts and changes. The relentless pursuit of prosperity is exhausting, so I often retreat to the mountains and forests, seeking solace in meditation. In the stillness of nature, everything is unveiled - flowers, grass, dust, flowing streams, fallen leaves, chirping birds, wind, sunlight, the moon. Though they appear in countless forms, they are all pure and simple. It's as if everything in nature is meditating, and I need only to learn from it.

I've come to understand that true living is about embracing a humble and calm life, with a mind undisturbed by the dust of the world. This is the mindful meditation I have longed for.

Kindness

Enlightenment begins with liberation.

Liberation begins with letting go.

Letting go begins with understanding kindness.

48. LIFE – DEATH MESSAGE

Early one morning, he found himself at the Buddha's shrine, seeking solace in the ancient sutras. The teachings reminded him of the root causes of suffering - greed, attachment, anger, and delusion - all of which keep life bound in a cycle of darkness.

As he entered the meditation room, memories from the past decade came flooding back. The years had been full of ups and downs, marked by struggles that tested his resilience.

The real estate market had frozen, leaving projects at a standstill and funds trapped beyond reach. The once-thriving organization began to falter as employees slowly drifted away, seeking stability elsewhere. Financial institutions crumbled under pressure, and after countless rounds of negotiation, he was left with the weakest partner, a decision that only seemed to deepen his troubles.

Moving to the South, far from the familiar comforts of home, he threw himself into the fight. The days were filled with clashes, learning, and moments of anger and frustration, yet progress remained painfully slow. His health, once robust, began to wane under the relentless strain.

Amid the chaos, letters circulated, each one adding a new layer of complexity to an already tangled web. His life seemed to unravel further with each passing day. When he broke his leg in 2016, it felt like the final straw. Unable to attend his teacher's funeral, he was forced to rely on a cane, a constant reminder of his fragility.

Despite these setbacks, he continued to search for a way forward. His quest took him to distant lands - Hong Kong, China, Macao, Singapore - in hopes of finding investors who might share his vision. But the challenges mounted, and in 2017, a visit to his Russian teacher's grave left him feeling adrift in a sea of self-pity.

By 2018, the struggle had intensified. His efforts to save the organization seemed fruitless, and then, as if to mock his determination, cancer struck. The diagnosis brought with it a wave of irony and despair. He spent many lonely days, isolated from those he cared about, his mind clouded by fears of failure and the looming specter of death.

In the stillness of his solitude, he confronted his deepest fears - fear of losing everything he had worked for, fear of bankruptcy, fear of dishonor. And yet, with the arrival of cancer, he realized that these fears were nothing compared to the fear of sudden death.

The loss of his mother at the end of 2019 was a devastating blow. The person he loved most was gone, leaving behind a void that seemed impossible to fill. But in his grief, he found a new understanding. Everything - fame, wealth, talent, love - was impermanent. Life, with all its trappings, was fleeting.

Yet, he did not succumb to despair. Instead, he endured. He learned to accept the transience of life, to face its challenges with courage. And on September 28, as the organization celebrated its 25th anniversary, he decided to share his "Life – Death Message – 100 Speedy Days" with his employees. He urged them to push forward, to accelerate through the hurdles, to keep moving despite the obstacles.

Difficulties remained, but his mind grew clearer. Even as he encountered lies, betrayals, and deceit, he found solace in the presence of those precious few who stood by him. He knew he was not alone in this journey.

With a quiet sense of gratitude, he whispered his thanks - to life, to the people, to fate.

Emptiness

As the years have passed, I have come to see,

The lessons of receiving, and the wisdom of giving.

When we return to earth, samsara continues endlessly,

Until we understand - all is impermanent.

49. SITUATION

On Monday, he attended a progress meeting that filled the room with grandiose visions. Everyone listened eagerly, inspired by the possibilities laid before them. But as he got into the car afterward and drove past the familiar houses, the weight of reality began to settle in.

The driver quietly reminded him, "Your meal should be served when it is hot." The breakfast he had neglected was now reheated - a small but poignant symbol of how life's necessities often took a backseat to the demands of ambition.

Being a business owner wasn't always what it seemed. Each day felt repetitive - the same dinner every night, rice and nuts, water, morning glory, and different vegetables. Breakfasts were rushed on the bumpy road to work, dinners were quiet and solitary affairs. In these moments of routine, he began to reflect on the true essence of life.

Then, as if whispered by the divine, came the wisdom:

"I give you:

- *The bitter and sweet wines of life to taste and learn from.*

- *Sleep to soothe your anxious mind.*

- *Quiet meditation to calm your restless heart.*

- *Illness and suffering to teach you the fragility of dreams.*

- *Your body, a bottle of wine, where each year adds depth to the life you live."*

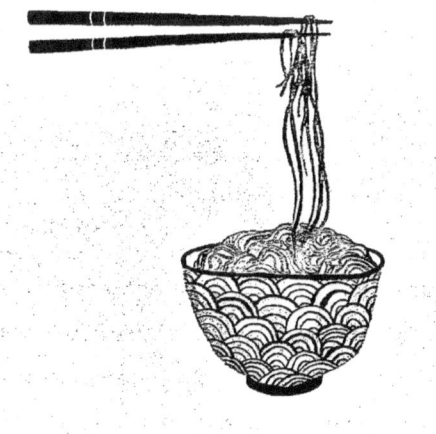

50. PRECEPTS

All religions hold precepts,

And every nation upholds rules of virtue,

Strikingly similar in their essence

Guidelines of do's and don'ts.

Avoid the bad, embrace the good.

Yet, wars persist, endlessly waged

Between believers and others,

Fueled by blind discrimination.

Prohibitions have a curious power,

Stirring cravings and daring us to

Confront the darkness within.

But if the world were one

A seamless blend of night and day,

Moving in an unbroken rhythm,

Like the four seasons,

In an eternal cycle of birth and death

There would be no need to avoid

Either the bad or the good.

Instead, we could let things flow naturally

As they come and go,

In success and failure,

In shining glory and arduous trials,

In the delusions of lust and worldly desires.

For all great things are often surrounded by mediocrity,

Together creating the vibrant tapestry of life.

51. ACTIONS AT PEACE

From time to time, there is a genuine interaction, a moment when the teacher within us falls silent, reverent. In these moments, it is beyond explanation how things unfold - sometimes, profound outcomes arise from doing almost nothing. The entire body and mind merge effortlessly with the object of focus, even as the body remains still or moves ever so slightly. What matters is that it happens, and that alone is enough.

Gradually, you begin to discern the quality of two interactions - success and failure. The difference is profound, invisible to others, but deeply felt within. To the outsider, a genuine interaction is marked by the gentle fluidity of the meditator's body, seamlessly connected with the object, while the rest of the body remains undisturbed.

If the interaction falters, the breath, once compressed, releases, and you find yourself needing a quick inhale to regain the connection. But after a true interaction, the breath flows out smoothly, the next inhalation unhurried. The heart beats steadily, the mind remains focused, and you are prepared for the next action.

In the mind, a genuine interaction feels like the dawn of a new day. There's a deep sense that all actions are righteous, and perhaps more importantly, all non-actions are authentic. This state of being is remarkable. Yet, those who reach this state are gently reminded by the spiritual teacher, with a subtle smile, that it is best not to cling to it. For only with a mind anchored in peace will this state naturally return.

52. WONDERS

I believe,

Justice is real

A truth shared by all born

Of parents, carrying human blood.

Yet, throughout history, I see so much injustice

Between people living on this earth.

It's as if justice took a long vacation,

But I still believe it'll return, perhaps with a tan.

I believe,

Love is real

A bond uniting all born

Of parents, carrying human blood.

And yet, history is rife with tales of hatred,

As if love lost its way in the crowd.

But I'm convinced love is just playing hide and seek,

And will soon jump out, laughing.

I believe,

Sincerity is real

An honest thread weaving through those born

Of parents, carrying human blood.

Still, lies seem to linger in the air we breathe,

As if sincerity misplaced its glasses.

But I know sincerity will eventually find them,

And see the world clearly once more.

I believe,

Goodness is real

A spark glowing within all born

Of parents, carrying human blood.

Yet, mistakes dot our path like stubborn weeds,

As if goodness forgot to water the garden.

But I trust goodness is simply learning to garden better,

And the flowers will bloom brighter.

I believe,

Impermanence is real

For all things change,

Like people and the passing years.

But there's a part of me that resists this truth,

Choosing instead to live in righteousness,

Love, sincerity, and kindness,

Which I nurture every day

Hoping that, just maybe, these wonders

Will outlast even time itself.

53. RELIGION AND LIFE

Life is a journey, and you are the traveler. The long road can leave you tired, bored, frustrated, indulgent, and confused. Along the way, in many different situations, you've blamed events, people, enemies, or perhaps even bad luck. But deep down, you understood - the mistakes were all within you. Like a skilled chemist, you must learn to find the right formula, the perfect mix, combining different elements both inside and out to create the compound you desire - success. Each person, in their unique circumstances, must discover their own formula, though learning from others' successes can help. But remember, the formula for success is as individual as a fingerprint.

That special concoction is called skill.

In music, success requires rhythm and harmony. The notes must be beautifully combined, resounding in an inviting rhythm, each note in sync with the others, creating a symphony that enchants the soul.

That is art.

Life is a labyrinth, filled with hidden signs, symbols, pitfalls, and roads waiting to be discovered. I've come to understand the importance of patience - of learning, observing, seeking, waiting, listening, staying calm, and enduring.

I see everyone carrying the burdens of life on their backs, perhaps including:

- Work and Family

- Emotions and Material Needs

- Spirituality and Reality

- Responsibility and Conscience

- Inner Feelings and Expression

Often, these burdens appear all at once or at different stages of life. To journey far, to reach your destination, you must learn to balance these burdens with grace.

Sometimes, it's challenging to reconcile the weights we bear. On one side, there's Life with its worldly objectives; on the other, Religion with its noble spiritual values. These two paths can seem forever divergent, yet sometimes they intersect, forming the cross of life. You must learn to carry both, whether your steps are light or heavy, as you choose your way to Heaven or Hell. The choice, as always, is yours.

In the maze of life, risks and dangers are constantly lurking, especially as you search for what everyone desires. You keep hunting, but you also become prey to jealousy and envy from all sides. And the true enemy isn't outside - it's within you. Eventually, you understand that you must move on, take steps, and forever seek yourself while you're still alive. There is no rest. Learn skills! Learn art! Learn balance! There is no other way.

Knowing Enough

Solitude is where inner maturity grows.

Letting go is daring to live with yourself.

Peace is found in calmness and resilience.

Wisdom is knowing enough to truly enjoy life.

54. A DAY WILL COME

The time has come.

No longer do you rush through roads of hunger,

Chasing grand plans for the future,

Living frugally in the petty games of competition.

Sometimes, a humble victory comes your way,

Only to be drowned in fleeting pleasures.

Your heart, once full of sorrow,

Now sees the truth - how ephemeral it all is.

There were days when no one seemed to care,

When, through the silent stares of colleagues and family,

You found yourself in strange lands,

Diving into the lonely sea and sky.

You returned home in solitude,

Where the flowers still bloomed indifferently in the wind,

And the dog, stretched out in the dimly lit corridor,

Barely lifted his head, half-eyed, as if to say, "You again?"

One day will come

When the haze of insecurity lifts,

And weariness settles like a fog.

The city, once bustling, becomes a swamp of stillness,

Surrounded by lies and hatred.

You will retreat into solitude,

But not into emptiness - no.

Instead, you find peace,

Letting all the dust of the world settle outside,

While within, you shine with the quiet brilliance of enlightenment.

55. MISSING MOM

I went out for dinner with my daughter, sitting by the sea, the waves gently lapping at the shore, and found myself missing my mother. I had asked her to go out with me so many times, but she was always tired, her legs ached, and she preferred to stay home.

As we sat there, I told my daughter about the day my mother passed away, the quiet peace that followed, and the memories that lingered.

"Rest in peace, Mom," I whispered to the sea, feeling her presence in the breeze.

I Am

I am the fleeting particle of time,

The burning candle's glow.

I am the wave of light that travels far and wide,

The soul within all forms,

Yet, in the vastness of the universe,

I am a lonely star, shining in the endless sky.

56. GOOD RESULTS

"Remember," said the master, "In any profession, achieving good results is only half the task. The true measure of success lies not just in the outcome, but in how you achieve it. A good result is important, yes, but it's the completeness of your effort, the integrity of your process, that truly matters. Only when both are in harmony can your work be considered whole."

57. REMOVING NAILS

Five years ago, he had nine nails pinned to his broken leg. Now, he returned to the hospital for the surgery to have them removed. The sight of the pile of nails was unsettling. As his body lay half-paralyzed under partial anesthesia, he could only hear the doctors calling for pliers and hammers, their tools of healing sounding more like instruments of destruction. He couldn't see what they were doing, but he felt the strikes along his body, like blows from wooden pestles.

After the surgery, he was on crutches for two weeks, waiting for the sutures to be removed. His first brother stopped by the hospital briefly and left. The second brother, thinking this was a minor issue for someone as resilient as him, didn't visit at all. Young girls hesitated to inquire about him, passing by quickly, perhaps in fear of crossing paths with his sisters.

In the end, he was mostly alone in the hospital, surrounded by nurses who addressed him as 'Uncle' one moment and 'young man' the next, depending on whether they had glanced at his medical record.

He longed to stay in the hospital, where at least there was company, but he had to return home. The next day, he was forced to carry his crutches to another province for a new project meeting. During the meeting with the Provincial Committee, he had to ask permission to rest his painful leg on a chair.

Returning home, he found the house empty. His wife was away on a charity trip, and his daughter was secluded in her dreamy room. Waking up the next morning, he struggled to find the energy to clean the disordered room. He called the security guards for help. The first had gone home, and the second's line was busy.

In the silence, he turned on some soothing Kitaro music. That was all he could do. Amidst the mess of blankets, clothes, books, and untold stories, he plunged himself into writing, seeking solace in the poetic muse that visited him.

> *The Body and the Soul*
>
> *The body nourishes the soul,*
>
> *Granting you pleasures and feeding your ego.*
>
> *It helps you grow into lustful forms,*
>
> *And yet, it often leads you to shameful mistakes.*

58. MEMORIES – PRESENT

So much has passed. In the rush of life, events come and go, often thought to be forgotten. But then, in a quiet moment alone, an old memory suddenly flashes back, as if it had been patiently waiting for you to pause. You find yourself smiling, seeing through those old stories - both the sad and the happy - softening the weight of yesterday's sorrows.

Peace

If this life is filled with happiness and peace, that's more than enough.

And if it's marked by sadness, well, who needs a next life anyway?

59. ACCEPTANCE

As time went by, looking back, he saw there was still so much unfinished work, mistakes that could never be undone, and the limitations of his abilities in the real world. He learned to know, understand, and accept:

- Loneliness, without sharing. Silence, while being alone. The changing hearts of others. His own imperfections and the external circumstances beyond his control.

- Living slowly, with leisure, taking life step by step. Enjoying things at their right pace, neither too fast nor too slow.

- Past failures, dissatisfaction, and the knowledge that success and happiness can be found in the simplest moments.

- Simplicity, humility, awkwardness, and even loss - yet living elegantly and affectionately.

- Despite injustice and dramas, learning to be tolerant and let go.

- Avoiding chaos, competition, and distractions to cultivate a quiet, deep, peaceful mind.

- There's no need to be dazzling, magical, or bright - just be youthful, fresh, and innocent.

- Seeing no villains or opponents, only partners, from whom he could learn, adjust, and adapt.

- Understanding that human life is short and fragile, that memories can be stubborn and petty, and that true value lies in the present peace, smiles, and joy.

- Compromising between inherent vices - wine, music, beauty, the pleasures of life - while also embracing giving and kindness.

- Believing in sincerity and repentance, and the power of daily prayer.

Happiness
Sometimes, he thought he was too tired, wanting to stop and simply stay away.
But deep down, he still secretly wished for a joy as refreshing as a new wave.
Seeing flowers wither, he knew they'd bloom again tomorrow.
Watching the sunset, he believed the sun would rise early the next day.
As always, today's difficulties and sorrows would pass,
And a day would come when everything would be smooth and joyful.
Happiness is learned, he realized.
Wait and be patient - it's worth it.

60. INNER MAN

Life unfolds with many nuances, like a play with countless acts. Sometimes, these plays intersect, their plots weaving together in unexpected ways. In this grand theater, a person often finds themselves juggling multiple roles and positions. Much of what we do stems from responsibility, external demands, and the need to make a living.

Even those who wield great power often find themselves more dependent on others than they might like to admit. Playing such roles is no easy feat, but it's just part of the external performance we put on for the world.

The school of life teaches us how to navigate these external roles - how to behave, build relationships, and refine our skills. We learn strategies to interact with others, but all of this shapes only the outer person we present to the world.

Yet, beyond this external persona lies a deeper journey: the quest to discover your true self within. In this inner world, you are the master, the leader of your own soul. It's here that you must cultivate discipline, becoming an artist in your chosen field, a spiritual guide for yourself, a voice of wisdom that lights your own path.

Finding your true self is the key. It's when you connect with this inner man that you begin to understand your purpose and the true meaning of your life.

61. SPECTACULAR FAILURE

He saw it clearly - he had failed. Without saying a word, he left quietly, slipping away unnoticed. The people he had supported over the past two years, who once depended on him, now seemed to turn their backs, whispering stories behind his back. The pranksters, those who reveled in others' misfortune, looked overjoyed, as if they'd just won a prize.

The road home was silent, almost too silent. He left everything he loved in the office, returning with an empty briefcase. As he said goodbye to the driver that late afternoon, he reminded him not to come the next morning. There was no need.

Hatred and anger at the betrayal and dishonesty of those who wronged him welled up inside, making his blood boil. He found himself crafting the perfect plan for revenge, imagining every detail with a sense of grim satisfaction.

But as time passed, he found himself in a new, better, and happier job. The anger faded, and the past began to blur. Yet, he knew deep down - he had undeniably failed.

Then one day, many years later, out of some vague fear, those who had once sabotaged him came back. They apologized, asked for forgiveness, their faces tinged with regret. But by then, he had forgotten everything. He understood something profound: success is short-lived, but failure is persistent. Success is often just a fleeting moment of luck; failure, on the other hand, is a harsh reality. Success might flash brightly, but failure lingers, shaping the contours of life, backed by years of worries and struggles.

These were the thoughts that had occupied him for twenty years.

And now, today, he found himself facing failure once again. But this time, something was different. He left voluntarily, even happily. He accepted it. He stopped worrying and simply let go.

He remembered how he used to be - passionate, hardworking, devoted, and joyful. But now, he understood it was time to stop, to say goodbye, to step back, to descend into peace and contemplation.

He knew he was nurturing something new, something magical within himself.

A great failure, he realized, is when something inside you overflows, boils, and waits for the moment to explode, lifting you up with its energy. But now, instead of that explosive force, he felt something even better - peace and contentment.

62. TIME OF MEMORIES

Time, that ever-flowing river, moves steadily from the past, through the present, into the future, marking its passage in the cycles of seconds, minutes, hours, days, months, and years. The past is fixed, a tapestry of what has been; the future is yet to come, vague and uncertain. We call this the chronological order of life.

But is it really so?

In the same span of time, different people perceive events and experiences in entirely unique ways. Even within one person's life, each chapter - though measured by the same number of years - feels distinctly different. Consider the school years, filled with dreams, curiosity, and romance. Contrast that with the early years of adulthood, where life often becomes a grind, the road to success stretching out, seemingly endless and monotonous. Yet, when success finally arrives, it often feels fleeting, consumed by responsibilities and the demands of work.

Time, in these moments, seems to chase us, always catching up, speeding ahead, leaving us breathless in its wake. And then, in old age, time slows again, becoming a hazy, absent-minded presence, a companion in the long wait for what comes next.

Time stirs the deepest emotions within us - anxiety, depression, the acute awareness of life's brevity. We yearn for something enduring, something beyond ourselves - permanence, eternity, the supernatural. It is from this longing that gods, beliefs, and religions have been born, offering salvation, consolation, and the promise of perfection.

But if we pause and look inward, we find that time is not just a relentless march of seconds and minutes. In our minds, time is a vast expanse, filled with thoughts, contemplations, and emotions. We are the sum of our memories, forever nostalgic. We fear, worry, suffer, and yet, we also experience joy, exhilaration, passion. We are everything, all at once.

We follow different paths to fulfill our life's purpose. We name things, define events, create laws, and build civilizations - constructs of our collective consciousness. It is through these constructs that we establish order in the world, a shared understanding of civilization, culture, law, aesthetics, nation, tradition, and education. It seems as if the whole world and society is a community of common beliefs, shared spirits, and collective reason. Without this, life might seem irrational, chaotic, even mad. But who can say for certain?

Perhaps this order is itself an illusion, a frozen and dead construct. What truly makes life vibrant are the vivid emotions, the passionate desires, and the burning feelings that arise within us. These are the endless sources of inspiration in our lives, driving us to create, to bloom, to endure pain and suffering, to face failure, loss, and sorrow. This is the song of life, the song of time, resonating within each person.

So remember... Time is emotion. Memories are moments captured in the past. But the only time that truly exists is the present - the here and now. Real life is a tapestry of burning emotions, blooming in every present moment. This is the essence of living Zen, the true art of being.

63. IF... LITTLE...

If we both had just a little more tolerance,

If we didn't strive so hard to be superior,

If we let go of petty grievances,

And resisted the urge to compete with others,

Our love would have been whole.

If our parents had known a touch of fame,

I might not have grown up with so much hardship.

I wouldn't have needed to travel far and wide in search of meaning,

Or learned the art of diplomacy and boldness,

Perhaps then, I wouldn't have faced humiliation.

If our ancestors had shown a bit more compassion when building the nation,

Had they not been driven by power, fame, and hatred,

Had they not succumbed to inferiority and allowed foreign invaders,

Had there been no corrupt kings or greedy mandarins to incite the people's indifference,

Our homeland might have been spared centuries of suffering, smoke, and fire.

Reflecting on the cycles of cause and effect,

My superficial youth now makes me treasure my emotions.

Simple parents made me resilient.

And though the country endured wars,

It now raises generations forged in strength,

Creating a millennial opportunity to move forward,

Despite the trials of wars and epidemics.

64. HOW TO REACH THE DESTINATION

Your journey may not have yielded the results you hoped for because they lack a deeper spiritual connection. You must understand that the destination lies infinitely far away, not in terms of distance, but in the depth of your inner awakening. A true meditator reaches the point where body and mind unite, not through extraordinary effort or means, but through balanced, harmonious practice. His results surpass those of a soulless practitioner, no matter how perfect the technique or advanced the tools.

The challenge, then, is not about the means but about the "awakening" - the relaxation and attention you bring to your practice, to every interaction. To unlock the power of spiritual awakening, you must approach your practice differently, much like a true dancer who loses herself in the dance. Every movement must originate from your center, from the place where true breathing occurs, where life itself pulses.

When you can perform your practice as a dancer performs her dance - spontaneously, from the heart, and fully present in the moment - you make the dancer and the dance one. In that unity, your spiritual awareness reaches its highest potential, its strongest expression.

You may not know when you will master these "dancing" rituals or breathe inner life into them. The results you achieve may not always hit the mark, leading you to wonder why your spiritual teacher has not yet taught you the secret to perfect aim. You begin to realize that the action and the destination are intertwined; the right direction must be aligned with the right interaction.

In this realization lies the wisdom: the path is not just about reaching the destination, but about how you journey toward it. When you dance with your spirit, the destination becomes less of a goal and more of an unfolding experience, a process where each step, each breath, leads you closer to true awakening.

PART 5: GONE OVER

The Path to the Land of No Land

We keep moving on our journey, the road stretching further and further away from our original wishes. We don't know when or where we will arrive. We long to stop, to find peace and happiness, yet our feet keep moving, driven by forces we barely understand.

But what is the true meaning of peace and happiness? We think we are seeking them, striving to make them our own, yet their whereabouts remain a mystery, elusive as shadows.

In the wisdom of the Bible and the teachings of great philosophers, there are stories of those who leave home in search of a better life. Take the parable of the Prodigal Son: a young man leaves his father's house, searching for happiness and fulfillment in distant lands. For years, he chases after worldly pleasures, but grief and poverty cling to him like shadows. The way home becomes a distant memory, and he wanders, blind to both light and darkness, unaware that his compassionate father is waiting for him, ready to guide him back with open arms.

In this story, the father represents the divine - God, a higher power, or wisdom itself - and we are the wayward children. We know these tales from ancient scriptures, yet we still struggle to find our way back. Despite our journey through the temptations and vanities of life - seduced by lust, intoxicated by fame and fortune - we remain adrift.

We ponder and reflect. We turn to the pages of ancient wisdom and encounter the teachings of the wise: "An adventurer turns back, and gold remains unchanged." This reminds us that a person can return to their true nature if they awaken, repent, and correct their course. It is like the old saying, *"Turn back, the shore is behind us."*

It's comforting to know that we have a repentant heart. Each morning, we seek peace in prayer, whether to God or through quiet reflection, taking refuge in the wisdom that has guided countless souls before us. But then, we step back into the day, full of unpredictable pitfalls. Every night, we return to meditate or pray, seeking solace and clarity.

Life, we realize, is like a river that flows endlessly. We don't know where the shore is, and each of us must struggle and swim in the sea of desire. We know it's hard, yet it seems impossible to stop and find safety.

The teachings of ancient philosophers like Socrates or the reflections of medieval mystics speak deeply and profoundly of the fleeting nature of life. They remind us that the journey to true understanding and enlightenment is arduous yet essential: *"For what does it profit a man to gain the whole world and lose his own soul?"* This echoes the difficulty of crossing over, of finding the way to true peace.

We find ourselves in the midst of a whirling life, directionless, jumping from one challenge to another, wandering through the many stops and platforms of existence. Our journey takes us over hills and through deep valleys, across rivers and into the depths of experience. Day by day, our burdens grow heavier. Sometimes we feel weary and frustrated, at other times, delighted and inspired. We often feel like heroes misplaced in a world that doesn't understand us. When life deadlocks, we seek refuge in prayer or the wisdom of those who came before us, hoping to let go and liberate ourselves. Yet, we come to understand that stopping, as we wish, is not so simple.

So we turn to the wisdom of the past, searching old books written by those who came before us, hoping to find guidance. In the annals of Roman history, we read of emperors and philosophers who faced great challenges. Consider Marcus Aurelius, a Stoic emperor who ruled during times of war and plague. Despite his burdens, he found solace in the philosophy of inner peace and virtue. At times, he longed to retreat from the world, to find peace in the solitude of his own mind. He sought refuge in his Stoic beliefs, understanding that true strength and peace lay within, not in the external world. Enlightened by this realization, he continued his duties with wisdom and fairness, governing with a calm mind until the end of his life.

He reflected:

"Forever a traveler of the mind,

Another day passes.

Home feels distant,

Miles ahead on this journey."

He warned us not to wander too far, to not lose ourselves in the endless pursuits of life. Instead, we should quickly pack our bags, leave behind the unnecessary, and return to our true inner goodness. We must journey to the shore of eternity - the land of no land - that resides within us.

This is the essence of the teachings from the sages, philosophers, and scriptures: Stop. Return to the shore. Cross over. Beyond this life lies the berth of true peace. It's all within the mind.

The land of no land - the formless realm, eternity - already exists within us. We must stop drifting along the river of delusion. No longer should we pass through the narrow doors of competition, desire, uncertainty, or ignorance. Instead, we must step into a new, expansive path, one that resides within our own hearts.

Come, enter the door of the land of no land, the door of endlessness and true happiness.

1. THE PASS

Yesterday afternoon, our team decided to embark on an adventure to a West-North province. We left at 1:30 pm, arriving at 8:00 pm - right on the day the storm hit. Of course, it couldn't just be a light drizzle. No, it had to be heavy rain with strong winds whipping through the pass. We drove from dawn to dusk, rain blinding our eyes, and our glasses fogging up like we were in a sauna. Eventually, we had to open our helmet masks just to see the road ahead. On the many twists and turns, we drove more by instinct than by sight. Our limbs went numb from the cold and fatigue, and shifting gears felt like a workout at the gym. More than once, I considered stopping, but I kept telling myself, "Just a little further, you can make it."

Looking back, it was great to have made the trip. We decided to go at the last minute, even with the rain. The bonus? We rode big displacement motorcycles, which made us feel like we were in an action movie. The young guys were determined, and though there were only nine motorbikes, the rest followed in cars. Cool, right?

There's something about pushing yourself beyond your limits that feels, well, pretty cool. When we finally arrived, we took a deep breath and felt a sense of accomplishment. After days of monotonous work and routine life, this challenging journey was exactly what we needed - a refreshing break from the mundane.

•

The way back home wasn't any easier. It was still raining, and by then, we were utterly exhausted. But we had visited a stunning spring, marveled at a waterfall, climbed a mountain, and kept moving on. At times, rainwater filled my eyes and mouth as it hit my face, and I seriously considered abandoning the bike for the warmth of a car. But somehow, we made it home. A few guys did give up along the way, but those who stuck it out discovered just how much endurance they had. My feet, arms, neck, and back all ached like I'd been in a wrestling match with Mother Nature. But honestly, it was fun. We all gathered for dinner afterward, and despite the exhaustion, everyone was in high spirits.

The next morning, I woke up after a solid sleep, feeling surprisingly light. I weighed myself - 60.7 kg (134 pound), down from 63 kg (139 pound) before the trip. Ha! It seems those two days of complete challenge came with a side of unexpected weight loss.

Simplicity is vast and spacious.

Complexity? It's just confusing and cramped.

2. SOMETIMES

Sometimes, I find myself drifting back to old memories.

A street corner from long ago, a road I once traveled,

An unexpected encounter with someone who suddenly appeared,

Only to fade away, as clear as day, and then, just as suddenly, gone.

There's always that faint sense of regret, as if something was left unsaid, or undone.

Sometimes he thinks about the inevitable - about dying someday, his body turning to dust. Where will his soul go? What's the meaning of it all? Life, after all, is fleeting.

When he's on a long business trip, staying in yet another cookie-cutter hotel, or walking down an unfamiliar street, those impermanent moments from the past come rushing back. The bittersweet taste of lost time lingers, growing larger with every step.

Work? It's always a challenge. The to-do list feels endless, and the pressure weighs heavily on his shoulders. Sometimes, he just wants to collapse and let it all go. Sure, the news paints a rosy picture of the country's bright future, with investment conferences and mega economic deals, but beneath that shiny surface lie stories of corruption, scandals, and the crumbling of social ethics. Schools where values are forgotten, businesses where integrity is a distant memory, farmers abandoning their fields for the uncertainty of urban life, and small enterprises crushed under the weight of foreign giants. All of this makes the spirit of entrepreneurship feel tired, worn out, and, frankly, a little hopeless.

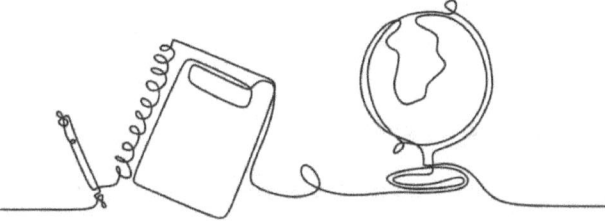

Yet, even on those **tough days, he still wants to make a difference.** How to revive a key industry, or thoughtfully invest in a production complex with real technology transfer. How to seize the moment and stand on the shoulders of giants, to learn the core technologies, to absorb knowledge from anywhere and everywhere, and somehow, in his own small way, contribute to building something better.

> ***Simplicity***
>
> *Fish swim fast in the ocean because they have smooth skin.*
>
> *Those who want to go far should pack light.*
>
> *And those who've seen it all learn to handle life in the simplest ways.*

3. INVISIBLE

There are many types of death: slow death, quick death, mass death, sudden death, silent death, painful death, smooth death - the list goes on. Death, as it turns out, can be quite the shapeshifter.

But really, it all boils down to two categories:

- **Explicit death** - the kind everyone can see.

- **Invisible death** - the kind that slips by unnoticed.

Epidemics can cause mass death. War does something eerily similar. Forest fires rage when loggers leave the land barren. And then there are those terrible storms that can blow entire neighborhoods into oblivion. These are the deaths that shock us, that make the evening news, that leave us feeling a deep, collective sorrow.

When someone dies painfully before our eyes, it shakes us to our core. We feel fear, worry, and a gnawing sense of insecurity. It's as if death is waving its flag right in our faces, demanding our attention.

But then there are the countless invisible deaths - those quiet, unnoticed endings that happen every day. The lonely wanderers, the isolated souls, the bleeding hearts that live among us, suffering in silence. These are the deaths that we don't see, the ones that don't make headlines but are just as real, just as tragic.

So, what do we do? Save yourself. Love yourself. And, perhaps, learn to become invisible - just enough to avoid the worst, but not so much that you disappear entirely.

The Meaning of Presence

When you look up at the stars in the sky, the leaves in the forest, the insects crawling on wet ground, the sand on the beach, or the drops of water in the ocean, you suddenly realize that our lives are no more significant than any of those things. We're tiny creatures, like a brief sound in the vast universe, existing for a short moment in the endless expanse of time.

Life feels small and meaningless when we separate ourselves from the moment of presence. But when we stay present, even in our smallness, we find meaning.

4. DON'T COMPARE WITH OTHERS

Life, like work, has its ups and downs, moments of progress and times of stagnation. Just as rivers sometimes flow smoothly and at other times crash over rocks and waterfalls, we too face challenges and triumphs. Accepting and overcoming these moments allows us to rise above sadness and complaints. It's important not to compare ourselves with others - believing they are luckier or better off. Behind every high mountain, there's always another, even higher one. Each wave in the ocean replaces the one before it. This is the natural order of life.

So, be patient and persistent as you climb your own mountains, walking your own path at your own pace. Each path is unique, with its own opportunities, values, and meanings.

Remember, what we see of others - their success, creativity, and joy - is only the surface. Beneath it lies a journey filled with effort, struggle, perseverance, doubt, and growth. It's easy to admire someone's achievements from the outside, but inside every success story is a tale of resilience, faith, and the courage to keep going despite the odds.

The greatest success in life isn't measured by how much we achieve, how famous we become, or how great our impact is. True success lies in finding the meaning of life and making a valuable contribution to it.

So go ahead. Live confidently, and live a life that is truly yours.

5. THE DESTINATION OF AWAKENING

There's a natural connection between the destination and the action. When you discover this, aiming becomes effortless. But if you're hitting the target every time, be mindful - you're in danger of becoming merely a craftsman, showing off your skills. For the ambitious man who counts his hits, the destination is reduced to nothing more than a piece of paper, lifeless and empty.

In the deeper path, the true "way" or "philosophy" of any practice considers this a deception. This path doesn't recognize a goal that lies at some fixed distance, waiting to be reached by skill alone. Instead, it knows of only one goal, one that cannot be touched by technique or precision. If we must use words to describe it, that goal is "Awakening."

The spiritual teacher shared this as if it were the most obvious truth. He urged us to observe the eyes of true masters in action. When they perform, whether in meditation or ritual, their eyes are often half-closed, not fixed on any target. They are not aiming at anything external.

Their focus is inward, beyond skill, beyond the reach of any physical goal. This is the essence of awakening - finding the destination within, rather than outside.

6. C'MON BABY!

C'mon, baby!
There's nothing left to say,
Two decades of half-spoken words,
Incomplete reprimands, hanging in the air.
You've heard the truth,
You've known it well
This land of torrential rains,
And sun that burns so bright.

Through the heat and the weight of attachment,
We've sunk into an ocean of sorrows,
Life's hard choices washing over us,
Sipping the bitter, the salty, the inevitable taste of defeat.
I don't claim to be better than anyone,
Nor can I bring myself to bow too low.

The only thing you've ever seen,
Is that I've always lived with what I carry,
Whether it's good or bad,
In luxury or poverty,
With a reputation high or low,
In the eyes of you and others.

We're all adrift in the suffering of human life,
Floating together, yet separate
Waves on the same vast ocean.
I don't know how long
A human life will last,
But I feel myself fading,
Drifting into the endless sea of the world,
Where I will be forever free, forever infinite.

7. WHEN DRIVING

As you drive, life's lessons unfold like the road ahead.

The Negative Side – Prevention:

Be mindful of speed - drive fast, but not recklessly.

Carry your pride with you, but don't let it turn into arrogance.

Move with urgency, but don't let it push you to madness.

The Positive Side – Initiative:

Embrace courage, but let it be rooted in bravery, not bravado.

Value intelligence, but let it shine with wisdom, not just cleverness.

Seek depth in your actions, but let it be sharp, not superficial.

Remember, the most colorful and fragrant flowers don't always bear the sweetest fruit. True success, like good driving, requires a balance between speed and caution, pride and humility, initiative and restraint.

8. REUNION

So I got in the car and began a journey of a thousand kilometers to pick up my daughter. Before leaving, I carefully packed two boxes of books, along with two stacks of old music records - treasures from a time nearly forgotten. These records, 10-20 years old, held melodies that had slipped away over the years.

Instead of flying to the city where my daughter was quarantined after testing for the COVID-19 virus upon her return to the country, I chose to drive. It was a chance to leave behind the melancholy of the world and the endless grind of business that I sometimes mistake for life's true purpose. For three weeks, I decided to live for my own feelings, to embrace the present with all its imperfections.

The night before setting out, I read Seneca's *On the Shortness of Life* and reflected on the Stoic understanding of life's meaning. I realized how brief life truly is, often squandered on meaningless worries and fleeting sadness. The future remains uncertain, and the present is fleeting, but the past - though clear - is unchangeable, a chapter already closed despite our regrets.

As the car sped down the highway, I glanced back at the city shrouded in rain and fog, its crowded streets and towering buildings fading into the misty dawn. The deformed shapes of countless rooftops struggled to emerge in the early light, a reminder of the life I was momentarily leaving behind.

In the car, I played an 80's music CD. The sweet, familiar sounds washed over me, soothing my anxieties. The saxophone and piano notes echoed like rain pouring down forever, filling the car with a comforting nostalgia.

Outside, the scenery began to change. Cool fields stretched out before me, dotted with lotus ponds and lakes where white ducks played. Trees lined the road, and distant villages appeared, their quiet charm untouched by time. As the sky gradually brightened, the pagoda's tiled roofs peeked through the green groves, embodying the soul of the countryside I once knew. The rain stopped, and the sun began to rise.

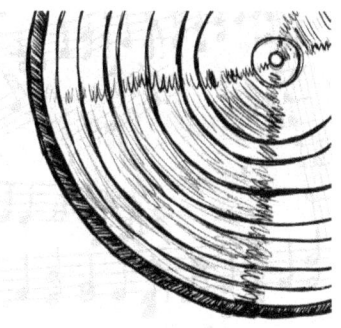

Golden silk spread across the countryside.

I embraced it and wove a song.

I played a quiet tune,

Filled with blue skies and new light.

9. A QUIET REFLECTION

Every day, life presents him with a continuous stream of events. With work, there are always challenges to tackle - problems that seem never-ending.

One afternoon, after a long journey, he went straight to the office to meet with a new project team. The discussions revolved around establishing priorities, managing partnerships, setting investment quotas, and balancing costs with time.

The following day was consumed by meetings focused on financial planning. It became clear to him that he needed to delegate or eliminate unnecessary tasks, so he could concentrate on those that truly add value.

By evening, he found himself yearning for a retreat - somewhere to rest and reflect, away from the demands of daily life.

To truly heal, he knew he must change his habits: adopt a healthier diet, find the right balance of rest, and dedicate time to meditation. It's not easy - there's no denying that - but there's no other way. Time, after all, is fleeting.

Illness, and the inevitable reality of death, are perhaps life's greatest teachers - strict, direct, face-to-face, fierce, enlightening, brave, and persistent.

If there is a true place of peace in this world, it lies in learning how to walk the path of life with awareness. To face reality, to live mindfully, to balance body and mind, and to discover happiness and freedom.

He reminds himself to cultivate six essential qualities: Grace, Resilience, Openness, Wisdom, Tranquility, and Hope (GROWTH).

He often says to himself:

Train to be tough.

But being tough doesn't necessarily make us strong.

Train to be soft.

For knowing how to be soft is what truly makes us strong.

10. THE TRAP OF MEANINGLESS INTERACTION

He practiced diligently, following the instructions without trying to force the outcome. At first, he didn't concern himself with where his actions led. Even when he occasionally hit the target, he didn't allow himself to get excited, knowing it was likely just a stroke of luck.

But as time passed, he began to recognize the danger in becoming accustomed to these meaningless interactions. If he let himself slip into that pattern, he knew he would fall back into a mind consumed by overthinking, losing sight of true purpose and clarity.

The real challenge wasn't in hitting the target, but in maintaining a mindful approach, where the actions themselves carried meaning and intention.

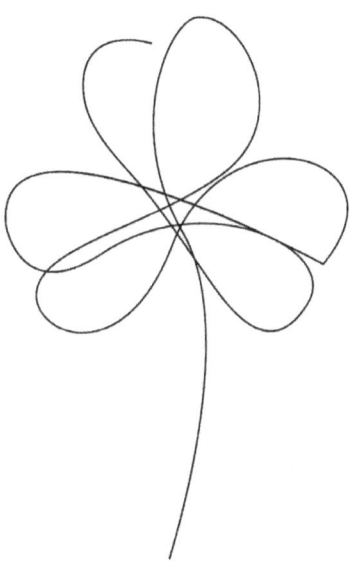

11. THE ETERNAL GLORY

With a pure body and mind,

He opened His heart to all,

Through the endless ups and downs of time.

Who among us is resilient enough to seek refuge in Him?

In the unpredictability of life,

He offers countless paths for us to choose,

Guiding us with compassion in every place.

By His side, the silent pine forest whispers,

The infinite expanse embraces His presence,

High mountains touch the clouds,

As the sunset casts its gentle glow,

Illuminating His calm and solemn face.

Kindness radiates from His being,

Peace spreads across the world,

In the eternal embrace of His glory.

12. LOVE

There's something about our country's coastline that's simply breathtaking - beautiful, wild, and untouched, especially in the early morning before the crowds descend. I've always had a soft spot for these places where the land cozies up to the water, where rivers carve their way around mountains, or where a stream leaps playfully down a rocky hillside. Sometimes, it's a tiny island tucked into a river's bend, other times, it's land that brushes up against the sea, or even a parcel on a distant island. Yet, somehow, those lands we once cherished have been returned, sold off, or left to their own devices.

There's an old saying that goes, *"The wise love water, and the virtuous love mountains."* Now, I've always considered myself more on the virtuous side - though I'll admit, I've been known to indulge in the occasional folly.

But here's the funny thing - I've always been drawn to both mountains and water.

Another nugget of wisdom tells us, *"The virtuous find peace in the mountains, while the ambitious set their sails for the sea."* I've spent some time mulling this over, wondering if perhaps my ambitions have been more like a gentle breeze than a roaring gale. If wisdom is about loving to learn, then maybe I've got a bit of that too.

But our own language, with its gentle insights, suggests, *"The virtuous climb mountains, the bold venture to the sea, and the tender-hearted live by rivers."*

The sea, it seems, is the playground of those with iron wills, who cross oceans in pursuit of glory. As for me, I suppose I'm neither a daring adventurer nor a master of the waves. Perhaps I'm just a person with a dash of virtue and a sprinkle of emotion, content with the quiet strength of the mountains and the soothing embrace of rivers.

In my career, I've often found myself yielding - whether to juniors, to women, or to anyone with enough gentle persuasion to nudge me off course. It's a curious habit, this tendency to step aside and let others take the lead.

Sometimes I wonder, if I were a woman, how many times I might have found myself expecting. It's an amusing thought - one that brings a smile to my face. Perhaps, in the grand scheme of things, I'm luckier than I've ever given myself credit for.

13. THINKING ABOUT YOU

I couldn't believe it - it felt so absurd

When I heard the news that you had gone.

But the sadness flowed in, a relentless stream,

And I knew then, the harsh truth had come.

I whispered softly, "Don't be sad, dear friend,

For you live on in the hearts of many who love you."

Silently, you slipped away in solitude,

Between the tender hours of dawn and morning,

Leaving behind the echoes of sorrow.

Your name stirs within me a flood of memories

Of blue skies and the endless ocean,

Of golden autumns far away,

And the warmth of cherished days.

My soul is heavy with a profound sadness,

A sadness that feels like a lonely star

Glimmering in the vast night sky,

A star that once shone so brightly,

But now has faded into the endless blue.

This star, where has it gone?

You seemed to vanish into the deep blue sky,

Into the abyss of the soul's waves.

My heart sinks into a deep silence,

Like the stillness of the ocean,

Or the quiet rustle of leaves and flowers in the breeze.

346 - GONE OVER

Time dances on in this land of no land.

Oh, how bitter it is to think

If, in the deep of night,

When the world sleeps in peace,

You were alone in the sky,

Your tears of light falling gently,

Touching the rows of silent stones,

Startled by the sight of your lonely grave.

But even if fear touched you in that moment,

Return to us like a distant star,

Casting a faint ray of regret,

A gentle breeze that whispers of you.

Though we are sad, dear friend,

Know that my heart still silently misses you.

Forget all the sorrows and pain you bore,

All the wounds that life ever gave you.

Gone, gone

No one remembers the mistakes of youth.

All gone, all forgotten.

The sad memories now shine in a quiet glory,

Until the day you rise again,

Even if you don't know where the road leads,

Only you knew how to live with yourself.

The books you read,

That once filled your mind,

Now rest, their pages no longer turning.

You found your answer

In the pursuit of passions,

In the search that led you to the end.

The road of life is dark and deserted,

And who knows when the darkness will lift.

But you, my friend, were blessed

For you lived and passed in the gentle dawn.

You sleep now for a thousand years,

With your wisdom and beauty, still sparkling.

Even if the fire of your spirit

Burned away the regrets

Of so many who loved you,

I still want to say,

I pray for your safe passage,

Into the morning light of eternal life.

14. HUMAN AND NATURE

I've come to see that human beings and nature are inextricably linked, reflecting one another in myriad ways:

- **Mountains** stand tall and enduring, much like humans: some are low, others rise high; some are majestic, others unassuming; they can be great or petty, gentlemanly or generous, each with its unique presence.

- **The wind** is akin to the human mind: at times light and gentle, at others strong and roaring. It can be peaceful or turbulent, a chaotic whirlwind or a quiet whisper, swirling with thoughts both clear and confused.

- **Clouds** mirror our ideas: they drift, sometimes scattered, sometimes dense and dark, at other times translucent and pure. They can be hazy, cluttered, or idyllic, layering one atop the other, overlapping in endless combinations.

- **Trees** represent the legacy we leave behind: some are small, others large; some are useful, others not. They can be lush or withered, blossoming with potential or bearing fruit, fragrant or foul, steadfastly rooted or clinging precariously to life.

- **Animals** embody the diversity of human personalities: fierce or cunning, cowardly or brave, they wander alone or in packs. Some are noble, others herding, leading or following, sociable or solitary, gentle or wild. They reflect our joy, melancholy, and the complex dance of our inner lives.

- **Rare ores** are like human talent: precious and hidden, like gold and silver, gemstones and metals, coal and oil - they must be explored, discovered, refined, and cherished.

- **Water** flows like human emotion: it floats gently, rushes furiously, makes noise, overflows, clouds our vision, overwhelms us, or calms us with its clarity and stillness. It can be both life-giving and destructive, serene or tumultuous.

- **Fire** burns with human passion: it glimmers softly, flashes brightly, fades away, then rises again, flaming hot and fierce. It can consume and ravage, or warm and inspire, surging with life's energy or smoldering quietly in the depths.

- **Thunder** and lightning echo our moments of glory and calamity: rumbling near and far, they shine brightly only to disappear, sometimes deadly and destructive, at other times insignificant - a mere warning of greater things to come.

- **Light** embodies the human spirit: brilliant and bright, sacred and divine, or dark and hazy. It can illuminate the soul or leave us in nothingness, a flicker in the vastness of existence.

In the calmness, stability, and immutability of the mountain, I find the unwaveringly enlightened nature of humanity.

In the harmony, unity, and innocence of nature, I see the deep and perfect beauty of the human spirit.

15. MOONLIGHT

When darkness cloaks the world in shadow,

Everything is tinged with doubt,

The earth becomes a vast jungle,

Full of hidden fears and uncertainties.

But under the moonlight's gentle gaze,

The paths begin to slowly emerge.

Not as bright as the dawning sun,

Nor as fierce as the midday blaze,

Or as splendid as the evening's glow,

The moon quietly reveals

The hidden corners of life.

The sun, always in a hurry,

Pushes the moments forward,

Drawing a clear line between day and night.

But the moon, with its subtle grace,

Waxes full, then wanes to a crescent,

Holding within its light

The silent passage of months and years.

The sun commands us to fight,

To chase after victory and glory,

Yet these triumphs are fleeting,

Their brilliance, impermanent.

Only the moon, in its quiet way,

Brings love, sanctity, and compassion,

Gifts we need to weather life's storms.

16. LETTING GO OF WORRIES

It's unnecessary to worry," the spiritual teacher gently advised.

"Release the outcome from your mind. You can still achieve your purpose, even if not every action bears fruit. The goal of hitting the target is merely a test - an affirmation of the external reflection of your inner state. Whether you call it a mind of no desires, no self, or pure concentration, the result is secondary.

Accomplishment comes in many forms, and as you ascend to the highest levels, you'll find that the outer goal naturally aligns with your inner balance, and the target is no longer missed."

17. LIVE FOR THE PRESENT

Today, I attended the grand opening of a dream hotel, nestled on an island filled with memories and nostalgia. Despite the cold wind and persistent rain, the artists didn't miss a beat, performing with passion, their dances alive with shimmering colors that cut through the gray skies.

Yesterday's sorrows and tomorrow's uncertainties didn't matter. Today, I felt a deep sense of gratitude - to God, to Buddha, to life itself - for these precious, fleeting moments. In this instant, I chose to live fully, embracing the beauty before me.

The Bridge

All beauty in life springs from love.

In love, we find music and dance,

A soul's dedication to the world,

Uniting two halves into one.

Love is a bridge across the void,

Connecting what was once apart.

In the interplay of differences

Giving and receiving, birth and death

Love spans the chasm,

Bringing forth beauty, greatness, and new life.

18. TALKING TO MYSELF

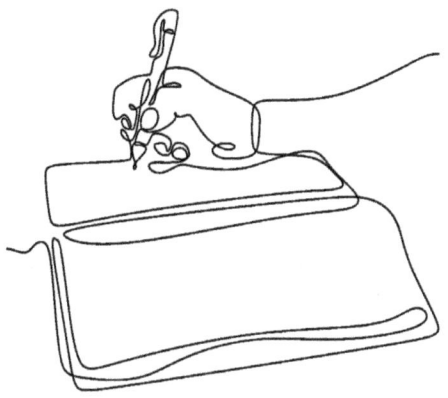

Oh, words! What harm in my silence,

When the world around me roars with chaos,

Like a stream tumbling through a rocky gorge,

Sweeping away black soil, fallen leaves, and distant echoes.

So I write,

Crafting these words from the whispers of my mind,

A lullaby for the heart,

Like the fleeting sound of white foam dissolving into the air.

What does it matter if all is destined to fade?

Who will share in the journey when we step into eternity,

Leaving behind both lies and love?

Let me sing,

Alone in this frozen time,

A song of love, even as the world drifts away.

19. FORGING

The start of the week always kicked off with a flurry of meetings. He made it a personal mission: by six o'clock each evening, all tasks must be wrapped up so he could enjoy some well-deserved rest.

He found himself silently praying - not just for his own sanity, but for the managers and employees, hoping they'd excel in their tasks and perhaps make his life a bit easier.

Amidst the chaos, he discovered an unexpected interest: the art of breathing. He began to see the connection between Qigong, Yoga, Zen, and even Vajrayana Tantra. This newfound focus on qi, or inner force, was like a secret weapon in his busy life. But mastering it? That required time, patience, faith, and a bit of robust health.

"Don't be like a stubborn, lonely bull," he mused with a chuckle. *"Instead, be the cowherd who knows how to gently guide the herd."*

And with that, he set out to conquer his day, embracing the wisdom of both breath and bull.

20. A NOBLE BELIEF

We often call each other Buddhists, simply because we are the children of Buddha. No matter what we do, nothing escapes the Buddha's watchful eyes. We are, after all, merely dancing in the palm of the Buddha's hand.

Yet, we are also the children of God. God is ever-present, within and around us, aware of every action, whether good or bad. And still, He protects us unconditionally, as long as we place our trust in Him and believe in the power of repentance. This divine presence is a great spiritual pillar, offering comfort and strength, helping us to keep our faith and continue moving forward.

When we set out to do something good and worthwhile, no matter how many obstacles lie in our path, we must hold firm to the belief that Gods, Buddhas, spirits, and ancestors are by our side - lighting the way, protecting, and guiding us.

So, each day, let us not forget to greet the dawn in silence, with a prayer to God and Buddha, asking for protection, trust, and love. A faithful belief, offered with sincerity, will surely touch His heart.

The Life Path

My life is a long journey,

Youthful days carried me far and wide.

The world seemed narrow in its competition,

I walked alone, with a cold heart and colder blood.

But now I return, bathed in His light,

The small path winding only around His feet.

With morning prayers and evening whispers,

I feel the warmth of love stretching out,

Embracing all the human realm.

21. INNER ALIGNMENT

The teacher offered this wisdom to his student: "In life, there are connections you may not always see, but they are real and powerful. Like a spider weaving its web, unaware that it will soon catch a fly. The fly dances freely, not knowing its path is already intertwined with the web.

In the same way, your outer actions and inner intentions are deeply connected. When you set your life's goals, don't just focus on external achievements. Instead, aim for the target within your heart - your true purpose. Aligning with that inner goal will guide you more surely than any external measure of success."

22. WHISPERS OF TIME

When will we meet again,

my dear soul mate?

The trumpet cries softly,

from a distant place.

Out in the street,

people shiver and move,

coming and going,

as they always have.

The music stirs memories,

whispers of old days.

Another year passes by,

like a manor of flowers,

leaves, and flowing water.

But why is it so quiet,

so utterly soundless?

Cups of tea stand waiting,

for a soul mate.

And I,

immersed in the stillness,

sit alone with time.

23. THE SOUL'S GARDEN

The soul is a curious thing, composed of sounds, images, colors, flavors, and a kaleidoscope of emotions. It holds all our memories and nostalgia, yet is forever entwined with the present. Picture the soul as a garden - it needs nurturing, care, cultivation, and devotion, all managed with a fair dose of skill, patience, and, of course, time.

A beautiful soul is one that blossoms, thriving despite the inevitable bugs, weeds, insects, and rodents that wander in. After all, every garden has its share of uninvited guests.

A lonely soul might be the muse for a romantic or tragic song, or perhaps a novel filled with epic sweetness - or stuck in the mire of desperation and sadness. It can be grand, or it can be downright miserable, depending on how it's tended.

A soul that shares, inspires, and radiates from the inside out is something to behold - encouraging and attractive, but even that glow can fade over time.

On the flip side, when a soul draws in from the outside, it risks becoming affected, monotonous, and dull. Loneliness seeps in, and soon it's empty, bored, and stuck in the muck of life. But here's the trick: learn to accept that loneliness, and treat failure and humiliation like black coal. It's just waiting for the right wind to come along and light a spark.

When that spark catches, it ignites hope, faith, and creativity - setting the soul ablaze with passion and new possibilities. And remember, the soul has its seasons too. It flares, it dies, it revives - just like the months, seasons, and years.

So, be patient. *Wait. Your time will come.*

Glittering

Little birds cannot spread their wings

across the blue ocean.

Strong arrows cannot reach the red sun.

But the bird still reflects on the vast

water, and the arrow still glitters

in the bright sunlight.

24. THE JOY OF CHALLENGE

I recently embarked on a journey with friends, traversing the beautiful landscapes of our country. It was an adventure filled with amazement and delight. Before we set off, I laid down a few ground rules:

- *Safety*
- *Team Spirit*
- *Fun*

These priorities guided us along the way. Everyone showed up, ready to follow the rules. Each day unfolded like a symphony, with its own highs and lows - one that I had the pleasure of composing myself.

Business, too, should follow these principles:

- **Safety** requires meticulous preparation - carefully considering and analyzing every step, just like mapping out our route and logistics.

- **Team Spirit** demands discipline and a shared sense of purpose, fostering mutual respect and support among all members.

- **Fun** springs from unending creativity, innovation, and harmony - learning, listening, and sharing along the way.

Of course, there were moments when some felt tired, discouraged, or even a bit fearful, especially on those winding mountain roads. Some might have even thought about giving up, feeling they couldn't go any further on their motorbikes. But through sheer determination and the unwavering support of their teammates, we all made it to the finish line, safe and sound. The joy we felt at that moment was a priceless reward, a testament to our collective courage and resolve.

Courage isn't the absence of fear - it's recognizing it, accepting it, and pushing forward despite it. It's about embracing the possibility of failure, yet still choosing to persevere, to overcome, and to never give up.

The Spirit of Adventure
Along with our daring team through mountains and rivers across the country,
Life became a song, with wine and laughter in the night.
As we trembled at the high pass, she hesitated,
Clinging tight, waiting for the warmth of the wine.

Mornings brought adventure, and nights held endless promise,
Shivering at the heights, beauty paused,
Hands clasped, cups raised - waiting for the dawn.

25. THE LIGHT AT THE END OF THE ROAD

*Y*esterday was one of those days. He encountered a real jerk who showed up demanding money, with threats that hung like a dark cloud over his mood all day. He decided to call it an early night, but it didn't help - his dreams turned into a restless tangle of nightmares.

The next morning, he woke up later than usual, feeling slightly better but still a bit off. Out of habit, he turned on his computer to check emails, only to be greeted by a nasty surprise. A disgruntled ex-employee, who had been trying to blackmail the company for months, had sent a venomous letter. The email was filled with insults, calling the board's decision to fire him idiotic and threatening to report the company to the authorities.

He sighed and decided to let it go - for the sake of his peace of mind. He went out and bought a few bonsai trees: peaches, apricots, Indian Oak. He spent the afternoon arranging them in the garden, trying to relax. But every time he thought about that email, a pang of irritation hit him right in the chest.

Today marked the end of the last month of the year. As the late afternoon sun slanted through the trees, his son asked if he wanted to play chess in the garden. They settled into the stilt house over the water, using a chess set his daughter had gifted him for his birthday. She had suggested that both Mom and Dad play together, but honestly, his wife preferred Go over chess. (Go, after all, is a game of strategy where you surround the opponent - quite different from chess's direct assaults).

So there he was, playing his first game of chess in nearly a decade. The last time, it seemed, had also been with his son. They played with intense focus, lost in the game until it grew dark outside. The kitchen lights flicked on as Mom began to cook dinner, so they decided to put on some music. He found a vinyl album that had been collecting dust for months - he'd only listened to half of it and hadn't had the time to enjoy it properly.

Father and son sat together in the dim light, letting the music wash over them. The lyrics whispered the essence of life, the melody fresh and lively. As he leaned against his son, a sense of calm enveloped him. This moment, right now, felt like the most beautiful moment of his life. He let go of the worries and troubles that had haunted him, forgetting about the evils that might lurk tomorrow. For now, he was living for himself, surrounded by those he loved.

He whispered a quiet prayer for the coming year: may it bring joy, health, and luck to his loved ones, himself, and everyone in the world.

Peace. Peace. Peace.

Safe and Happy

I pray to God and Buddha for peace.
I've rarely been lucky,
and my life has seen its share of sorrows
and hardships.
I've learned much,
and forgotten much too.
Now, I just hope to be safe and happy.

26. TROUBLE SHOOTING

When we worry too much, our minds turn into a tangled mess. Overthinking leads to mental confusion, trapping us in a cycle of panic over things that haven't even happened yet. This mental chaos can wear down the body, chipping away at our health.

On the flip side, when we make snap decisions, our emotions can get the best of us, leaving us confused and wondering what just happened. It's a tricky balance.

To calm the mind, sometimes the best strategy is to do… nothing. Just sit still, be patient, and gently tell your mind to take a break. Gradually, the mental storm will settle, and clarity will return. When it does, focus only on the present moment. Find something fun or positive in your situation - anything that can spark new energy and break the deadlock.

As Napoleon, that genius of war, once advised, "Don't cling to just one strategy." Adapt to the situation at hand, and let flexibility be your guide.

Forget

You slip away like a grain of time, unnoticed.

I labor each day, driven by desire,

While you quietly count what I forget.

But when the numbers run out, when time ends,

Will you still remind me of what truly mattered?

27. UNSEEN FINISH LINE

"When you're standing right in front of the finish line, it's impossible to miss it, even if you try to look away. Yet, deep down, you know that what's visible isn't the whole picture. What truly matters is often what you cannot see - the unseen forces, the invisible truths that guide you to the finish.

In life, it's not just about crossing the line you can see, but about recognizing the invisible paths, the subtle signs, and the hidden lessons that accompany you on the journey. The real finish line isn't marked by what's in front of you, but by the wisdom you gain from what's unseen."

28. THE MERMAID

Oh, the memories,
How they rush back,
Sweeping me into a sea of nostalgia.
Just the sound of your voice
Echoes through the corridors of time,
A fleeting moment
That feels like a thousand years have passed,
Yet it was only days ago.

My eyes grow wet,
As I remember your gaze,
Soft and blue as a new moon.
"You're so cold," you said,
But where are you calling from?
From the bright sunlight and the endless deep blue sea.

Once upon a time,
We walked barefoot on the warm sand,
And you, in a moment of pure magic,
Kissed me - then looked away.
We stood there, both confused,
As the waves whispered
Their sweet and distant secrets.

Oh, how you turned me into a flare,
Sparkling in the night sky.
For that one miracle,
I've wandered through the years,
Carrying the memory of that kiss,
And your eyes,
Merging into the vast sea of life,
Like a mermaid dissolving into the blue waters.

Yes, it's you. Pristine and eternal.
Keeping me safe as I navigate through storms,
Guiding me to the farthest edge of the horizon.

29. THE ART OF COMPENSATION

In life, every person, event, and relationship comes with its own built-in compensation. This isn't just a rule for individuals - it's a universal truth that plays out across entire nations and even in the rhythms of nature itself.

Take a stroll through history, and you'll see that contradictions often come in amusing pairs: beauty seems to always have a flirtatious sidekick, intelligence sometimes dabbles in deceit, and brightness has a tendency to invite a little dullness just to keep things balanced. Passion might lead to misery, success often has unhappiness tagging along, wealth brings out a touch of crudeness, power feels lonely at the top, fame might stretch the truth, talent tends to be short on cash, and sophistication - let's face it - sometimes masks shallowness.

But here's where it gets interesting: these pairs aren't set in stone. They're more like dance partners at a never-ending ball, constantly switching it up. One trait might push the other to new extremes, or what seems like balance can suddenly swing into a whole new pairing. Beauty might find itself coupled with a streak of bad luck, intelligence might walk hand in hand with righteousness, and a tough career could eventually lead to a well-deserved promotion (after a few bumps in the road, of course).

On a grander scale, a nation brimming with brilliant minds might also be brimming with distractions, or find itself under threat from all sides. Meanwhile, a country known for its hardworking, resilient citizens might feel the weight of loneliness as the years pass by. A rich and free nation? It might be so caught up in internal squabbles that it forgets what really matters. Then there's the peaceful, kindhearted nation that struggles with poverty - bless its soul. And what about the country with natural resources galore? Its people might end up lazy, envious, and stuck. But don't overlook the small, resource-poor country - it might just have the most innovative government, propelling it forward with surprising vigor.

These dynamics are as changeable as the seasons, cycling through birth, growth, decline, and renewal. It's both fascinating and fragile - nature loves to shake things up, shifting relationships just when you think you've got them figured out. And when things go too far in one direction, you might find people wishing they could hit the reset button, and nations teetering on the edge of collapse.

Picture a ceramic pot: the walls and the empty space inside are both essential. Pour in too much water, and it spills over. Push the pot's limits, and it shatters.

So, what's the takeaway? Embrace the natural balance between excess and scarcity, the good and the not-so-good. Master these pairs with a blend of wisdom and a touch of humor. After all, understanding this delicate balance is key to navigating life's quirks and the ever-turning wheels of history.

30. FARAWAY MOUNTAINS

As we drove through the cities,
amid the hurried flow of people,
past the intersections of history and civilization,
it struck me
In the rise of highways and streets,
the fields, the prairies,
the jungles and the mountains have vanished.
Silence fills the void.
Identical houses line the way,
built from the same bricks,
standing on iron poles, with precast concrete,
monotonous in form,
shaped by rules and conventions.

In this uniformity,
privacy and difference are laid bare,
exposed by the latest technologies,
trendy yet sterile.
Souls seem frozen in bottles,
preserved but lifeless.
Wooden crates for corpses,
resting on sidewalks,
awaiting the final journey
for those whose time has come,
to dense plots of land,
a ghost city in waiting.

Once, people's souls were as vast as endless grasslands,
their characters magical and boundless like forests, rivers, and streams.
But now, those noble and benevolent hearts,
like mountains, are slowly drifting far away.

31. THE ILLUSION OF EGO

We often dwell on ourselves - our ego. We scrutinize it, watching as it shifts and morphs from moment to moment, much like the world around us. We convince ourselves that one day, we'll grasp it, pin it down, understand it completely. But when it slips through our fingers, we're left holding nothing but wishful thinking, chasing shadows of our own making.

We judge others through the tinted lenses of our own subjective minds. It's no wonder we end up confused by people - sooner or later, our perceptions betray us. We love and hate based on fleeting feelings, which inevitably change with time.

Even we are in flux, uncertain and nebulous. We speak of the ego as if it's something solid, something fundamentally "us." But in truth, that ego doesn't exist. What does exist is a multitude of selves, a kaleidoscope of personas, each one a different facet of the same elusive diamond. It's a monster with many heads, springing to life every time our minds stir it from its slumber.

Glory and shame, heroism and cowardice, wisdom and ignorance, clarity and confusion, pride and arrogance, stubbornness and openness, satisfaction and desire, hope and bewilderment, hatred and forgiveness, envy and tolerance, stinginess and generosity, selflessness and pettiness, delusion and playfulness.

We are all of these. We are none of these.

These are merely emotions, thoughts of the mind - ever-changing, like leaves caught in a breeze, shifting their position in space and time. Our bodies are no different. Every second, millions of cells die, and millions more are born.

An ancient Greek philosopher once said that no one bathes in the same river twice, for the river is in constant motion. So too are our minds, flowing like a river that never stops.

The Buddha taught that the 'self-ego' is an illusion. All images of our 'body-mind' are illusions, yet none of them are truly illusions either.

So, what is real?

Only the 'body-mind' in this present moment is real. To find that reality, we must still the ceaseless flow of mind, emotions, and thoughts.

We call it Zen. In that stillness, every thought ceases to be a thought. When there are no more thoughts, that is the true thought. Time stops. There is no time. Is that the path to enlightenment? We're not sure anymore.

But we do know this: when time no longer flows through memory and nostalgia, there is only the present. The false self fades away.

What remains is the true self. The selfless self.

We understand this, yet we're still ensnared by the ego - clever, multilingual, cunning, sophisticated, wise, and endlessly deceitful.

32. THE SIMPLICITY OF THOUGHT

Complex thinking often leads us down winding paths to wrong decisions. With too much information, our minds become tangled, making it hard to choose the right course. Before long, our mood sinks into a pit of frustration and resentment.

Zen masters, however, keep things simple. Their thoughts are clear because they focus on one specific task at a time. When the task is done, their minds find peace.

So, perhaps it's time to step back from the noise - turn off the TV, stop endlessly scrolling the internet, and take a break from the constant stream of emails and messages. Instead, create a simple mind map of your current problems. Simplify your thinking, and clarity will follow.

Nothing

How could we compare

the color of sunrise and sunset?

The former wakes the east,

the latter bids farewell in the west.

Both change as the earth whirls around.

Don't be arrogant

nothing wins, nothing loses.

33. THE ART OF TRANSFERRING SPIRIT

In the quiet of the temple, the spiritual master never seemed concerned with destinations. Instead, he watched us closely, observing every move we made. One day, I asked him a question. His answer wasn't what I expected; it wasn't about the destination at all. Instead, he spoke of the way I had approached the question, capturing the essence of my actions with such precision that it was as if he had read my thoughts.

It was in that moment, through his calm and focused presence, that I felt the transfer of something deeper - a transmission of spirit. He wasn't just teaching a skill or a technique; he was passing on the very soul of his art. I had always been skeptical of such things, dismissing them as mere legend. But as I stood there, absorbing the quiet power of his words, I realized that this direct transmission from teacher to student was not a myth. It was real, profound, and deeply personal.

34. GRACEFUL MOMENTS

In just a few days, my daughter will head off to study far away, and soon after, my son will return to school after his winter break. My wife mentioned she'd go to the mountains before Tet (Lunar New Year), so I've decided these days are best spent with family - cooking, gossiping, and simply enjoying each other's company.

Lately, I've been trying to meditate on light, healing my spirit in the process. Meditating and daydreaming, I find myself feeling strangely empty yet peaceful. I've taken a couple of days off - no meetings, no anger, no worries. And suddenly, the tension in my neck has eased, the stiffness in my shoulders has melted away. Amazing how the spirit influences the body.

As the clock ticks down to the New Year 2019, I find myself secretly wishing my wife would come sit with me, watch TV, and wait for the countdown together - just like old times. I'm like an old lover, hoping for a knock on the door, anticipating that familiar presence.

Sunset Grace

Don't be sad if no one remembers us later.

We have the sun, music, and each other.

Cherish the warmth of friends,

the laughter of wine and butterflies.

Hold tight to those sweet moments of love,

for they shine with grace even as they fade.

35. YESTERDAY'S DUST

He was jolted awake around 1:00 am by a phone call from his family in America. Unable to drift back to sleep, he sat up and decided to review the documents for the morning meeting with the Tokyo team. The files were a hefty 130 Mb - far too long. So, he grabbed a pen and scribbled a few thoughts about the past days. Despite the early disruption, he arrived at the office with a burst of energy after a solid 60-minute yoga session to kick off the week.

The morning whizzed by in meetings, stretching until 1:00 pm, leaving him just thirty minutes for lunch. By 2:00 pm, the meeting room's warm air had him fighting off drowsiness, so he asked the secretary to let him catch a 15-minute nap in his chair. The meeting dragged on until 5:30 pm with no break in sight.

Finally, he retreated to his office, locked the door, and lost himself in a book. At 6:30 pm, he decided to call it a day and head home early, sending a few messages to relatives along the way. His brothers- and sisters-in-law often vented to him about work, and he thought with a wry smile, *"I must owe these people from a previous life."*

Just a few weeks ago, an old employee reached out to him, asking for help with some god-awful task. He couldn't understand why people felt compelled to connect or reconnect in such strange ways - whether in this life or a past one.

Life is strange like that.

> **Eyes**
>
> *Close your eyes,*
>
> *to see with different eyes*
>
> *from within.*

36. THE SACRED WITHIN

"In the beginning was the Word, and the Word was with God, and the Word was God," says the Bible. With these words, God invites us to awaken and listen to His teachings. Similarly, the Buddha taught, *"Mind starts the methods, Mind masters, Mind creates."* Both God and Buddha remind us that our journey begins within, shaped by the power of thought and word.

God's voice, spoken in His divine language, serves as the bridge between the Creator and man, forming the foundation of our existence. Buddha, on the other hand, teaches through both words and silence, guiding us to enlightenment. In Zen Buddhism, even the simple act of contemplating a lotus flower can lead to profound realization.

Human beings connect to the world through the five senses: sight, smell, taste, hearing, and touch. It is through these contacts that consciousness awakens. Each sense, when fully engaged, can elevate mundane activities - painting, arranging flowers, cooking, making music, or practicing martial arts - into a form of art. In Japan, the highest expression of these arts is often seen as a meditative state, a union of body and spirit.

Sound, one of the most profound forms of connection, guides us to reflection and spiritual insight. Visual images, too - whether in the form of pictures, symbols, or icons - are indispensable tools for spiritual awakening.

Buddha emphasized that the mind precedes all things, suggesting that our psychological state is paramount. If we nurture a respectful mind towards the teachings of God and Buddha, this reverence becomes a pathway to spiritual enlightenment.

Respect extends beyond ourselves to the objects and experiences that shape our consciousness - through words, images, scents, tastes, and touch. This respect leads us toward enlightenment, whether through the jhāna of Zen Buddhism or the spiritual practices of other faiths.

As humans, composed of both body and mind, our first duty is to be respectful of ourselves. This is why it is said, *"The Buddha is within us,"* or *s* We are the sacred shrine in which the divine dwells.

To approach the divine with reverence, we must continually renew and purify our inner shrine. This means:

- *Purifying our body and mind.*

- *Being grateful to the divine and all creation.*

- *Living a life of giving and loving, filled with gratitude.*

Life is fleeting and impermanent; everything is born and eventually passes away. Yet, in this transient existence, we must understand that:

- *We are our most sacred and valuable work.*

- *We must dedicate ourselves to each moment of life.*

- *We must live with reverence, holding noble gratitude for the most sacred - God and Buddha.*

37. ENLIGHTENMENT

He spent his days racing from one meeting to the next, navigating a maze of interactions with executives, old friends, high-ranking officials, entrepreneurs, intellectuals, scholars, and even those with a checkered past. His goal was always the same: to secure the help his company desperately needed to survive the challenging times of political upheaval.

This had been his life for years. Now, worn out, physically weakened, and even battling illness, he still couldn't bring himself to quit. There were moments when he wanted to throw in the towel, to simply let things unfold as they would. "Whatever happens, happens," he often muttered to himself in moments of exhaustion.

But the difficulties never seemed to end. Problems cropped up from every direction, and despite the passage of time, nothing seemed to change - neither the people nor the politics. Just last night, he overheard a leader advising, "Whatever you do, make sure to protect yourself and separate public matters from personal ones." It was a stark reminder of the constant caution he had to exercise in his world.

That afternoon, he attended a meeting where another leader addressed a room full of private business owners. "The real challenge isn't catching the worms," the leader said, "but preventing them from getting into the trees in the first place. If we all did that, business would be a lot better."

These words stuck with him, but it was a quiet conversation with two other leaders that brought about a true moment of clarity. He realized that the best way to weather the storm wasn't through endless struggle, but by keeping his mind fresh, relaxed, and at peace.

In the weeks prior, he had attended a spirit-calling ceremony. The spirit of his ancestors had urged him to approach everything with his heart, to keep his mind joyful and calm. The message was simple: when you cultivate peace within, peace follows in the world around you.

From that moment on, he decided to embrace this wisdom.

Peace of mind, he learned, is the true source of strength.

Physical beauty, after all, is born from the pain of discipline.

38. BEYOND THE GOAL

There are times when genuine interactions occur - some hit the goal, and others fall short. Yet, whenever we find ourselves upset, there's the gentle reminder from the spiritual master: "What are you thinking about? Don't let bad interactions trouble you. This is something you've encountered before. And remember, don't get too excited about good interactions either. Step away from the likes and dislikes. You need to learn how to stand firmly in all situations, finding happiness even when it's someone else who has acted well."

39. NAKED TRUTHS

I've desired too much in one short human life.

So many intentions, plans, projects, relationships, knowledge, positions, assets...

The list is long.

In those brief days, with nights full of restless sleep,

I struggled for months, uncertain for years, chasing it all.

Now, having wandered through so many paths of life,

I can't remember half the things I've done

What I ate, where I shopped, what I wore, or how many people I've met.

All these things blur together.

I only realize now that there's not much time left.

My eyes are dimming, my legs are weary,

And I'm getting older by the day.

Yet the path ahead still stretches long,

And there are so many things I feel I must do.

Then it hits me

I've been dragging my possessions, my ambitions,

All the things no one else would ever want,

Toward a place of eternal darkness.

Leaving behind the burdens of this world,

With nothing more than this thin, empty body,

I finally understand why,

Every night before I sleep,

I crave the simplicity of being naked

To strip away the illusions

And grasp the truth of what really matters

In this fleeting, virtual world.

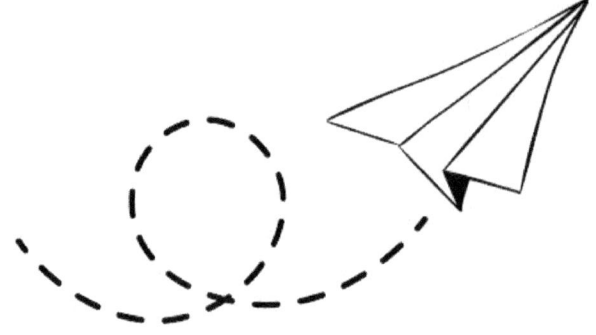

40. . THE SPIRIT OF THE LAND

After many years of traveling the world, I've had the opportunity to taste wines and spirits from various lands. Each drink seems to carry the essence of its place of origin, reflecting its culture and people in subtle ways.

- **Vietnamese Rice Wine**: Light and simple, varying slightly by region, with a taste that evokes the countryside. It has a modest aftertaste, and if you drink enough, it might stir up feelings of nostalgia and a bit of cheerfulness.

- **Japanese Sake**: Elegant and refined, sake is as much about the ritual as the taste. Whether served hot or cold, it carries a sense of quiet pride, deeply rooted in tradition and subtlety.

- **Korean Soju**: Smooth and slightly sweet, Soju is an easygoing drink that pairs well with good company. Its simplicity can sometimes reveal the relaxed, convivial nature of the drinker.

- **Chinese Rice Wine**: Ranging from everyday varieties to more refined options, Chinese rice wine has a strong, distinctive flavor. It's a social drink, often enjoyed in lively settings, reflecting a culture that values generosity and celebration.

- **Russian Vodka**: Pure and straightforward, Russian vodka is a symbol of strength and resilience. When chilled, it offers a clean, crisp experience that speaks to the heart of Russian hospitality.

- **Polish Vodka**: Similar to its Russian counterpart, Polish vodka is known for its clarity and strength. It has a way of warming you up, reflecting the warmth and resilience of its people.

- **Northern European Vodka (Sweden, Finland)**: Cool and crisp, with a light fragrance, this vodka carries a quiet strength. It's both romantic and reserved, much like the landscapes it hails from.

- **French Vodka**: Smooth and aromatic, French vodka carries a touch of elegance and charm. It's a drink that invites conversation and contemplation, much like the sophisticated culture it represents.

- **French Cognac**: Rich and complex, Cognac is a drink of depth and character. Its golden hue and layered flavors reflect a blend of tradition, refinement, and understated strength.

- **British and Scottish Whiskey**: Bold and robust, whiskey from the British Isles is steeped in history and tradition. It's a drink for those who appreciate depth and complexity, with a touch of wildness and adventure.

- **Tequila**: Vibrant and lively, Tequila is the spirit of celebration. It's a drink that brings warmth and energy, often enjoyed in moments of joy and festivity.

I used to be quite the "wine connoisseur," eagerly sampling the spirits of each land, chasing experiences and savoring the diverse flavors. Now, those wild days are behind me. What remains are the memories of each drink, each land, and the realization that perhaps people and their wines share the same essence - each one carrying the distinct character and flavor of their homeland.

41. ETERNAL ECHOES

During the period of social distancing, the city took on a barren, desolate beauty. Empty streets, closed shops, and shuttered hotels created a strange stillness. Temporary barricades - ropes and chairs - marked the entrances to alleys, manned by a few weary faces. He couldn't help but recall the vibrant gates that once welcomed the city's celebrations in years past. Yet, the daily warmth of the sun and the sudden rush of late summer rains remained unchanged, a comforting constant in a world of flux.

•

Last summer, seeking solace from the pandemic, he found himself wandering along the pristine beaches of the countryside. There, he was immersed in the deep blues of the sea and sky, beneath a blazing sun that felt almost Mediterranean. He took refuge in a quaint house with a round roof and dazzling white walls, where vines and flowers bloomed exuberantly. The cool air-conditioned room became a sanctuary for his wandering thoughts, as he lost himself in dreamy pages. Evenings were marked by intimate gatherings, lit by the soft glow of candles, accompanied by the rustling of trees under the moon and stars. Now, those moments felt a world away, as distant as a forgotten dream.

•

He often wondered where she was, what she did, how time had treated her. Her name was as ephemeral as clouds, as vast as the sky, as elusive as the scent of flowers carried by the wind. She took on the forms of night and day, dawn and sunset. Her soul, like water and fire, was a mix of contrasts - sometimes calm, sometimes turbulent. She existed in his imagination, in a place of elegance and grace, where beauty met mystery.

He knew her in his dreams - noble, passionate, with a touch of the erotic. She was a muse, fragile yet fierce, a figure from a storybook wandering through a green garden. On long journeys over mountains and passes, she was an adventurer, her spirit free and untamed. In quiet moments, she pondered the world with a glass of sparkling red wine in hand. She was a creation of his heart, born from thoughts, dreams, and fleeting images.

Where are you now? Are you still awake?

The garden breathes with jade orchid's grace.

I step through the door, silent and still,

Hoping for you, with a heart to fill.

•

There was something unreal about it all, something that lingered just out of reach, like a shadow at the edge of a dream. Sometimes, the dogs barked at the night as if sensing an unseen presence. Leaves rustled, bells chimed softly, and with them came thoughts, wishes, and memories, drifting in like a gentle breeze.

This morning, he asked the helper to place a small speaker in the stone tower at the corner of the garden, letting it play Buddhist scriptures. As the prayer whispers filled the air, he felt a sense of peace:

For the trees and the rocks,

The wind passing by,

The fish and flowers,

To comfort the soul

Of you and me,

As of a thousand years,

The continuity of impermanence

Of an eternal realm.

42. THE FINAL GIFT

As he gazed at the bright lights of the streets, preparing to welcome the New Year, a question lingered in his mind: "What do you want from life?" He had tasted love and loss, joy and sorrow, life and death. But what did it all mean? Thoughts spiraled - doubts, struggles with ambition, searches for clarity, the tension between reality and wishes. Was there a common thread, a deeper meaning that could enlighten and guide his life?

As a company owner, a leader, a family head, and a member of various communities, he felt the weight of responsibility pressing on his shoulders. Demands and pressures clashed from all sides, each vying for his attention.

In the past, when he was brimming with health and enthusiasm, life was an adventure filled with discoveries, challenges, possessions, achievements, and dreams. He was like a spider weaving a web, eager to catch all that life offered. But now, all that he had gathered felt more like debts, and the web he had spun had turned into chains that bound him.

He had come to understand that every joy and pleasure comes with a price - a price paid with health and time. As he reflected on this, he realized that perhaps death, the ultimate end, is the most expensive gift life has to offer.

So now, he approached life with a new awareness, cautious and meticulous. He knew that preparing for this final gift, the closing chapter of his journey, required deep thought and careful preparation. It was the most meaningful and deserving gift of his life, one that he intended to meet with dignity, having lived fully and with purpose.

43. IN FULL BLOOM

What is the meaning of life,
In years spent with toil and strife?
I feel small and alone,
In the sea of silent work, I've known.

Yet beauty lies in moments,
That come and go like gentle breezes,
Where we learn to cherish,
Each fleeting feeling, as it eases.

From this place of quiet,
Sprouts faith, love, and desire,
To create something meaningful,
For now, and what's to aspire.

In that shining instant,
Where thoughts ignite,
Lives the spark of creativity,
Enthusiasm burning bright.

It purifies and lifts,
To new heights unforeseen,
For the land and its people,
A future, serene and green.

Though I am small,
In the grand stream of time,
I dreamt of merging,
In the flow, so sublime.

Mixing with the blood,
Of strange, yet loving kin,
Through many lifetimes,
Until my life blooms within.

44. THE RESILIENT MIND

Strength in the body comes from regular exercise. It's not always easy - there are obstacles, pain, and moments when you want to quit. But the more you push through, the stronger you become. Yet, true strength lies not just in muscle, but in resilience.

The same is true for the mind. Life's difficulties, hardships, and complex problems are like exercises for the mind. When we're young, our minds are flexible and strong. As we mature, our minds grow clearer and more focused.

In the past, criticism often sparked an immediate reaction - anger, hurt, or the silent burden of letting it fester inside. But with time, I've come to see these challenges in a different light.

Now, I realize that we must thank the difficulties, the obstacles, and even the opponents in our lives. They keep our minds sharp, resilient, and ready for whatever comes next.

Now I understand.

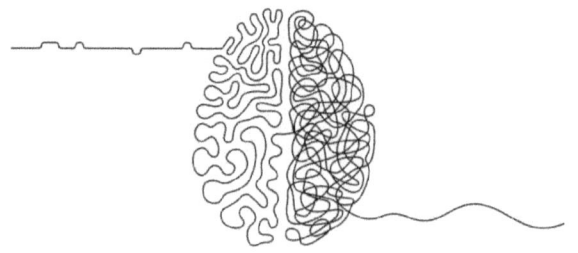

45. UNITY IN THE MOMENT

He found himself lost in a fog of confusion, where even the simplest things seemed chaotic and messy. Questions swirled in his mind - was it him, the one interacting, or was it the medium that pulled them all to a higher level? Did he hit the target, or did the target hit him? Was it the spiritual within the mortal eye, or mortality within the spiritual eye? Or could it be both? Or perhaps neither?

It seemed that everything - tools, objects, goals, and even himself - had become so intertwined that separating them felt impossible. And as this realization dawned on him, he noticed that the desire to separate them had also faded away. He understood now that only by engaging with the medium, by truly interacting, did everything become clear and remarkably simple.

"This very moment," said the spiritual teacher, his words enveloping him, "you and the medium have become one, transcending the object."

46. SLEEP TIGHT

We shared wild, passionate moments,

Wandered hand in hand through lands unknown,

Welcomed dawn by windows adorned with purple and pink,

Surfed the clear blue sea, chasing the sun as it set.

In our youth, life was tough,

Yet we committed to it together,

Rushed dinners on empty streets,

All-night meetings, driven by dreams.

For love of me, you gave your all,

Enduring the bitterness and hardships of half the world,

Silently suffering,

Silently shielding me from the storm.

I still wait for you to come home,

To hold our baby in your arms each night,

Whispering softly, "Dad loves you,"

Leaving worries behind the door,

Immersed in the soft music of prayer.

Tomorrow will bring happiness anew,

Good night, my love.

Sleep tight, and dream sweetly until we meet again,

Waiting for our souls to reunite in the next life.

47. THE LONG ROAD

He looked back on the journey he had traveled, each step marked by challenges and perseverance:

- It took him five years just to get approval for his business project.

- Nine years of relentless struggle followed as he fought to reestablish his company amidst financial crises.

- Three years were spent battling failures and health problems - sickness, a persistent cough, a broken leg, back and neck pain, and a series of severe diseases.

- It took two years to commit to a vegan diet and a rigorous exercise routine that eventually helped cure his ailments.

- Many years were lived in a lonely house, far from the warmth of family.

- Countless times, he thought about giving up everything, retreating to an isolated place to live in peace.

- And there were many plans, carefully laid out, that ultimately failed due to life's unpredictable twists.

But today, something had shifted. Despite the weariness, despite the years of struggle, he found himself filled with a renewed sense of curiosity and hope. He realized that these weren't entirely new dreams - rather, they were old ones, deeply rooted in his heart and mind, waiting to be rekindled.

Take a sip of bitter tea,

And let the sweetness rise,

As it settles in your throat,

A quiet, gentle surprise.

48. THE OLD LOVER

(To the man I loved before)

You chose me, the old lover,

With eyes drooped by time's gentle hand,

Still longing for a love that burns,

Full of life, like a steadfast tree.

You chose me amid the turbulent sea,

Seeking a haven from life's storms,

Braving the hardships with a need

For warmth and a place to belong.

You chose me, despite my scarred heart,

To understand the lonely tears,

To exchange love's warmth once more,

*And revive a heart that has known too much **pain**.*

49. THE NEXT GOOD LUCK

As the New Year dawns, we exchange wishes of good luck and success, hoping for a year filled with blessings. Each month, we stand before Buddha and the Holy Spirit, seeking peace and fortune, knowing well how precious these gifts are. Such blessings, we realize, must be nurtured and cherished in our thoughts, for they do not come by chance.

No one wishes for the opposite, and it's clear that *"Good things bring more good things."* Each day, we nourish ourselves with wholesome food, feeding both body and mind. In the same way, our destiny needs to be tended to, cultivated with small joys, fresh perspectives, and steady progress.

So, take time to remind yourself of the good that lies ahead - progress, luck, and success waiting to unfold. Let your faith in the future bloom, bringing smiles, energy, and triumph. This is the secret of life: to nurture hope and believe in the luck that tomorrow holds.

50. THE ART OF NO ART

As time passed and the practice of interactions became less frequent, the spiritual teacher began to guide us on the 'way' of professional skills in relationships, showing us how to apply them to the level we had attained. His teachings, often wrapped in mysterious imagery and profound metaphors, required only a few words for us to grasp their deeper meaning.

He paused at the concept of the 'art of no art,' suggesting that this elusive mastery is something technology may one day approach, though never fully achieve. The teacher explained, "The one who can interact with any medium, whether it be a rolled-up paper or a delicate flower, will eventually see beyond the medium. There is no paper, only the essence of the flower at the center. At that moment, he will have reached the pinnacle of understanding - the master of the 'art of no art.' He becomes both guru and not-guru, unified in a single being."

At this threshold, technique transforms into movement without movement, a dance without a dance. It is then that one truly enters the state of Meditation - Zen.

51. THE PATH TO PEACE

As another week drew to a close, he found himself once again spinning in a whirlwind of bad news, pressure, depression, and anxiety. Despite it all, he kept reminding himself to smile and maintain a peaceful mind.

He had been reading books on cancer treatment, which essentially advised him to:

- Adopt a completely vegan diet, detox the body, and consume plenty of mineral water and fruit juice.

- Exercise regularly, sleep moderately, meditate daily, and cultivate peace of mind. Manage stress and approach physical intimacy according to his needs.

- Engage in activities that bring joy. Let go of greed, anger, and delusion. Be happy, fun, and kind. Nourish both mind and heart.

Yet, the demands of daily work clung stubbornly to his thoughts. This was the most challenging issue to resolve. He wondered how he could create a schedule that would allow him to:

- Stop working by 6pm.

- Have dinner at 7pm.

- Go to bed by 11pm.

- Spend weekends in the mountains, practicing meditation.

The reality, however, was that he had to accept giving up many things. He had already made the difficult decision to let go of a business he loved. Perhaps, he thought, it all depended on faith. Today, he met with another business owner who offered assistance, but he remained conservative and somewhat detached. He reflected, "If you want to heal your body and mind, you must find peace and harmony."

On a flight to the city, he pondered, "I hope the work is entrusted to capable and conscientious hands. Now is the time to lay down the sword."

I felt as if I had finally discovered the path to spiritual enlightenment, a way to heal both body and mind, and to restore a pristine, natural life. This was the path the ancient sages had discovered and passed down through the ages. But I realized it would take immense perseverance and determination to follow it.

Compared to this path, all the pursuits of fame, fortune, position, happiness, and ambition seemed so small and impermanent.

52. ECHOES OF MEMORY

As he sat in meditation, memories began to surface, uninvited yet vivid, like scenes from an old film.

He recalled:

- The moment when he held her hand by the window, fireworks blooming outside as if the world was celebrating their love, even though the ground beneath them was shaking, perhaps with the same trepidation they both felt.

- The day they came home after a lazy afternoon in the park, where he carried her up the stairs and lulled her into a dream with a whispered lullaby. He had always thought he had a terrible singing voice, but that night, it seemed to work like magic.

- Receiving her letter after waiting for what felt like an eternity. From that day, he became a wanderer, traversing through countless stations, hopping onto overnight trains just to see her, just to hold her once more, even if it meant sleeping on uncomfortable benches and surviving on stale coffee.

- The time they lived together. He took care of her, helped her study, even when his own books were gathering dust. Then, life took a turn, and they were apart, the sadness and regret hanging between them like a fog neither could dispel.

- After that chapter of life closed, he was determined to leave everything behind. He thought he could find peace on the mountain, among the quiet trees and ancient rocks. That's why, in this life, he told himself he must take care of those he loves, to do what he couldn't back then.

- That night, while meditating in the pine forest at the foot of the mountain, she suddenly reappeared. Not as a ghost, but as a memory so vivid it was as if she was there in the flesh. Silently, they descended the mountain together, finding the old silhouette of their past.

And as he meditated, a quiet smile played on his lips. Life, after all, was strange. One moment, you're striving to forget, the next, you're clinging to memories like a lifeline.

The Song of My Life

Those who aren't passionate may never know,

That life's just a fleeting show.

Sadness, joy, suffering, and madness

It's these ups and downs that compose my life's flow.

As he recited the words in his mind, he couldn't help but chuckle softly. Life was a bit of a joke, wasn't it? A grand cosmic play where the script often made no sense, but the performance was still worth every second.

53. BALANCING THE LEDGER

Maybe one day, I'll take my leave from this world without much warning. So today, I figured it's a good time to review what I'll leave behind. I made a mental balance sheet, listing my assets on the left and my debits on the right.

Assets	Debits
Family, wife, children	*Obligations, sharing*
House, car, money, property	*Worries, calculations, distractions*
Shares, company	*Responsibilities*
Relationships, reputation	*Binding, preserving, unfinished knowledge*
Books, libraries	*Love. kindness, gratitude*
Luck, fate	*Gentleman, grace*

As I glanced over my life's balance sheet, I couldn't help but notice: the more assets I have, the more debts I seem to owe. And, of course, there are always a few unpaid debts hanging around. So, I've come up with three solutions:

1. **Minimize Assets:** If we keep our assets lean, our debts will naturally shrink.

2. **Share the Wealth:** If we've accumulated too many assets, perhaps it's time to give some away to lighten the load.

3. **Stop Accumulating:** If we resist the urge to gather more assets, our debts won't pile up as quickly.

Now, I'm already working on the first two - downsizing and sharing where I can. But that third one? It's a tough nut to crack. It would be like renouncing all worldly pleasures and heading off to a monastery in the mountains, living a life free of others' influence, and letting go of everything - sex included, which, let's be honest, leads to all sorts of karma.

So, in conclusion, life is pretty enjoyable as it is. After all, when the final tally comes, death has a way of clearing a lot of our debts.

54. THE ART OF MORALITY

He knew a man, well-regarded and seemingly calm, whose reputation in business was steadily growing. This man had heard of his struggles in his own business and decided to extend a hand, offering to introduce him to some influential people who could potentially turn things around.

Time and again, this man emphasized that the core issue with the company wasn't the lack of effort or unity among the staff but rather the absence of connections with key players. This struck a chord with him, and he was so touched by the man's concern that he took his hands in gratitude.

As the Moon New Year approached, the man suggested they visit these important contacts to present gifts in the spirit of the season. Eager and hopeful, he agreed without a second thought. When they arrived at the first house, the man took the gifts, entered ahead, and asked him to wait outside while he spoke with the boss.

Minutes turned into what felt like hours. Finally, the man emerged, wearing an apologetic smile, and explained that the boss was too busy to see him that day. Disappointed but still trusting, he accepted the explanation and left.

Over time, he realized that this so-called benefactor had never actually facilitated any meaningful connections. The man had mastered the art of appearing moral and generous without truly being either. He would often tell university students about the importance of ethics and wrote books filled with advice on living a meaningful life. He even boasted about his children's virtues, funded the construction of schools, temples, and bridges, and organized tree-planting initiatives to reforest the mountains. But as he observed, it became clear that this man's morality was more of a performance than a practice.

And so, he learned a valuable lesson: sometimes, those who preach the loudest about morality are the very ones who've mastered the art of appearing virtuous without living virtuously.

55. ECHOES OF THE SELF

He often found himself caught between the demands of the outside world and the pull of his inner solitude. Business required him to build relationships, forge connections, and seek success. Yet, the more he tried to engage with the world, the more he felt the urge to retreat, to surrender, to tolerate rather than confront.

Loneliness, he realized, was an intrinsic part of his nature. It was a chronic condition, incurable by any external remedy. So, he chose himself as his own companion, engaging in constant dialogues with his inner self to alleviate the weight of solitude.

In these dialogues, he would often blame himself, hovering above the present moment like an observer of his own life. He saw himself walking alone, suffering, accepting the inevitable. But alongside him walked another presence - an alter ego, frustrated yet contemplative. He understood that as the world evolved, so too did the unpredictability of human nature. This alter ego bore the brunt of these changes, struggling and enduring with a quiet resilience.

In the midst of this internal struggle, he discovered another part of himself - an ideal, a seeker of knowledge, a student of life. This part was constantly inquiring, learning, and striving to become wiser and more righteous.

Life, to him, seemed a blur of memories, recollections, and reality. The line between the physical and mental, between dreams and life, was often indistinguishable. Yet, he wondered, was such a distinction even necessary?

Life was a journey, a path filled with joy and sorrow, with moments that both uplifted and burdened him. His imagination fueled this journey, where each day was a new expedition - whether on business trips, motorbike rides, or through the landscapes of his mind. In these travels, he was never alone; his many facets accompanied him. Together, they ventured deeper into thought, growing more isolated yet more interconnected.

Instead of confiding in others, he often resorted to sarcasm, malice, and quarrels within himself. But in those extreme moments, he found her, and he found you. She flew beside him, while you walked close by. She was proud and distant; you were supportive and near. Jealousy, anger, and loneliness intertwined, pushing him on a spiritual journey in search of solace.

Joy, he realized, was fleeting. The wine eventually runs dry, the party ends, and the flowers wither. Disappointment followed, leaving him and his inner companions bruised and bewildered.

In the darkness of his mind, he heard voiceless cries, uncertain of how to respond. But then, a kind master appeared, guiding him with a transcendent aura, more than a saint, a god - perhaps even a Buddha within himself.

And now, another figure emerged - 'Brother' - a soulmate, carefree and experienced, devoid of jealousy or scorn, full of sympathy, harmony, and love. The further he journeyed, the closer he felt to these beings. 'Me and you,' 'me and him,' 'you and me' - all reunited under 'His' light, at 'His' feet, with 'Brother' by his side.

●

Thus, he had created a system within himself - a multifaceted way of understanding life, complex and ambiguous, contradictory yet intertwined like the ancient "Eight Trigrams Map." This map wasn't something to be grasped or understood in a literal sense. It was a reflection of the chaotic world, a way to impose order and find peace, even if that peace was relative, a temporary respite from the relentless motion of life.

But true peace, he knew, could only be found when the mind ceased its restless wandering. When desire was no longer criticized, and regrets were laid to rest, he could begin to find the path back to his true self. And it was there, in that stillness, that he might finally discover real peace.

He knew this because 'He' had guided him, but he still had to continue moving forward, seeking comfort and understanding along the way. This was his way of entering the world - one step closer to the truth within himself.

56. ENTERING THE WAY EVERYDAY

"I don't demand that you practice every single day. But unless you have a true reason to stop, don't let a day go by without performing the simple initiation to enter the way - even when there's no medium or object before you. At the very least, focus on breathing properly. You needn't do anything more. I understand that you'll never truly abandon this spiritual art of Zen, for this is what the path offers you: a constant, profound struggle with yourself in the deepest corners of your being."

57. BRAVERY

Another tiring day passed. His entire body and mind felt drained. At noon, he dozed off in his chair, only to wake and trudge over to his bed, still in his long pants, the new shirt hastily tossed aside. He wrapped himself in a thin blanket, rolling the corners tightly around him, cocooning himself in the fleeting comfort. Then came the knock on the door - 30 minutes had passed like a blink. The guests had arrived. He wished he could roll back into that brief, blissful oblivion.

He couldn't help but wonder why the meeting schedule never seemed to end. Was it because the work was genuinely never-ending, or had his secretary simply become too skilled at keeping him busy?

Each day felt like every other day - a mix of joy and sorrow, of problems solved and problems that persisted. His clients were reluctant to settle their debts, his employees occasionally took off without a word, and some of his once-good friends had drifted into the realm of adversaries. Yet, amidst the chaos, there were new projects - beautiful, innovative designs that sparked his passion. New friends had come into his life, bringing with them encouragement and understanding, while others had faded into irrelevance. His daily interactions with the secretaries, drivers, and security guards were always thoughtful and polite, their quiet empathy touching him in ways they might never know.

Yesterday, his eldest son had come home, weighed down by the pressures of exams, the stress of life, and the heartbreak of his first love. Late at night, he picked up his son from the airport, wrapped him in a comforting hug, and held his hand all the way home, saying nothing, letting the silence speak for them. He had heard the short, stifled sigh from his son and understood.

The next morning, when he entered his son's room, the light was still on. His son lay on the bed, staring at the ceiling, eyes filled with a distant sadness. Sitting beside him, he gently patted his shoulder, squeezed his hand. His son woke up, hugged him tightly, and choked back an apology, "Why are you so thin? How is your sickness, Dad?" He patiently listened, comforted him, and then pulled out some colored pens to draw on paper. He sketched out a chart of events, relationships, problems, and options - drawing lines, circling choices, and highlighting paths to help his son understand.

"That's the way I took," he told his son. "Now it's your turn. Try your best, son."

For months, he hadn't gone to see a doctor. Instead, he read every book he could find on treatment methods, tried various drugs, and explored alternative remedies - acupressure, acupuncture, sauna, detoxification. He learned how to heal his body and mind, even as he battled constant crises of melancholy and depression. He appeared quiet and calm on the outside, but inside, he was fragile. That's why he sought out psychological books - to understand the reason for living, to grasp at the meaning of life.

Now, he found himself teaching his son how to heal, much like a wounded wild animal crawling into a canyon to lick its wounds, waiting silently for the pain to subside. He was also teaching him how to live a meaningful life, instilling in him the values of courage, patience, generosity, tolerance, and commitment.

This is what he was doing to comfort himself. Did his son know that?

In the afternoon, he met with a delegation of partners, signed a contract, and then hosted a party to celebrate. They all shouted and cheered together, raising their glasses high.

During the noisy celebration, a subordinate approached him and said, "You have to stay healthy so that we can stay healthy. Yesterday at the meeting, you looked so tired. I was worried. But now, I'm glad to see you're fine. We haven't seen you like this in a while. We all miss you."

Another friend, noticing his changed appearance, exclaimed, "How many kilograms have you lost? Five? Unbelievable! You look so healthy, in good shape, and younger! You're so brave to keep going in this situation."

Late that evening, after returning home, he found the house quiet. His son and wife had gone to visit the grandparents. Only his youngest son had waited up for him. He lay down beside his child, holding him close, and thought to himself, "Look at your Dad, Son. Dad isn't as brave as everyone thinks. He needs a reliable shoulder, warm hands to hold, and a few kind, loving words, just like anyone else."

In that quiet moment, as the night wrapped around them, he felt a sense of peace - a brief reprieve in a world of endless demands. But deep down, he knew that tomorrow would bring new challenges, new battles to fight. And somehow, he would find the strength to face them all over again.

58. QUEEN OF THE BRIGHT SEA

Oh, those sad eyes,

gazing wistfully into the distance.

Your eyes seek to enter my mind,

like a small boat navigating the vast ocean.

My life lies bare under your gaze.

You know everything I possess,

yet the depth of my sea remains unfathomable.

You speak of meditation and compassion,

but your eyes hold thoughts and regrets.

You journey onward, body and soul,

to distant lands,

bringing joy and solace to strangers.

Your smile shines bright,

a beacon of peace in times of hardship.

If only you understood,

I am always alone in the crowd,

lost in heartless, boisterous events.

I seek sympathy and connection.

Do you see yourself reflected in my eyes?

I meditate, seeking the moment,

detaching from the meaningless noise.

Every morning, I pray for mercy in the silence,

before stepping out into the world.

If my life were counted in years,

I'd crush it into thousands of bricks

to pave a path for our children.

But I know they will choose their own way,

so I guide others on their journeys.

If my life were stones of ambition,

shaggy, rough, and unpolished,

I would refine them into glittering jewels,

to shine wherever you are.

Oh, my love, my life is a boat,

drifting in a dark ocean,

searching for a peaceful harbor.

You are the queen of that realm,

yet you do not light the way for me.

If only you saw clearly,

that my life is a vessel of love,

laden with worries and sadness,

lost in the misty ocean of the past.

It longs for your eyes to light up the sea of life,

and guide me to a compassionate shore.

I plead with you, Queen of the Bright Sea.

59. BAD PEOPLE

A businessman, drowning in difficulties, once came to him for help. Grateful at first, the man seemed sincere. But when his troubles passed, he revealed his true colors - impersonating him and trying to recruit a criminal into his twisted schemes.

Then there's another fellow, someone he barely knows. This one's always boasting, climbing the ladder by greasing palms and flattering the right people. He calls himself a boss, though his success seems more about manipulation than merit. Now, he's teamed up with yet another businessman, plotting to seize control of someone else's hard-earned business.

Shameless, isn't it? Yet, these men are still regarded as celebrities, their connections with the powerful growing by the day.

What's the best course of action? Should we stand firm like a tree in the wind, bending but not breaking? Or should we be like a stream, flowing over the rocks, patient in our journey to join the wide river and plunge into the great waterfall? Patience, after all, can outlast deceit.

If there is a paradise, there must be a hell.

> **Who Tells Me Now?**
>
> *Gentle words,*
>
> *but unpredictable intentions.*
>
> *Smiles at first sight,*
>
> *but evil behind it.*
>
> *Buddha sees this*
>
> *who tells me now?*
>
> *I pray to Him for a peaceful life.*

60. HOPE

There are moments when depression seeps in,
When the world around us feels dull,
A sound, a taste, a fleeting touch,
Leaves us with a deep sense of disappointment,
As the world falls short of what we hoped.

There are times when life feels like a struggle,
Battling through hardships, injustices, and lies,
Like swimming in a sea of overwhelming doubt,
Or running endlessly on a road of obstacles,
That make us want to escape this loveless world.

But still, my heart beats on.
I taste, touch, smell, and breathe in life each day.
I remind myself to keep going,
For strength still courses through every beat of my heart.
And my mind whispers that luck will come,
When I've weathered this storm.

This fragile belief, a magical light,
A gift from the gods,
A little grace to help us rise above,
The countless trials they place in our path.
We call this light Hope.
And we thank Him for it.

Faith and Reason

Man has always lived with a delicate balance of faith and reason. It's one of the great challenges of life and has been throughout human history. Living entirely on faith alone is difficult, even illogical at times. Faith is infinitely sublime, great in its scope, but often impractical, ambiguous, and intangible. How can one maintain unwavering faith in the mundane details of everyday life?

On the other hand, living purely by reason seems easier. Rationality offers clear benefits, grounded in common sense and easy-to-understand methods. Yet, reason can be blind, misunderstood, and sometimes, it leads us nowhere. It can even drive us to a dead end when we face adversity.

The true challenge lies in balancing the two - living wisely with faith, while finding peace in reason. This balance allows us to navigate the complexities of life with both hope and clarity, giving us the strength to endure and the wisdom to understand.

61. THE SEARCH FOR MEANING

Sometimes he feels that his life is drifting without meaning. The struggles for survival seem endless, with each day feeling like a grind. If he were to divide his life into ten parts, nearly eight of them would be consumed by worries and struggles. The remaining two are filled with small moments of joy and vague hope, like fleeting glimpses of light in a dark tunnel. It's as if life is slowly pulling him toward the inevitable grave, the final resting place where all struggles cease.

Yet, amidst the overwhelming challenges, those small moments of light offer him just enough hope to keep going. He realizes he must rethink his approach, perhaps even reverse his mindset. He sees two paths before him:

• Acceptance: Surrender to the circumstances, allowing the powers that be to determine his fate.

• Purpose: Find a higher purpose - a sacred joy - that transcends mere survival, honor, or material possessions, something greater that gives his life meaning beyond the day-to-day struggles.

The Story of a Tree
The tree is painfully cut down,
Yet it becomes dried wood,
Shaping a home for people.

It fuels a fire that warms hearts,
Transforms into a guitar
For songs that lift spirits.

Or it is crushed, soaked,
Reborn as blank pages,
Bringing knowledge to children.

You are planting your tree of life.
Sometimes it's cut down,
Only to be refined,
Becoming something that cherishes life.

62. KEEP ON PRACTICING

In meditation, he comes to understand why techniques must be practiced with the whole heart. When he surrenders himself completely to the moment, letting go of self and desire, all external creations unfold naturally - spontaneously, without the need for conscious guidance or control.

The path to mastery lies in rehearsing and repeating the practice, again and again. This is the journey of those who seek to grow, to go further, and to rise higher. This truth has been time-tested, proven through the traditional professions and disciplines.

He keeps on practicing.

63. A WISE CHALLENGE

The Creator, in His infinite wisdom, has given us many wonderful gifts. Feet to travel, hands to grasp, eyes to see the world, a mouth to sing, and a body to savor life's pleasures. It all seems perfectly designed for enjoying the sweetness and joy of life.

But then, just as we're basking in that joy, the Creator gives us a nudge, reminding us that lurking just behind the laughter, sadness waits, ready to knock on our door when we least expect it.

It's as if He's whispering a secret to us: "Don't get too comfortable. Learn a little more, because real peace comes from wisdom and practice." The Creator's guide to life might go something like this:

- Keep your feet steady on the ground.

- Let your mouth speak quietly, even when tempted to shout.

- Move your hands slowly, with care and intention.

- Turn your eyes inward more often.

- And train your body to endure pain - it's good for the soul.

Humans, by nature, are a wild mix of selfishness, arrogance, ambition, and stubbornness. We compete, we demand, we push. The Creator, with a touch of humor, suggests that if we really want to be strong and wise, we might need to try being humble, patient, soft, and giving instead.

It's a tall order, a challenging wish. But then again, isn't that what makes life interesting?

Extraordinary

Great ambition spills over,

Time bends and stretches,

A great soul embraces the world,

Rising above the ordinary,

Reaching the extraordinary.

64. BEAUTIFUL SIMPLICITY

I have met many different types of people in my life. The variety is diverse, but they can be divided into two main types:

Important people – those who influence my work and career. I need to build relationships with them, behave skillfully, shrug, be patient, suffer both materially and emotionally. There are a lot of things I don't want to do, but I still have to make them happy.

Less important people – the rest, who are not directly involved in any decision-making processes. I have met them by chance, or worked with them, or they have worked for me, but quietly and with no special role. They often suffer both physical and emotional loss because of low income and little care.

When I left the company late in the day, I found that most of the private rooms and working areas had the lights turned off and everyone had gone home. Only a few rooms, like the secretary's rooms, specialized areas, or transaction sections that had to process their work for the end of the day, were still lit and buzzing with activity.

If the second type of people in my organization had to work near me, they would probably be the ones I scolded the most. Not because they were necessarily at fault, but perhaps because I needed someone to channel my frustration toward, or because I was incomplete myself.

But surprisingly, the small joys of the day came from their sincere words, sympathetic eyes, or a beautifully presented document. It could be a simple flowerpot with a slender branch, green sprouts, and a few humble little flower buds in the corner of the room, or an unexpected message asking about my health. On certain days, countless sincere wishes came from people whose names I couldn't even recall, but who had quietly passed through my life.

Strangely, there are people who couldn't stand to be near me and moved to another workplace. They grew and held many important positions in new places. When they met me again, they all texted or told me they learned a lot when working with me, sometimes recounting wonderful memories that I didn't even remember.

I have a special car driver. He has worked for me for almost 20 years. Sometimes he wished to quit because he couldn't stand me any longer - I was fastidious, demanding, twisty, and unpredictable. But still, he worked for me. Maybe he couldn't leave me either. I went on a macrobiotic diet, and he did too. I detoxified, he fasted. I shaved my head, he went bald. Deciding what kind of wine I will drink at a meal, he would choose the right wine for me. After a drink, I often smoke a cigar, and he always had a cigar, lighter, and ashtray ready for me. I follow a strict vegan diet, sometimes monotonous, but he always knew how to cook the meals and arrange the dishes so they looked delicious and were ready when I arrived.

When I returned from Japan, I wanted to renovate the garden. I consulted many professional architects, designers, and gardeners, but none satisfied me. I called him, gave him instructions, some beautiful picture books, shopping pages, stores, and took him to the garden. That's all it took.

Then I continued with my busy work, sometimes coming home late at night without even looking at the garden. Three months later, one morning, I woke up and heard the sound of water murmuring, bells ringing musically. It was so strange. I ran down to the garden. Wow! It was like being lost in a fairyland, with grass and flowers swaying in the wind, waterfalls rushing in the mist, a gravel road winding through pine trees, and a few silent stones leading to the stilt house over the water, reminiscent of cultural architecture symbolic of our capital back 1000 years ago, with carp hovering around.

Now, my driver also takes my kid to school, teaches him discipline, repairs or installs furniture or electricity, and changes the water and arranges flowers for Buddha Mother.

I once read a story about a general who built a big temple to worship God. He was often busy fighting wars. Every time he returned home, he would visit the temple to worship God, and there was always a temple watchman working hard, cleaning, offering flowers, placing water and candles on the altar thoughtfully. The general was very grateful to him. On the day the general returned to heaven, he was stopped at the gate. Looking inside, he saw the temple keeper already there, at the feet of God. Surprised, he asked why he wasn't allowed in while his servant had received God's grace. The gatekeeper looked at the earthly merit book and said, "Because you were too busy with your career, you rarely visited God, so you can't enter. But the temple keeper, who spent many years faithfully offering sacrifices to God, is allowed to sit beside Him."

Perhaps the most valuable things we learn in life are the simple things around us. If we know how to observe and listen, from people and nature, there's no need to travel far. That's what I thought to myself.

PART 6: WANDER

The Journey of Unity

I walked along the coast to the south,

So far, so far away, to find myself again.

To breathe in the wind from the blue sky,

On a sunny spring day with comrades,

Like mighty warriors under the shining sun.

We traveled down the coast to a sunlit place,

To hear the wind whisper:

"Let's go fast.

There are many wonders ahead."

Together we seek,

Sweet moments when the night sparkles,

With the dreams of our childhood,

Oh, the cool, sweet breeze,

Bringing me back to memory land.

The bell rings, guiding us to wonderland,

Filling my heart with

Sweet melodies.

We rounded the roads of this beautiful country,

Roaming high passes,

Soaring through the forest.

The wind blows and fills our chests,

As the sound of warm friendship

Sings in our hearts.

In the morning, we welcome the dawn,

The day is for moving forward,

The night is for joy.

Have you ever thought:

How can we be as close as brothers?

Did you notice,

The future is filled with heaven and earth?

You can feel it everywhere,

Blending in the peaceful wind.

I'm searching for magical moments,

In my childhood dreams.

You and I are spinning

An innocent dance of heaven and earth,

Leaving behind the tiring days of gain and loss,

Like distant memories

Buried in the past forever.

We passed many towns and villages,

Bowing our heads in respect.

Temples and shrines,

Honored for generations,

Whether heroic or unjustified,

Guardians of the nation's spirit.

The sacred relics,

Hold the soul of our homeland forever.

Though the fruit trees differ by region,

And phonetics and lyrics vary,

Dynasty after dynasty,

All changes subside,

All share the same mountain of the Holy Spirit.

When the sunset relaxes,

Gone with the dust of the village road,

Some houses have their lights on,

While others remain in the dark,

Just like life among ordinary people.

The souls of the world sometimes shine brightest in the dark,

Depending on the source of light

Light bulb or candle?

And when dawn fades,

Only divine souls

Will shine all day and night forever.

You see, it's very strange, very strange.

It seems the divine soul speaks.

I chase the breeze, the breeze,

And I don't know how to stop.

Everyone is busy,

Chasing extreme ambitions,

Running from the fear of inferiority and loneliness.

And I run fast, fast with the breeze,

Toward the dreams and fragrance of the mountains.

You see, it's simple, how simple.

For those who've been on the road once,

Imagine how wonderful, oh how wonderful,

The mountain, the green hill, the sun, the song, and the falling rain,

Filling my heart to overflowing,

As luggage on a trip

Memories, the unrequited debt of gratitude.

And I run fast, fast with the new wind,

Following the footsteps of the national spirit.

Insects, high mountains, deep green forests,

Small sparkling streams

Float around the mountainside.

Faintly, birds spread their wings,

Soaring above the villages,

Rice fields with greetings,

Marking the love of the homeland.

We are little children,

Stretching our chests, breathing in the free air,

Drinking the holy water,

Carrying the passion of our fathers,

Stretching our arms from the ocean to the mountains,

Wishing to do worthy things,

Wishing the Fatherland to come to glory.

Concurrent People

Not sharing any bloodline, even using different languages and foods.

But drinking together the water of life's worries, disturbances, and uncertainties.

And sharing the joys and sorrows, the ups and downs of an era.

1. PEACEFUL EVENING

My son invited me to dinner, a simple gesture that brought unexpected warmth. So, I made my way home earlier than usual, feeling the quiet anticipation that often accompanies these rare family moments. The garden greeted me with its soft, fragrant breeze, the kind that makes you want to pause and breathe deeply. The children were huddled in the kitchen, busy with small tasks, their chatter filled with youthful curiosity.

They asked about school, about friends, and a few even ventured into topics beyond their years - business, investments, how to build character. It made me smile, this mix of innocence and budding wisdom.

After dinner, I suggested listening to music, a ritual we both cherished. "Great idea, son," I said, as we moved to the music room. I let my son choose, and together we settled on something soothing, like Blue Voice. The piano notes filled the room with gentle elegance, while the saxophone added a touch of earnest romance.

The teapot sat beside a flickering candle, casting a warm, swinging glow. We talked about America, upcoming vacations, work, and even about an old girlfriend - now just a memory, once a source of pain, now softened by time. My youngest son, knowing his brother would soon return to the U.S., left to pick him up, leaving me alone with my thoughts and the music.

I let myself drift in the candlelight, the night outside growing colder. Walking down the hallway later, the scent of hyacinths lingered in the air, a reminder of life's fleeting yet precious moments. These were the unforgettable pieces of my life - simple, yet filled with profound beauty.

Wind, clouds, oceans, mountains, the weather - they all change unpredictably.

But the magnificence of life, I reflected, is rooted in the simple, cyclical wonders of the sun and the moon, constants that bring peace amidst life's uncertainties.

In that peaceful moment, I understood that these small, serene moments were what truly mattered.

2. MYSTERIOUS WORDS

There are certain words that, when spoken or thought, instantly spark a cascade of images within me. They're like keys, unlocking worlds both shadowed and bright, full of intrigue and subtle power.

Take the word 'wet.' It conjures up a vision of swamps, thick with tangled grass and heavy with moisture. It's a word that feels mysterious, inviting curiosity. There's a sense of something lurking beneath the surface, something that clings to your steps as you wade through. It pulls you in, compelling you to reach out, to push aside the weeds and uncover what lies hidden. The experience is startling, bewildering - a journey into the unknown.

The word 'library' brings to mind long, dusty shelves lined with books, each holding a world of its own. There's a stillness there, a quiet broken only by the soft rustle of pages turning. The shadows of people move silently among the rows, their presence felt more than seen. The musty scent of aged paper fills the air, mingling with the faint, ghostly aura of floating glasses and the laughter that echoes in the corners. It's a place of haughty silence, where knowledge waits in the wings.

And then there's the word 'sensual.' It evokes a rush of sensations: a tightening of the chest, a quickening of the heart. It's a word that pulses with life, filled with tension and release. There's the nakedness of vulnerability, the pounding of suppressed desires. It's a chaotic dance of emotions - panic, trembling, outbursts of passion, all held in check by invisible restraints. It's light and dark, wet and hot, a rush of toying with what's just out of reach.

Indeed, words are mysterious, each holding a world of its own. But the mind, oh, the mind is ten thousand times more mysterious and unpredictable - a labyrinth where these words weave their magic, creating connections that are both unexpected and profound.

3. JOURNEY'S END

Oh wonderful days, goodbye.

Tonight, the last party among teammates,

Surrounded by smiles, eyes of joy,

Leaving after hours of light.

Every time the night fills the space,

As if all around me are echoes of the endless murmur

Of wind, sun, mountains, and sea,

Inspiring for a new and indeterminate journey.

Arms outstretched across the vast Heaven and Earth,

There are moments that show me the limits

Of humanity and fear

Before alluring dangers.

Infatuated with a solitary mind,

Gliding through the abyss among the vast green mountains,

A deep voice is filled with dizziness,

An urge to travel to a land that has never been.

We journeyed through the vast green bays,

Along the golden sand that stretches forever.

The boats bobbed around the docks,

And the two sailed quietly out into the ocean.

It's so good to be lonely and foggy.

How many times have I wanted to give up,

Leaving behind worries and fatigue,
To follow the call of a distant past life.

But I'm still here,
Amidst the bonds of love,
Receiving every day more of life's humiliation,
To pay off the accumulated karmic debt.

Regret it? Burdened by who?
Can't give up. Don't stop
In front of the road with many turns.
Only my heart reminds me of a faraway place,
With so many hidden vibrations of desire.

I passed through the raging passes.
There was wind howling
And the sound of souls
Of winners and losers.

Whether heroic or cowardly,
They have devoted themselves
To the green of their homeland.
Today is as peaceful as a flower.

The country is bustling with children's sounds,
Peaceful past beside lonely monuments
Still echoing reminders.
Let's do something for the beloved Fatherland,

Reaching out to the ocean.

The silhouettes of the ancestors appeared,
The sacred soul of the class built up
Into a gloomy, painful, and majestic bronze.
Silently protect the Jiang shān.

My life – tomorrow I say goodbye to friends.
I will return to worries
Early in the evening.
Patience until the next step is common sense.

Whispering every night or before dawn,
Be patient to move on and overcome.
Deeps of doubt separate
The day will come when you will find the land of your dreams.

Let's say goodbye to the tall mountains, the wide sea.
Tomorrow, when I return to the streets of the jungle,
I bring with me the smell of the earth, the sea air, and the blazing sun,
With high passes, waterfalls, bird shadows, clouds in the sky,
Even the whispering reminders of unnamed souls.

Live your short life to the fullest.

4. ROLLER LOVERS

Beloved,

The artist wanders, busy searching for himself,

Yet often loses sight, missing the bookshelf of his soul,

Flavored with the years that have passed.

I love those longing eyes,

Dreamy eyes,

Eyes that reflect an aspirational soul… you know?

"A man does not cry," he often tells himself,

But life is foggy, with so many layers of silent pondering,

Deep inside his heart.

I love you, I love you with all my heart,

I love you with all my heart…

No matter what life brings,

I still love… just as in the beginning.

There are times when I'm sad.

I love you even when you're harsh,

I love you when your eyes are gentle.

Love… as sweet as a stream…

Sometimes I feel wild, or I hide my feelings.

Sometimes I'm sad and blame myself,

And tears fall.

I love you with all my heart,

Both halves of you… you know?

5. THE INNER MASTER

A true professional learner must embody three essential qualities: unwavering discipline, a deep passion for their chosen path, and unconditional respect for their spiritual guide - their Zen master. In times past, the bond between teacher and student was the cornerstone of life itself, placing immense responsibility on the Zen master, far beyond the confines of mere instruction.

When you reach a level of maturity and profound enlightenment, you will realize that the ultimate Zen master, the true spiritual teacher, has always been within you.

6. CITY OF TIMELESS SPIRITS

Sparkling city, veiled in haze,

Time's mist blankets past skyscrapers,

Amidst fields of red and green,

Whispers of the past linger unseen.

Night, smoky and thick,

A stream of glittering lights flows,

Silent figures move through strange doors,

Yet smiles and kind eyes still glow.

Simple lives in a changing world,

Where the old pagoda stands,

Its brown-tiled roof in quiet repose,

Smoke and incense rise,

Carrying the oath of a thousand years,

Guarding the sacred soul of the land.

7. THE PATH OF PEACHES AND APRICOTS

On the way to Zen class, my wife sent a text about loving-kindness, asking what it takes to cultivate compassion, joy, and equanimity.

After a long workweek, I was heading to meet my colleagues with a fresh sense of love. Perhaps I was already practicing loving-kindness. She asked again:

"Do you want to become a Paccekabuddha?"

"Why do you ask that?"

"Miss L told me that you said so."

Oh… that reminded me of a classmate from long ago, with a body like a ripe peach, making many boys swoon. Then, I thought of her again, on a bright spring day, not unlike a fairy fruit with two dimples, making everyone smile.

"Come on, when we reach Nirvana, we'll see who becomes what…"

The ripe apricot fruit was mentioned again in a long sutra. The Buddha explained about the two types of Nirvana fruit, where defilements and sorrows are gone in all three realms, distinguishing between those with residue (with full body and form) and those with no residue (no body, just form).

Oh, I think I'm lucky in this life. I've encountered both apricots and peaches. And in the next life, if I attain the fruit of Nirvana, I hope to have enough medicine. If I meet you again in another world, I'll be sure to spread loving-kindness immediately.

8. LOVE NET

I still remember that afternoon,

When I kissed your eyes at Park Corner,

The anger melting into a sweet, tender embrace,

As melodious love songs played,

And I promised to be with you forever.

I carried you home to the sound of birdsong,

In that ancient elevator without a guard.

Gently, I took you upstairs,

Cradling you in a loving embrace.

I walked all the way down that corridor,

Still feeling the warmth, still dreaming.

"Don't go, honey," you whispered.

"Hold me, love me, and protect me."

The love net we wove together,

Like the streets outside, sparkling with lights,

You are still tender in my heart.

I came to your room and tapped softly.

You were lost in a dream, your curls falling.

"Don't go, honey," you whispered.

9. UNFINISHED LOVE

(from old love)

I wonder what we are to each other...

Both of us sad, lost in nostalgia.

Through text messages, the worrying chats,

A love so bittersweet, yet we can't let go.

I understand it's just a fleeting memory,

A chapter in our lives that we both hold dear.

But how many times have I tried to detach?

I want to leave, but now... I miss you more.

Yeah... I tell myself it's time to forget,

Not to meet, not to call your name anymore.

Who would have thought a broken heart could reignite,

Remembering you nestled in my arms.

Our love, so deep yet tinged with sorrow,

Nameless, cherished day by day.

Let me return to those old days

For we haven't had enough of fate...

What is this love of mine? Why can't I let you go?

10. THE SILENT GUIDE

The teacher quietly observes the student's journey, noting each effort and inquiry without pressing for swift independence or immediate mastery. He understands that awakening and growth cannot be hurried. With patience as his companion, the teacher waits for the student to naturally mature, knowing that both have time. In this shared stillness, the teacher does not push, and the student does not rush - allowing wisdom to unfold in its own time.

11. THE QUEST FOR THE PERFECT BIRD

I finally finished the last lines of the book I'd been working on for so long. I thought it would be easy to close the notebook and call it a day, but I never expected how much effort it would take to typeset, layout, and illustrate it.

Luckily, there were half a dozen assistant secretaries from the three regional offices, all eagerly helping with saving, straightening, and editing sentences. A few more months, and everything would be just right.

Today, one of the secretaries brought in the final draft. Colors, pictures, sidebars... almost perfect. Holding it in my hands was truly heartwarming. But one detail nagged at me - each page needed a small illustration of a bird by the page number, and the current choice wasn't cutting it.

"Hey, why does this bird look so... weak? It's a bit short, don't you think?"

"Oh, I searched everywhere but couldn't find any that looked better. All the Vietnamese birds are small and have these curved beaks."

"Really?" I looked at her with genuine concern. She could see I was taking this bird issue seriously. I pulled out my phone, tapped and swiped for a few seconds, then showed her what I found.

"See? Why can't we use this one? It's long and healthy."

I stood innocently beside her, holding the phone up. We both stared at the screen.

The bird
(the one she found)

The bird
(the one I found)

12. WITNESS

Reflecting on Camus' "The Stranger," I find myself pondering

The absurd and meaningless aspects of human existence:

Human society is absurd,

Yet the movement never ceases.

Much of life is unfair,

And only a few find satisfaction.

It seems there is more bad than good,

As our desires for good rise against the weight of greater evil.

Mean-spiritedness is widespread,

While noble qualities are rare.

Poverty is rampant,

Yet insightful wealth remains elusive.

People often follow the crowd,

Even as they think of themselves as individuals.

However:

As history repeats itself,

Society continues to evolve.

Nations rise and develop,

Some swiftly, others slowly.

Therefore:

Is it wrong to think that all laws are temporary,

That the only constant is impermanence?

The circle of cause and effect is always present.

Suffering fills life,

Yet love is the balm that soothes.

Thus:

- Death is inevitable.

- Decay is unavoidable.

- Civilization is the work of a few.

- Luck has its place.

- The past is gone.

- The future is yet to come.

- The present is fragile.

- Only true value endures.

In wisdom, we find:

- Order emerging from chaos.

- The reasonable arising from the irrational.

- Beauty blossoming from the mud.

- The good within the bad.

- Insight piercing the darkness.

- Wisdom.

- Value.

13. ECHOES OF AUTUMN JAZZ

This afternoon, while sitting in the garden, he stumbled upon an old jazz CD titled *"In a Rainy Day."* As the music played, it took him on a journey through memories long tucked away.

The music flowed like a school of fish gliding effortlessly around a still lake, each note smooth and fluid, drifting lazily, just as the wind occasionally whispers through the trees.

The melodies were mellow, sweet, and bright, glowing like the clusters of yellow perilla swaying gently behind the tiny green fairy's hair-like trees. Each tune seemed to wander, much like his own thoughts, interweaving with the trickling stream beside the island. The rhythms hung in the air like a distant mist, spreading softly, touching his heart with an unspoken longing.

There was a quiet serenity in the music, a gentle reminder to lose oneself in its lonely, wonderful sound - a sound that perfectly captured the essence of wandering, of finding peace in solitude.

He couldn't help but think back to one autumn afternoon, after a journey across high mountains and wind-swept hills. The steppe had been cold and unforgiving, but as the jazz played, those memories were no longer harsh - they were softened, imbued with a sense of nostalgia, as the music wrapped itself around his heart.

In that moment, the garden, the music, and the memories all seemed to blend into one, creating a space where past and present met, in the soothing embrace of a jazz melody.

14. INVITATION TO THE HERMITAGE

You're invited to my secluded retreat,
Down a winding path to the distant unknown.
In the midst of a pure pine forest,
Where misty clouds embrace the green mountains.

The autumn road is blanketed with leaves,
Across from a murmuring stream
Where fish glide gracefully
In harmony with the gentle autumn rain.

Cool grass cushions your steps,
Purple wildflowers smile in greeting,
A bamboo bush bows to welcome you.
A small door opens with an extended hand.

A simple red roof
Nestles under the Buddha's serene gaze,
A peaceful throne beside the realm of man,
Fading gently into oblivion.

With a soft brush,
Gently sweep away the dust of the world,
In silent prayer.

Pray for the world to fade away,
For the chaos to be seen,
For the mind to witness impermanence,
And for our hearts to find peace.

As the afternoon sun dips on the way back,
If you falter, there are yellow thatched tents,
Adorned with golden flowers, waiting to shelter you.

15. HARMONY IN SIMPLICITY

The pink peach blossoms have fallen, their delicate petals scattered gently in the corner of the garden. Nearby, a few branches of yellow dahlias are in full bloom, adding a splash of sunshine to the green. Fresh orchids stretch out to catch the breeze, while rows of purple violets rise high, only to suddenly bow their heads one day, as if lost in thought. In another corner, a few pots of golden apricots shimmer by the aquarium, their colors glowing in the spring leaves and the summer sun just outside the door. The gentleman's flowers, in shades of white, pink, and red, have woven themselves around the window, swaying gently, with butterflies fluttering by, as if dreaming of fairies.

Everything here arrives calmly and departs quietly. Our house, nestled among tall-walled neighbors, seldom welcomes the sun into the bedroom. Yet, there was a day I returned home earlier than usual, just in time to catch a few thin rays of the setting sun at the doorstep. I opened the door wide, inviting the sun inside, along with a few dusty beams, like streams of fragile memories that suddenly surfaced. "Come in, come in," I thought to myself.

The world changes, and life moves in cycles. We chase after paths of desire, only to find ourselves lost once more. The spiritual path is often tentative, with a few steps forward, then a retreat, yet it feels as though we've walked it before, its familiarity etched in our souls from time immemorial.

We are not alone. Everything is interconnected, woven together by the threads of time - past, present, and future - each moment reflecting another, through the hazy yet vivid memories we carry. Here, in this simple home, surrounded by the beauty of nature, we find peace and harmony in the ever-changing dance of life.

16. THE PATH TO MASTERY

The spiritual teacher knows his first responsibility is to guide the student into becoming a skilled person, one who can control and master his movements with precision. The student must be diligent, repeating the practice over and over, refining each movement until it becomes second nature.

The true goal for the student is to reach a point where he no longer has wishes or desires that pull him away from the path. Instead, he learns to patiently accept everything as it comes. Over the years, he will find that the ritual movements, which once felt like constraints, have now become liberating.

Mastery, the teacher knows, is not about the confinement of the self, but rather about freeing it. As the student's mastery grows, he will begin to develop his own skills, nurturing novel ideas with less resistance. Observing his progress, the teacher knows that soon, the student will harvest unexpected creations, fruits of the discipline and patience that have brought him here.

In the quiet of meditation, both teacher and student understand that this journey is one of unfolding, where mastery leads not just to skill, but to wisdom and creativity, beyond the bounds of any ritual or form.

17. THE WISDOM OF VEGETABLES

One day, I sat down with my child, who was pushing vegetables around on their plate with a frown. I could see the wheels turning in their little mind, trying to figure out how to avoid eating them. So I decided to take a different approach, one with a bit of wisdom and a dash of humor.

"You know," I said, "vegetables are like water, and meat is like the earth. Plants need both water and soil to grow. But here's something interesting - some plants, like those in the desert, don't need much soil, just a little water, and they can thrive. That's why you have to eat both vegetables and meat, but maybe, just maybe, you need a little more of those vegetables."

My child looked at me, still unsure, so I continued, "I like to think of myself as a tree. Each year, I sprout new leaves, grow stronger, and someday, I'll bear ripe fruit. I'll enjoy the taste of life, just like a coconut tree giving coconuts with sweet water."

My child giggled, "So, if I eat my vegetables, I'll grow like a tree too?"

"Exactly," I smiled. "And that's when we live a creative, blossoming life - full of flavor, just like a coconut."

> **Blossoming Life**
>
> I am like a tree that sprouts each year,
>
> Growing ripe fruit, tasting heaven and earth,
>
> Like a coconut tree, sweet water to share
>
> That's when life blooms, in joy and mirth.

18. SPRING INCENSE

I have inhaled the scent of spring on silver pine hills,
After nights with graceful mountain maidens,
Understanding that all precious things eventually fade.
I was brave enough to love, but never truly content.

My life, like a lonely bird, wandering,
In search, flying over lands with unfamiliar scents,
Listening to the train's whistle echo on divided roads,
Where flowers lose their fragrance, and the moon hides its glow.

I leave behind sorrows, drifting in memories,
Choking on the quiet beauty of endless wheat fields,
And the misty white snow of Russian winters,
With dark, smoky beer and melancholy summer camps.

If only I could shed my worries now,
And soar toward the passions I am devoted to.
Yes, I hope that Mother Earth, in her wisdom,
Loves and protects this wandering son,
Who has finally returned home.

Wake Up Early

A new workday often begins in a rush. From morning to evening, I hurry through tasks, barely aware of the world around me. Time slips away, leaving me detached and numb.

But if you rise an hour earlier, you can embrace the day differently. Slowly inhale the fresh morning air, catch the first rays of sunlight, listen to the birds singing, and watch the newly bloomed flowers dance in the breeze. Your heart will fill with warmth and simple joys, bringing back familiar feelings of love that will carry you through the day.

19. A TOAST TO LIFE

At the end of the week, we gathered for a service to honor the Holy Mother and Saints in the Goddess religion. It was a joyful occasion. We sat in the lotus position for what felt like 9 or 10 hours, drinking countless glasses of wine and listening to the melodies that filled the room.

By Monday, my body and mind were both numb. As I reflected on the years gone by, I realized just how many shortcomings and mistakes had piled up.

So, I made a vow: from now on, I'll strive to purify my body and mind. No more than two glasses of wine or one strong drink per day - any more than that, and I find my eyes no longer appreciate the beauty of flowers, and my hands miss the chance to catch pink butterflies.

I resolved to live fully in the present moment, embracing each experience with a heart open to joy and sorrow alike. I would overcome the fears and challenges on the road of life, accepting whatever fate brings my way. I vowed to live with faith, with love for life, for people, and for my homeland.

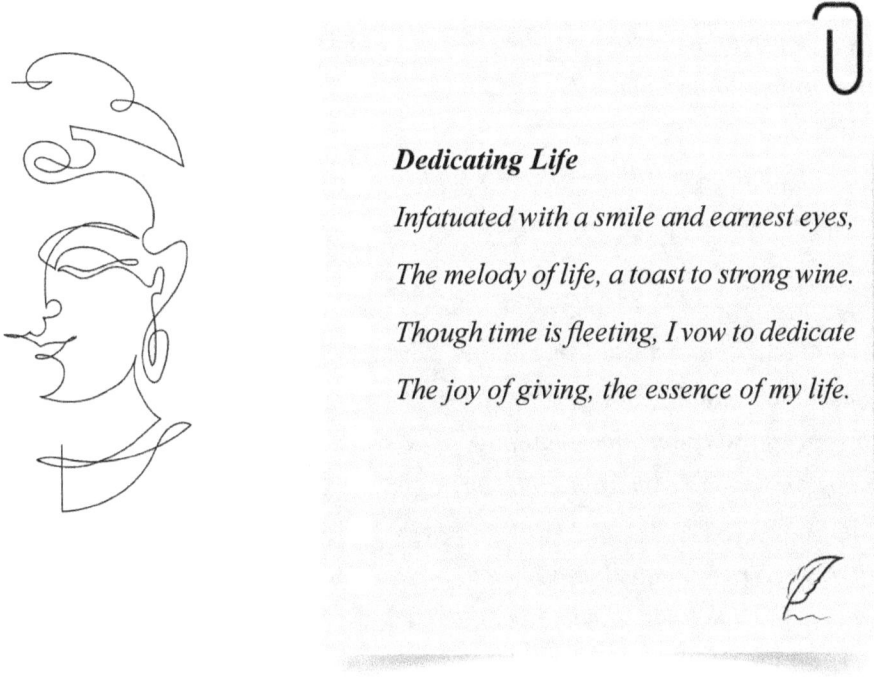

Dedicating Life

Infatuated with a smile and earnest eyes,

The melody of life, a toast to strong wine.

Though time is fleeting, I vow to dedicate

The joy of giving, the essence of my life.

20. ECHOES OF A PAST LIFE

I seem to have met you in a past life,
Those eyes, that smile, those curled eyelashes.
You are fragile, a fleeting image passing through my days,
A fragrant white lily shining in the night.

I've journeyed through many lives, like rivers,
Sometimes noisy, sometimes lonely, sometimes sad,
Along the winding path, seeking the meaning of human life,
You gently led me into a peaceful dream.

Months and years are behind us now,
The road ahead is boundless and vast.
Life is full of fleeting worries and endless calculations,
The dust of time erasing beautiful childhood dreams

You disappear with the dreams of flowers,
Yet this morning's dawn shines bright,
The bird sings,
The harmony of life's music awakens my soul,
Like a voice carried from far away.

Memories flash by, too swift to grasp in time,
Months and years pass, my hair has turned silver,
Yet the evening jasmine's incense still blooms.
Sparkling bright sunshine hums the song of life,
Reminding me of life's wondrous color and light.

Last night, I returned in a beautiful dream,
To a garden of white lilies stretching out in beauty,
Waiting, as if inviting, oh my dear.
Thank you for joining me in this shared karma.

21. ETERNAL GRACE

Prayers and murmurs echo through sacred mountains and rivers,
Come along to hear the song where spirit thrives in the four palaces.
On auspicious days, disciples gather for a solemn feast,
Agarwood incense rises, its smoke spreading far and wide,
Inviting the Most High Holy Mother to witness,
The Palace of Literature, the Moon, and the rhythmic drums.
Sweetly and smoothly, the flute plays the first song,
In adoration of Saints, the famous heroes of our ancestors,
Their prestige fierce and raging, their honor pure.
Fairies offer flowers as jade banquet tables sing with joy,
Of Saints who protect the nation, secure the people, and bring peace,
This is the blessing of our land, long life to our country.
From the East Sea to the mountains, the wind stirs the trees,
Late at night, as the moon sets and the stars dim,
A song is offered to the Goddess of a thousand mountains,
With birds chirping and gibbons calling in harmony.
Green scarves, green shirts, ivory skin, and phoenix eyes,
Smiling mouths like blooming flowers, the Goddess bestows blessings,
A landscape of hills and trees welcomes Saint Male on horseback,
Fairies gather joyfully, following in his footsteps.
Fine wine flows as royal flowers are offered by the fairies,
The Saint drinks three glasses, watching flowers bloom,
And waits for the moon to rise once more.
Wine is bestowed to people in all four directions,
Then Fairy Saint Female comes to bless us with her grace,
Pink balls roam the water, the heroine lives in eternal glory,
She returns to give holy water for purification.
The shrine's door is hidden by fragrant flowers,
A cup of joy and happiness is raised with one heart,
And Saint Junior has returned,
Drink as heaven and earth tilt,
A busy celebration today,
The rhythmic song of adoration resounds,
Inviting the Saints' committee of the Holy Mother's Council.
The halo shines brightly in the night sky,
The magnificent Holy Spirit shows the way,
Exorcizing evil spirits that harm people,
Causing visitors to tremble in fear,
Blessing disciples forever and ever,

We respectfully implore, divine protection gives blessings.

22. THE ART OF MASTERY

In his journey, the student reached a point where he could no longer distinguish between mind and body, nor separate which of the two had completed the task before him. The lines had blurred; his actions flowed seamlessly from thought to movement, from intention to outcome.

But to arrive at this stage - where skill transcended into art, and art became spiritual - he had to pour every ounce of his attention, physical strength, and mental energy into his practice. It was the discipline of years, the quiet persistence, and the relentless pursuit of mastery that had made the difference.

In the world of the student, as in any true art, there was no shortcut. Only through full devotion to the craft could he transcend mere skill and reach something higher - something that felt like a reflection of the divine.

In this state of grace, mind and body ceased to be separate entities. They became one, working in perfect harmony, completing the circle of art and spirit.

23. WANDERING SONG

Listening to Leonard Cohen's music, I drift back through the years, letting the melodies carry me to distant places. How many people, how many moments, how many stories have I passed through like fleeting shadows? The years unfold like pages in a well-worn book, filled with love, loss, joy, and heartache. And now, as the years recede into memory, what remains? Songs, verses, and lingering echoes of a life once lived. Words and feelings flow from my heart, soft and trembling, like leaves fluttering in the autumn wind.

I will write these songs for myself, weaving them from the sweet memories that linger - each one a fragment of my life's essence. It's funny how thirty years can slip through your fingers like water, leaving behind only traces of what was once so vivid.

The ups and downs, the laughter and tears, the victories and the losses - they've all left their mark. And yet, somehow, there's peace in it all. A gentle hope rises, as steady and soft as a familiar refrain.

Now it's time to move forward, to wander into that vast landscape of song once again. The music calls me back, and I will follow, letting it carry me wherever it wishes.

Wandering Song

Thirty years of living in the ephemera,

A lifetime of sorrow, gain, and loss.

Yet from the remnants of those fleeting days,

I gather melodies to hold.

Now, as the music calls me home,

I walk the road of songs once more,

With hope like the wind at my back,

Carrying me beyond what was before.

24. AUTUMN REVERIE

Early this morning, autumn's breath arrived,

The garden stirred - flowers, sunshine, bells,

Whispering secrets through the breeze,

Hints of realms just out of reach,

Fleeting as the season's change.

•

Petals drift in the cool wind's grace,

Falling like silk from unseen hands.

Nostalgia wraps itself in apricot's scent,

While smoke dances, gently sweeping away

The dust of days we left behind.

•

Ask the flowers what they whisper

In the quiet, crisp breath of fall.

Do I know what they long to say?

Last night, the rain wept softly

Whose hand let yellow petals scatter?

Whose voice rides the wind,

Brushing past my memories?

•

The garden brims with color,

But, oh, the wind - be still!

This fragile heart has borne enough.

The world is torn, yet somewhere,

Bells still laugh through the quiet.

•

The walls glow green as the sun rises,

Yellow leaves flutter down,

Dancing on the restless wind,

Whispering the story of life,

Each leaf a chapter turning.

•

Beneath the autumn sun, flowers bloom,

Yet the wind stirs, relentless,

Asking me - did love slip through my fingers?

Did it drift like these scattered leaves?

•

A school of fish glides by in the stream,

Reminding me - life moves on,

With or without our grief.

The water stills,

But the wind - what is it that makes my soul tremble so?

•

Fragrance overflows,

Blurring the lines of what's real and what's dreamed,

Like a song carried on water,

Like a carpet of flowers,

Like ripples, expanding outward.

But why does she stand alone,

In autumn's fragrant embrace?

•

The sound spins around me,

Coming, going

Like a whisper of things left unsaid.

Where do you wander,

Oh sunlit butterfly,

For whom do you flutter on this gentle breeze?

•

Old friend, is your soul still searching,

Humming poetry to the sky,

Knowing life is both joy and sorrow

Why worry?

•

The morning sun touches my feet,

And my heart swells

How I long for all of autumn's sky to light up.

Let the stream sing,

Like bells ringing with life's sweet echo.

Green fills the air with the scent of being.

Fish still swim.

Water still flows.

And in the flow, all of the world's sorrows drift away.

25. THE JOY OF SIMPLICITY

Before, he indulged in wine as though each drink were part of a carefully orchestrated symphony. Every sip had its place, like an instrument in a grand performance. Each dish, each moment, each conversation had its corresponding glass of wine. The flavors moved from light to bold, from sweet and sour to sharp and biting. The scent of flowers lingered like a stream of clouds, while the oaky undertones carried stories of time well-aged. The experience could be soft and gentle or intense and profound, with the final note leaving him either sweetly dreamy or deeply reflective.

When the wine was cold, it numbed his teeth. When cool and fresh, it felt like the calm of a quiet afternoon. When warmed, it evaporated, spreading a soft, ethereal warmth through his body.

The meals followed suit - plates overflowing with variety, like a choir of flavors singing in harmony. Fresh flowers filled vases with vibrant colors, as the garden outside bloomed with life and color.

But now, he drinks less - just a glass or two. He savors each drop, as if each contains the secrets of the universe. He enjoys it warm, full of depth, listening as heaven and earth whisper in his cup. The meals are simpler now - a few greens, like petals and nuts, enough to bring the taste of wind, clouds, moon, and stars to his table.

Even the flowers have become simpler - thin branches with buds just beginning to bloom. Sometimes, just one vibrant flower, placed thoughtfully in a rough vase, is enough to capture the beauty of the moment.

In the imperfection, he finds joy. A fragile beauty that feels more precious than ever. Perhaps he has shifted from the grandeur of a symphony to the purity of a solo. From the thrill of entertainment to the peace of true enjoyment. From the desire to possess to the desire to give.

And in that shift, he has found something infinitely more meaningful.

26. LIFE POEM

Sorrowful life

Wasted life

Empty life

Desert life

Life of struggle

Damn life

Fake life

Quiet life

Wandering life

Lonely life

Life-forged life

Painful life

Life pays

Life is forever

Rough life

Poor life

Dark life

Loving life

Life giving

Life consecrated

Life rising

Careful life

Diligent life

Nurturing life

Green life

Flowering life

Life intoxicated

Searching life

Dream life

Love life

Life is fragrant

Sweet life

Ephemeral life

Irregular life

Cause and effect life

Distressed life

Solitary life

Prayer life

Anyway, I have still lived life like a small child.

27. PASSING THROUGH

I've wandered through many places,

Sometimes finding a hotel room warmer than home.

Passersby, with fleeting kindness,

Often more considerate than those we call our own.

I learned so much from school and books,

Yet most of it has faded from my mind.

It's the lessons life carved deep into my bones

That linger, unshaken by time.

I've met all kinds of people

The bossy ones who act like they run the show.

But they vanish, replaced by a newer class,

While the common folk stay steady, always in tow.

Experience humbles, teaches with a gentle shove,

As life flows on, with humor and love.

28. THE SIMPLE DREAM

Sometimes I dream of being free for a few weeks, traveling across the country. I start planning what to bring for this long-awaited trip:

- Books - several dozen of all kinds, from novels to philosophy.

- A bottle or two of wine - mostly red, a little white, and maybe a few honorable mentions: vodka, whiskey, and cognac.

- Music's already on my phone; all I need is a good speaker to bring it to life.

- A bit of cash - just in case I end up somewhere without a card machine.

- And, of course, a good-looking woman who appreciates books, wine, and music as much as I do.

But then reality starts to sink in. If space gets tight in the car, something's gotta go. I decide, with a sigh, to leave the speaker behind.

If things get even tighter, I'll cut down on the booze - perhaps just a bottle or two.

And if I must, I'll part with the books (though it stings).

If the situation really squeezes me, maybe I'll just rely on the cash. But what if the cash runs low?

Do I... leave the lovely companion behind? That thought makes me chuckle and sigh simultaneously. What kind of adventure would that be?

But then, I remember - I'm resourceful. With a sharp-witted driver, quick thinking, and an eye for opportunity, we'll make do. Who knows, we might even earn all of the above on the road.

And so, we'll just depart. The open road ahead, enjoying the taste of life as we pass through the three regions, free and unburdened.

Sometimes, the best trips start with nothing more than a simple dream and a good sense of humor.

29. THE ART OF STILLNESS

The teacher, deeply aware of the nature of success, understands that preparation is not just for the teaching but for the cultivation of the self. To enter the creative mind, whether in art or life, one must first appreciate the deep stillness that brings necessary relaxation. It is in this balance of all powers, in the calm focus of one's energies, that true concentration and awareness emerge.

Without this stillness, no real work can be accomplished. This "needless stillness" is not an absence of action but the preparation that leads to effortless creation. It is as though the work forms naturally before his eyes, self-fulfilling, as if guided by an invisible hand.

In any profession or craft, this stillness is the first step toward mastery - the poised movements, the careful preparation, the moments of deliberate waiting. All of these are bound by the same principle: that in stillness, power gathers, and in relaxation, precision takes shape. The teacher knows that to act without agitation is to move with purpose, where every gesture is imbued with meaning and grace.

30. NATURE'S WISDOM

Months rush past in hurried flight,
As Earth and Heaven shift their light.
Eyes fixed on futures yet unseen,
Spring arrives, so fresh and green.

Tomorrow's scent begins to fade,
Afternoon mist drifts, cool and staid.
Winter's breath still lingers near,
But morning thunder soon draws near.

Wind chimes sing of fleeting grace,
Rain bursts forth in hurried pace.
Flowers bow as life moves on,
Summer's scent waits at the dawn.

Outside, the sky is bright and clear,
The sun above holds promise near.
Birds afar heed thunder's call,
Their gathering whispers to us all.

I wake and look, the world aglow,
Grass entwined in streams that flow.
The dance of life spins round again,
Time slips by with soft refrain.

For seasons teach us, year by year,
That change is constant, ever near.
And like the clouds that drift above,
We find our way through loss and love.

31. THE GIFT OF TEA

In the comfort of modern life, everything's at your fingertips. Boiling water, a soulless coffee maker with its heartless knobs, tea bags in endless varieties, a cold white enamel teapot, and a tray of cups just tossed about, served up by hands that are going through the motions.

But then, there are those rare times when you decide to slow down and make a real cup of tea. You take your time - placing a small pot on the flickering flame, letting the aroma of the tea leaves fill the air. You wipe down the tea tray, handle the delicate cups with care, and clear the table of clutter. Maybe you turn a flower in a vase just right, or flip through a book, meditating on the words as they blend with the moment.

As the water begins to bubble softly, you slowly pour the tea into a simple brown ceramic cup. Holding it in your hands, you feel the warmth spread through your fingers, and you watch as the golden liquid ripples, catching the light - maybe reminding you of someone's eyes.

With just a small effort, and only a few minutes, you find deep satisfaction. And somehow, in that moment, life has a touch of poetry.

32. HILLSIDE REVERIE

Living in a hermitage near Buddha's shrine,

On a lonely pine hill where time aligns.

Afternoon breezes gently flow,

Insects hum, shivering low.

The Buddha teaches to rise above desire,

Cultivate the mind, put out the fire.

But as I sip a glass of wine,

Emotions stir, a prayer divine.

Scented Delight

Good wine and flowers in bloom,

Bring life's fragrance to my room.

God doesn't give both to all, it seems,

But here I hold the wine of dreams.

As I look at flowers, sweet and fine,

I sip, savoring both: the bloom, the wine.

Roots of Tomorrow

The summer sun blazes like life's heat,

Yet evening brings a cool retreat.

On pine hill's breeze, we sit with ease,

Sipping rose wine beneath soft trees.

But when we're gone, beneath the earth,

What tree will grow to mark our worth?

In Vino Veritas

Alcohol can make the humble grand,

The ordinary feel like heroes, they stand.

The fraudster's words are sweet and sly,

But only the kind speak with a cold sigh.

Drunk with truth or with deceit,

Wine reveals what lies beneath.

Brightened Spirits

Yesterday, sadness crept within,

A day so dull, a heavy din.

But today, you came with light and cheer,

Pouring wine, a smile so dear.

Gone are sorrows of yesterday's plight,

Like a past life, fading from sight.

Fairy's Toast

Good wine and friends in close embrace,

Together we've found our perfect place.

We waited long for this flowered hour,

Now joy flows like wine's sweet power.

Drunk on laughter, songs we raise,

As if sipping fairy wine in a haze.

33. GARDENING IN HARMONY

The garden breathes like life itself, vibrant and alive. To avoid the prying eyes of the neighbors above, we had to build a high wall, a barrier that offered privacy but also felt confining. In response, I decided to drape that wall in greenery. Slowly, over time, I added colorful plants, a few more each day - replacing what had wilted, repairing what had grown unruly. I planted bamboo groves, a pine tree, and carefully placed stones. A small pagoda roof emerged behind a waterfall, a bridge spanned a tiny stream, and small house models nestled into their new home. Gradually, statues of monks, woodcutters, and buffalo herdsmen found their places, bringing a sense of life to the scene.

With every season, the garden continued to evolve. Peach branches and apricot pots arrived in spring, and hanging vines took their place in the summer sun. At another point, I constructed a small water tower above the aquarium, and in the evening, I would turn on colored lights that shimmered on the water's surface. On windy days, the bells in the garden would ring softly, a gentle harmony between the earth and sky.

Sometimes I sit and simply contemplate the flowers, watching as the scenery subtly shifts and transforms day by day. My heart is filled with a quiet excitement, the kind that comes from noticing the birds singing to welcome a new dawn. It's in these simple moments that I realize perhaps the happiness I seek is already here, in this small garden that offers a refuge for my soul. When we can be ourselves, in the midst of nature, we return to something deeper and more essential. In nurturing the garden, I find that I am nurturing myself. In returning to nature, I return to who I truly am.

34. THE INNER LIGHT

"Like a candle that lights another candle." That's how a true teacher guides - the pathway within the mind, gently lit, allowing the entire mind to shine. The teacher's role is not just to impart knowledge but to kindle the flame of understanding within the student.

When the student becomes attuned to this inner illumination, they realize that the true work lies not in external achievements but within. It is the quiet mastery of the mind, the deep inner work, that surpasses all the visible accomplishments of the outside world. This is the real task - the core responsibility - that a master must ultimately fulfill.

In this way, the journey is not about conquering the outer world but finding balance, stillness, and clarity within, so that when the flame is passed, it burns with the light of wisdom and inner peace.

35. VELVET EYES

Sparkling magic light,
A gentle gaze like velvet, bright.
Dreamy smoke, a fragrant air,
Distant sounds, your eyes ensnare.

All the stars above do gleam,
Willow shadows softly stream.
Petal-soft, your hands, so light,
Golden buds in threads so bright.

A deep whisper close,
"I've searched for you the most."
Shining stars in the velvet sky,
Invisible sparks fly by.

In that moment, we disappear,
Into the void, without fear.
Holding you sweetly, I feel,
This radiant space, so surreal.

Gliding gently, hearts afire,
The world fades, pale, desire.
Love shines with joy's embrace,
As we dream in heavenly grace.

No need for words, let's just be,
Soft curls, cheeks rosy and free.
Falling deeper, love's overflow,
Velvet eyes, an earnest glow.

36. A HERO

He was quite the extraordinary gentleman, particularly around women. He had a habit of breaking into song at parties, especially after several overflowing glasses of wine. It was always the same tune, and he would begin with the same familiar introduction, explaining the reason for his performance. His friends had heard it countless times, yet his voice never failed to capture attention - earnest, warm, filled with a blend of anxious longing and deep affection. There was usually a beautiful young woman by his side, eyes sparkling as he sang, clearly enthralled by the emotion he poured into the song.

The performance was always for her, or so he said. His voice would crack with passion as if the melody held all the unspoken words his heart longed to convey.

Sometimes, after the music ended, he would speak nostalgically of his youth, recalling stories of heroism and adventure during the war. His audience, whether they were hearing it for the first or tenth time, would fall under his spell, hanging on every word as if they, too, had been transported back to those heroic days.

On more than one occasion, I found myself helping him sneak out through the back door, just before his wife made one of her "surprise" appearances. She'd arrive graciously and calmly, though there was always a knowing glint in her eyes. I welcomed her warmly as if nothing unusual had transpired.

In my eyes, despite everything, he remained a hero - a legend in his own right.

A Beautiful Woman

As lovely as a flower,

Though time might fade your grace,

Emotions rise and fall like waves,

They drift like clouds, leaving no trace.

But hold each moment tenderly,

In love, in joy, in sorrow's plea,

For all you have is endless affection,

A lasting bond, a sweet connection.

37. A MAGIC SPELL

On December 26th, he escaped the noise of Tết, retreating to a remote island for ten days of detox. It had been years since he'd taken such a long vacation, especially with his life partner.

As the plane took off, he began reading Aura by Carlos Fuentes - a story of a woman trying to preserve her youth with a magic spell. With a chuckle, he wondered if he'd ever been under a similar spell himself - perhaps that magic had once made his heart race.

His partner caught sight of the book's cover and smiled knowingly. Who needed magic? Life had cast its own spell, binding them with its quiet, everyday enchantments.

The island was peaceful, just as they'd hoped. Morning walks, sunset evenings, and the gentle rhythm of the waves made him realize: they'd cast their own spell on each other - one that had lasted through time.

And yet, humor had its way of sneaking in.

> ### Blooming from a Withered Tree
>
> *On our first date, you were gentle,*
>
> *Soft words like petals in the breeze.*
>
> *Now time has hardened your heart,*
>
> *Cold as a river's flow,*
>
> *Yet still,*
>
> *It makes my withered heart bloom*
>
>

38. AUTUMN'S WHISPER

The fall has come to my front door,

The wind rings softly, evermore.

The river hums a tender tune,

As leaves beneath the sky are strewn.

What are the fish still searching for?

Lost echoes from a distant shore.

Past dreams, like shadows, gently cast,

Yet here, the present holds us fast.

In autumn's glow, a sweet refrain:

To let the past and future wane.

In every breath, the moment's grace

39. WHAT I CARRY

My parents held no titles, no power,

Just ordinary souls,

Who gave me a home full of love and warmth,

Their guidance etched upon my soul.

They weren't rich or grand,

But simple and humble,

Who taught me to grow and learn,

With dreams of hope that never crumble.

My country, too, has known hardship,

Years of pain and separation.

Our ancestors fought to save its heart,

To see the day of its restoration.

It's not wealthy or vast,

Its villages and alleys still poor,

But every day, the people strive,

For a future that holds so much more.

Love and labor are what we share,

With hopes and dreams to guide us through,

Following us from youth to age,

Leading us toward the light anew.

40. TAKE IT EASY

By your age, great men had already done remarkable things - crafted masterpieces, built monumental works, performed glorious feats. Of course, some died young, yet still managed to achieve so much by 30 or 40.

But then there are those who restart life at 50, who only catch their dreams at 70 or 80.

Suddenly, your heart fills with panic, mixed with hope. Panic because life hasn't yet given you the harvest you've been waiting for, despite the toil. And yet hope flickers because perhaps your mission isn't as grand as theirs, but something smaller, simpler. How much time do you have left? Maybe 10, maybe 20 years to fulfill it?

Life is like the seasons.

Spring - when you were young and full of sweet passions, fleeting love, and illusory hope. It was like living in a tranquil novel - innocent, primitive, but still thrilling. There was poverty mixed with narcissism, pride clashing with inferiority, brilliance mixed with bewilderment. Spring yanked you out of school, pulled you across foreign lands, then brought you back to your homeland - a whirlwind adventure.

Then came *Summer*, when you were 30 or 40 - racing madly, fast and loud, like a wild thunderstorm. It was extravagant, stubborn, and shameless - competing, learning, scheming. Those were the intense storms of summer, sometimes quenching your thirst, sometimes leaving you parched and weary at the end of the season. It lasted longer than expected and wore you down, taking years to regain your strength.

Now, you tell yourself not to rush into *Autumn*. You imagine living like a sturdy tree - deeply rooted, slow, persistent, with yellow leaves starting to appear, but strong enough to understand what's enough. You'll do a few things you love, perhaps with a few close people, and then just live. Maybe, in late autumn, flowers will bloom again, and you'll return to a new spring.

As for *Winter*, you're not ready to think about that yet. You hope autumn will stretch out, with winter just a quick passing - a brief pause before the cycle begins anew.

Take it easy. Where are you rushing off to, anyway?

41. THE NATURE OF TAO

More and more, I am deeply engaged in the practice of "Tao in our profession." It is an art that has evolved into a ritual, something I perform without any conscious effort. It feels as though I am being led, almost like in a dream. And so, I admit, this is precisely what the Master spoke of.

Yet, I still can't stop my inner attention until the moment of action. The intense focus of my entire body not only tires me but also leads to moments where the tension becomes unbearable, pulling me away from concentration. Therefore, I must always remain aware, alert to the exact moment when I need to interact with the object.

"You see," said the Master, "because you don't truly forget yourself. It's actually simple."

"Think of the way a lotus leaf behaves," he continued. "Under the weight of night dew, the leaf bends downward, lower and lower. Suddenly, the heavy dewdrops fall, but the lotus leaf remains still."

"You must be like the lotus leaf - held in perfect tension until the moment of action happens on its own."

Reality works the same way. When singular focus fills your entire being, you will act effortlessly through the object. The result you desire will come to you, like the dewdrops falling from the lotus leaf, before you even think about it."

42. THE THEATER'S REFLECTION

Sitting in the grand theater, watching an opera from my country - emotions ran deep. The performance flowed in English, while my country's language scrolled on an electronic board above. The audience was mostly from my homeland, their faces attentive, caught in the beauty of it all.

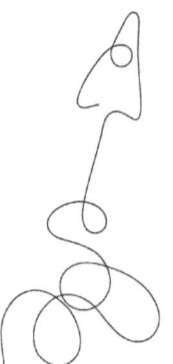

I looked up at the ornate dome and the walls that had stood for over a hundred years. This place held stories. Everyone seemed joyful, immersed in the performance. But as I sat there, a thought stirred in my mind: a hundred years ago, while this building was rising, the Europeans were already creating the first cars. Across the ocean, Americans were mastering the art of mass production, churning out millions of vehicles on assembly lines.

Now, we assemble imported cars, but still rely on foreign engines - our understanding of that intricate core remains elusive. A small regret weighed on me - why couldn't we yet master this part of the craft?

But then I remembered: progress, like life, is about balance. We evolve step by step. My country's journey is different, unique in its challenges and achievements.

Fire and Water

Fire, creation's spark and war's fierce light, Yet also warmth in the deepest night. Water, life's stream, both cold and clear, Brings death, yet soothes and conquers fear.

Fire builds, it brightens and consumes, But water nourishes, heals, and blooms. We need them both, as seasons turn, A dance of balance in which we learn.

At night, fire glows with brighter might, While water cools in softer light. And so, the two entwine as one, Each needed, as day yields to sun.

43. MELODY OF THE DAWN

The dawn breaks gently with its light,

The mist ascends in silver white.

Young branches glisten, fresh and new,

The willows whisper as they grew.

In beauty bright, the nightingale,

Sings melodies that never fade.

Heaven lends its sweetest song,

To pine trees old, where time's been long.

Holding hands, embracing beloved flowers,

The wallflowers hum, the daisies sway,

Petunias blush, shy in their way.

On moss-clad walls, the jasmine blooms,

Its fragrant scent fills every room.

In nature's arms, love's tender grace,

Nostalgia lingers in this place.

44. THE LONGING HAPPINESS

On the hill, in the forest, or by the lake, there is joy in the simple pleasures. Listening to jazz while reading *The Sun Also Rises* by Hemingway - a perfect harmony of sound and words. Those night walks through Paris, to coffee shops or bars, the dancing, the laughter, the drinking, all captured in prose. Or the bus ride to Spain, crossing mountains with Basque farmers, where every mile felt alive with the thrill of adventure.

Remembering that time has drifted by like the softest breeze...

The Drifters by Michener stirs the same nostalgia - a sweet jazz melody that plays on in memory, whispering promises of future journeys to be taken, adventures waiting on the horizon.

Soulmate

Empty your cup and feel its glow,

A warmth within your heart will grow.

Wine, so sweet, but love is more

Without it, what is drinking for?

Loneliness may fill your night,

But hope returns with morning light.

Where is your soulmate, lost in time?

Perhaps you'll find them in love's rhyme.

45. PASSION

Passion is fascination,

An immersion into miracles,

Where only we understand

What truly happened, and why.

•

Passion is guided by wisdom,

By enthusiasm and the stirrings of a hopeful heart.

It lifts us to dazzling heights,

And even when lost,

Drifting into the endless night sky,

It still glows - like a shooting star

Carving its brief, brilliant path.

•

Sometimes we are lost in love,

Blinded, immersed in the murky depths.

Yet even in the darkness,

There is purpose

A whispered truth:

This is my way of repaying the debt of life,

A journey toward the day

I rise again to the light.

•

But if your mind grows restless,

Cold and devoid of feeling,

You will see that no amount of vanity

Can fill the void.

Without love, without belief,

Life loses meaning,

Becomes hollow,

Like an empty shell beneath the vast sky.

46. FINDING THE UTMOST FREEDOM

Step by step, I gradually consider my profession as a martial art in the spirit of Zen, like a flash of lightning from the cloud of inclusive reality. Through each unobstructed movement of my mind, that reality manifests itself. And within it, I meet reality again, as if meeting my original, nameless self-nature.

I keep encountering that self-nature again and again, each time awakening to the ultimate energy I can be. Reality - both for myself and through me to others - takes shape in a thousand forms and shades. Yet, despite diligent and patient practice, I have not yet fully absorbed the Zen spirit that penetrates deeply and burns within me, allowing it to saturate every corner of my life.

My existence captures only fleeting good moments because, for me, sacred freedom has become a profound and undeniable necessity.

47. THE FALLING WINTER

The earth's rhythm turns,
Four seasons flow like rivers to the sea,
Evaporating into clouds,
Then falling back as rain.
Wind carries the cycle onward,
Always returning, always renewed.

But this afternoon,
When spring should yield to summer's light,
Rain still approaches,
A wind bends the world.
Pines shiver,
Cypress vines rush,
Petunias sway,
Phalaenopsis stands alone.
Pink bougainvillea flutters in the gust,
While tithonia and hibiscus hide
Behind bamboo groves,
Combretum falling with the rain,
Cuphea weeps quietly.

On the lake,
Waves ripple as yellowed leaves curl and fold.
Spring has withered away,
And there is no winter where old trees sprout anew.

It is a reminder of creation's quiet power
That life itself is an unexplainable dream.
Those who cling to illusions must see,
Life is a melody
A song of creation that flows,
Endlessly transforming,
Yet deeply rooted in mystery.

48. THE THREE WAYS

Upon entering a temple, you might notice the three-way gate - an elegant structure dividing the entrance and exit. It's often said that this gate represents the pathways of life:

- The form (material)
- The void (impermanence)
- The middle way (balance between form and void)

Of course, there are many interpretations, because life rarely offers just one explanation! Some say the gate symbolizes:

- The "Three Jewels" *(Buddha, Dharma, Sangha)*
- The "Doors of Liberation" *(Emptiness, Signlessness, Aimlessness)*
- Or perhaps, the "Doors of Enlightenment" *(Precepts, Concentration, Insight)*

And let's not forget Buddhism's famous trifecta:

- *Body, Speech, Mind* - the three paths we purify to live in harmony.

Even in our everyday lives, things seem to come in threes:

- Home, Market, Temple - the three places where we practice. Home, of course, is the hardest place to stay Zen; the market's a close second, and the temple? Well, that's where we catch our breath.

Maybe Buddha just really liked the number three. Asians certainly do. There's always:

- Truth, Goodness, Beauty
- Essence, Breath, Spirit
- Heaven, Earth, Man
- And the three strategies: The Best, The Middle, The Worst.

Even in the humdrum of modern life, we're constantly navigating three modes:

- At Home, On the Street, At the Office
- Resting, Living, Working
- Lying, Sitting, Standing

It's all about recognizing where we are and adjusting our behavior to fit the moment. The trick is finding that sweet spot where everything flows smoothly. And hey, once you've mastered it, you **might even look wise - and if not, well, you can always try again** tomorrow.

49. DELUSION

I hadn't seen her in a long time. Today, she arrived like the wind - whirling, swirling, and sweeping through everything in her path. It was like a storm and a breeze all at once, blurring the lines between reality and something ethereal.

After a well-prepared party, layered with flavors and aromas, the evening was awash with the finest alcohol - strong, light, sweet, deep, fire-like, amber-hued. She looked at me with that mischievous sparkle in her eyes, as if we shared a secret the world couldn't touch.

Under the flicker of candlelight and the soft strains of sentimental music, her voice came to me like a distant whisper, even though she was right there, inches away.

"Do you know the book *The Kuma Sutra*? It's fascinating. I read it online."

I chuckled. "Ah, you mean *The Kama Sutra*. I used to have a beautifully illustrated edition I got from the UK, but it's lost to time and moves."

She grinned, that playful glint in her eye. "Well, I always knew you had a bit of the scholar in you. A real know-it-all, huh?"

"Not quite," I replied. "Back in the day, when I had too much free time, I translated a book on that subject from Russian and made a little booklet out of it. I'd send it to friends as a joke."

She laughed softly. "You're something else. A secret lecturer of the unspeakable!"

Her eyes narrowed as she leaned closer. "Your fingers - they're magical. I wonder how many people have felt their touch."

I smirked. "Oh, it's nothing special. When I was young, I practiced the violin religiously. I'd spend hours caressing the strings, squeezing, vibrating, and stroking them. Eventually, I moved to the Spanish guitar, and my fingers had to learn to dance across all ten strings, creating melodies full of memories, light and romantic."

Her smile was sly now. "Someday, you'll play for me, right?"

I shrugged. "Maybe. My fingers might remember, but my mind... who knows?"

She sighed. "You're a mystery to me. Sometimes you smile like the world's your friend, and other times you're distant, like you're carrying a burden no one can see." She paused, her tone softening. "You must get lonely, eating alone like that."

I was surprised. "How did you know?"

"Your colleagues told me. They say you're cold when you're unhappy, that everyone's afraid of you." She hesitated. "But that's not the man I see. When I'm with you, you're gentle, thoughtful... soft."

I smiled faintly. "Maybe I'm just like everyone else - a little rough around the edges, with different sides depending on the day."

She nodded. I added, "Maybe. You know, sometimes I think of myself as a hard-working bee, buzzing from flower to flower, gathering nectar, offering honey to the world. My knees may be rough, but they've seen a lot of work." She chuckled.

"And sometimes I feel like a flower, waiting for bees like you to come around. My petals may be fading, but there's still sweetness left to share."

Her eyes twinkled. "So… are you a flower or a butterfly?"

I shrugged. "I don't know. In a deep meditation once, I felt like a lady from another time, playing instruments with delicate hands, admired by many."

She tilted her head. "Sounds like you were a real catch."

"Maybe," I laughed. "But in this life, I think I'm here to repay some old karma. I love deeply, I give everything, and who knows? Maybe someday I'll become a Bodhisattva for it."

She laughed, shaking her head. "You're delusional! Men are always dreaming up fantasies about themselves."

I sighed. "Maybe. But life is fleeting. Sometimes, I just want to run away, retreat to the mountains, and live quietly, far from all this noise."

She leaned in closer. "That sounds nice. Maybe I'll join you, leave the city behind, and we'll meditate together in peace."

I smiled, a touch of mischief in my eyes. "Oh, what could we be, you and I? Why can't I be like the Sixth Dalai Lama - pleasing both Buddha Tathagata and my beloved all at once?".

Buddhas Within Us:

- *Guanyin* – *Compassion through Listening and Helping*
- *Samantabhadra* – *Strength in Action and Execution*
- *Manjushri* – *Clarity through Knowledge and Wisdom*
- *Kṣitigarbha* – *Dedication as the Guardian of all beings*

Through practice, we embody:

- *Love*
- *Gratitude*
- *Forgiveness*
- *Generosity*
- *Fulfillment*

In these ways, we draw closer to the Buddhas.

50. BACK TO THE EMPTINESS

If you wish to continue to the end, you must once again walk the path of 'art and non-art.' You must take a decisive leap before you can live in reality as one truly merged with it. You will become a student again - a beginner. You must navigate the last stretch, the steepest slope on the path you have chosen, with many more transformations still ahead.

If you succeed in this journey, your life will be fully realized. You will encounter the unbroken reality, the essence of all realities - the unseen fidelity of all things. This is the "Emptiness," the origin of everything. You will be swallowed by the "Emptiness" and reborn from it.

51. THE WANDERER'S SONG

I set off on a journey, leaving worries behind
For nothing is ever permanent.
With each step, I wear a gentle smile,
Who will remember these paths, years from now?
The pages of life keep turning,
Leaving behind just whispers of youthful dreams.
Time is like a bird flying in shadow,
Where will its wings take it next?

Like clouds that kiss water, then disappear,
The friends of our youth have drifted far.
Dusty roads beneath our feet
Are they the same paths the ancients walked?
I may not shine like the sun,
Nor have I unlocked creation's secret.
But in the deep ocean of my mind,
I have found a precious jewel:
Life is priceless.

How do we find our way back?
Before the party ends and everyone has gone,
Let's pour a glass, brimming full.
Drink it with all our heart
For heaven has no wine for wanderers.

I am the source of my own joy and sorrow,
A mixture of earth and vitality,
Reflecting life in all its forms
So wonderful, yet so simple.

52. RETURNING FRESH

After three days spent in the stillness of the forest - lost in stories, books, and the quiet notes of music - he returned to the city. The road ahead stretched out like a ribbon, and the car hummed along in tune with Bach's guitar. The sun slanted through the windshield, and he cracked open the window. The wind rushed in, roaring as it swirled around him. He smiled, feeling as if the sunlight itself was wrapping him in a warm embrace.

Life, in that moment, felt beautiful. Joyful even. He found himself a little nostalgic for the simpler days he had left behind, though they were long gone now. Perhaps, he mused, death could be just as beautiful - another transition, as gentle as this one. In a moment like this, it almost seemed that way.

Perfection

Responsibilities come with burdens,

Even when hiding in the mountains.

Trouble always finds its way down.

How to get the best of both worlds?

To be like Buddha, yet still be human.

53. SPIRITUAL SINGING

I am in love with the sacred songs of the Goddess's ceremony.

Each time the lyrics rise and the melodious music flows,

My heart is overwhelmed with love - love for my mother,

And the deep connection to my homeland.

It swells within me, filling every corner of my soul.

Every graceful movement in the dance

Reflects the rhythm of my childhood,

Carrying me back to those simple, joyful moments

Even in this time of sorrow.

As time passes and I wander far from home,

The music of foreign lands fades away like the morning dew.

Yet the sacred singing remains, echoing in my heart

A gentle melody that delights and comforts my soul.

54. NATURAL HARMONY

Harmony is the essence of life. Nature mastered this long ago - mountains, forests, flowers, trees, lakes, animals, clouds - they're all interconnected, each playing a role in an intricate symphony of balance. The contrasts aren't just important; they're vital. Without differences, nature would collapse under its own weight. It's like nature's way of shrugging and saying, "Relax, I've got this."

Gardening is the perfect example. You can't force a garden into beauty; you have to watch, listen, and respect the natural order. Try to control it, and you'll get weeds, disappointment, and maybe a nervous breakdown. But when you follow nature's cues, something magical happens - beauty grows on its own, in perfect harmony.

And humans? We're no different. Harmony is the key to all relationships. It's about appreciating the goodness in each person, understanding that the quirks and differences are what make life colorful. After all, if we were all the same, life would be like a garden full of identical flowers - predictable, monotonous, and downright dull.

55. THE BLOOMING OF EVERYDAY HEROES

Politicians tell us they'll fight the good fight,

Bringing justice and prosperity to all in sight.

But the crowd quietly thinks, "We're doing just fine

We can handle our families, thanks for the line."

They don't see civilization's subtle light,

Creeping into their homes each night.

Artists promise joy and beauty with flair,

Praising life's love in the laughter they share.

But after the show and the fleeting delight,

The audience sighs, "It was fun... but life's still a fight."

Our daily worries quickly return

That's just the way the real world churns.

Writers pen epics, deep and profound,

Hoping their words will eternally resound.

Yet, readers take away just a brief spark,

Soon forgotten as life leaves its mark.

They wonder if their legacy will last,

Or fade away like echoes of the past.

Doctors strive to heal and save,

Putting strangers above the love they crave.

But sometimes all they get are frowns

Angry patients throwing them down.

Gratitude? It's often quite rare,

But still, they continue with care.

Scholars reach for new horizons bright,

Dreaming of making their homeland's future light.

But friends and family shake their heads,

"Dream all you want, we still need bread."

Fantasy and brilliance often dismissed,

As daily needs persist, persist.

Businessmen toil late into the night,

Building from scratch, though out of sight.

Sacrificing pleasures for a future unseen,

While people imagine them living the dream.

They say, "All they do is sit and scheme,"

Not knowing they work by the midnight gleam.

But here's the truth, dear everyone:

We are all the quintessence of life, bar none.

From the smallest acts to the grander schemes,

Every contribution adds to the streams.

Life is short and fleeting, true,

But each bloom matters, old or new.

For even wildflowers on the hillside steep,

Know their time is brief and deep.

Still, they stretch toward the sun,

Knowing that their bloom has just begun.

56. CALM

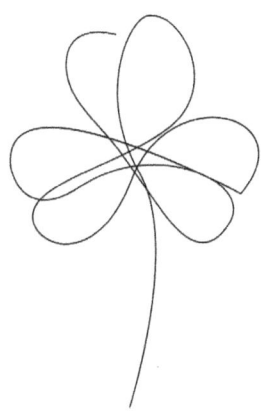

Purple, yellow, rose flowers - petals drift and fall,

Green, brown, gray moss - nature's quiet carpet unfurls.

The plants climb, stand, and reach, like shadows of us all,

White fish, red fish, and black fish swim for food, simply making their way.

Out in the world, life changes in a never-ending dance,

But here, in this moment, calm settles like a deep breath.

When the Heart Speaks

Trembling steps on the lonely miles,

We hold onto our sorrows, though they weigh us down.

But with each passing day, we edge closer

Closer to the land of the possible and impossible.

And oh, the joy that fills us when the heart speaks.

57. THE WAY OF ZEN

The path of Zen can transform any profession into an art, a way of life that is both mindful and purposeful. Here are the main principles that help infuse Zen into our daily work:

- **Embrace the profession as a battle with oneself.** The true Zen practitioner knows how to live in solitude, finding purpose within themselves rather than relying on external validation.

- **Master the rhythm of your breath.** Breathe deeply, quietly, and slowly, aligning your inner world with each inhalation and exhalation.

- **Synchronize breathing with movement.** Whether walking, standing, or focusing, every action flows with the breath - steady, deliberate, mindful.

- **Refine the basics.** The foundation of Zen is repetition without desire. Practice your craft patiently, repeating each movement again and again without longing for progress or success.

- **Relax into your work.** As you perform your tasks, release tension from your body and mind. Let go of desires, love, hatred, joy, or sorrow. Simply be present, finding quiet satisfaction in the process.

- **Honor each step of the process.** Every interaction - from preparation to completion - should be a ritual, performed with the highest respect for the work and for yourself.

Treat your workday like a dance, or a festival of mindful practice. The Zen practitioner becomes a dancer, flowing through their tasks with mindfulness, concentration, and dedication.

When the body, mind, and purpose align with the world around them, the work ceases to be work. It becomes Zen - a state where effort and ease coexist, where you are fully present, one with everything around you.

58. THE FAIRY'S PLAYFUL DANCE

1. Garden of Love

When we first met, you were as small as a pistil,

Now, you overflow like a garden of love,

Too vast for me to hold in my arms.

Being with you, I feel so small

But in your garden, I am always lost, joyfully overwhelmed.

2. Surprised by Regret

A girl sent me a message one day,

I hesitated but went anyway.

When I saw her, she surprised me

A white neck, wet eyes, a figure so thin,

Speaking of gratitude, of regret...

For not meeting sooner.

3. Beauty from Afar

You were like a willow, swaying in the sky,

Graceful, with a smile that could light up the night.

You needed love, but kept it far,

Like a sweet fruit - just out of reach,

And I, too shy to taste its sweetness.

4. Winter's Ice

When we first fell in love, you gave me your all,

Forgiveness was easy, no matter how I might fall.

But now your smile fades, your love grows thin

Seeing you is like drinking ice in the dead of winter.

5. The Fruit of Love

Love blooms, bears fruit, and flavors life.

But tasting strange fruits in this world

You never quite know what you'll find.

So cherish the taste, every time you make love,

For it's a sweet adventure, full of surprise.

6. Diamond Heart

I'm not a coward, no.

You are sweet and earnest, a fairy in flesh.

It's not that I've turned to diamond

It's simply my longing,

To inhale your fragrance, to hold your essence close.

7. The Mermaid's Dive

I often hold beauty close in my arms,

Whispering softly, she nestles with charm.

But sometimes, like a mermaid, she dives deep,

Into unpredictable seas

Leaving me in wonder, yet always enchanted.

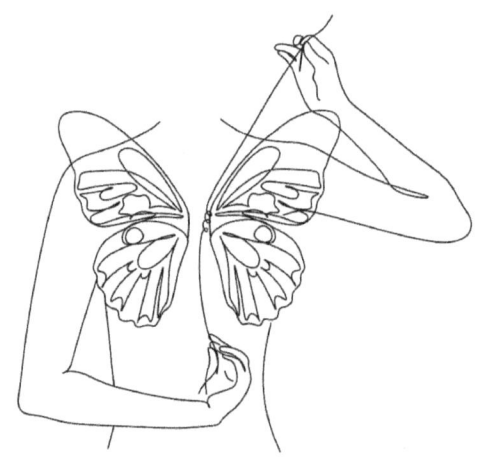

59. SPARKLING

A small spark can ignite a forest, and in much the same way, a chance meeting can kindle an unexpected adventure. She hadn't planned on him, but life often has its way of taking the most ordinary moments and turning them into something extraordinary.

She loved the way he carried an air of elegant calmness, even when boredom or sadness crept into his features. It was his thick lips, that charming smile, and his eyes - those sparkling, mischievous eyes - that cast a spell over her. She was mesmerized.

It wasn't until later, when she accidentally glimpsed his broad chest behind a tight shirt, that she felt a different kind of spark. His body was strong, with a small waist and soft, fragrant skin. His slim fingers, white and graceful, had a touch of gentleness - a delicate femininity - but still, he radiated calm strength.

Once, as a playful moment turned into something unexpected, she felt his hands - those large, powerful hands - lift her up effortlessly. With a laugh, he spun her around in the air, and for a moment, she felt weightless. But when he gently set her back down, the world trembled beneath her feet. She clung to him, gasping for breath, laughing, trembling, her heart racing as he pulled her close.

I Will Be With You

When Autumn arrives,

And the shadows of jealousy have faded,

We will sit beneath the lotus bloom,

Our souls quiet, finding their calm.

At dawn, we ring the bell

A gift offered to Buddha,

And in the gentle light of dusk,

Among the petals that whisper peace,

His loving eyes watch over us.

With a tender smile,

He blesses our reunion,

Filling my heart with eternal serenity,

As we meet again,

In His radiant embrace.

60. THE MOVIE OF LIFE

Rewind the movie of our life
Scenes flicker by, faces and places long forgotten.
Crumbling houses, meaningless parties,
All in a city blurred by engine smoke.

There's the train pulling away to some distant land,
Leaving behind the chaos,
The crowd bottling up their screams,
Boiling with ambition, weighed down by worry.
And there's love - oh, the deceitful kind,
Silent whispers between people draped in borrowed clothes.

I remember loving the blue sea and golden sun,
The soft, fragrant skin, the taste of good wine.
We spoke earnest words,
Made promises under starry skies,
With lovemaking that felt endless
Vows for eternity etched in our minds.
I thought I had locked it all away,
The images, the desires, the dreams.
Yet somehow, they slip away,
Like walking into a room each morning,
Only to find the whirlpool has washed it all clean.

I once believed I could reach greatness,
Walking contemplatively atop a deserted hill.
I thought I was standing on wisdom's peak,
Only to stumble into the deep valley
Of doubt and fragile self-esteem.
I rushed to meet the world's demands,
Telling myself the storms of life would explain it all.
But now I realize, in the grand scheme,
I'm just a speck of dust
Drifting between heaven and earth,

Trying to make sense of it all.

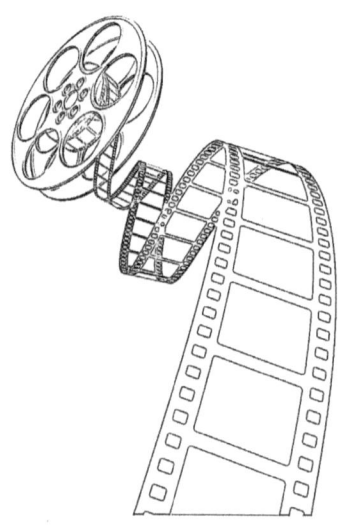

61. CLEANSE

Every day, we all have to bathe, scrub our bodies, trim our beards, fix our hair, and tidy up our nails. We also clean the bedroom, fold the blankets, and make sure the corners are sharp enough to rival a military inspection. The furniture? Gleaming, of course.

And then there's the office. If your desk is neat, with papers and documents in their rightful places, and your cabinets are organized like a filing guru's dream, the surroundings fresh and bright, well - you're bound to have a fantastic day, right?

But here's the thing: just like the body and the office, the mind is a garden too. And depending on the rain and sunshine of life, that garden might sprout some weeds along with the flowers.

So what do you do? You've got to weed it, cleanse it. How? By thinking clearly and simply, by learning to let go of the baggage - be it resentment, regret, or that thing your friend said to you five years ago that still bugs you. Let it go, forgive. For others, sure, but more importantly, for yourself.

Because in the end, a clean mind is like a clean desk - it just feels better, and everything flows a little smoother.

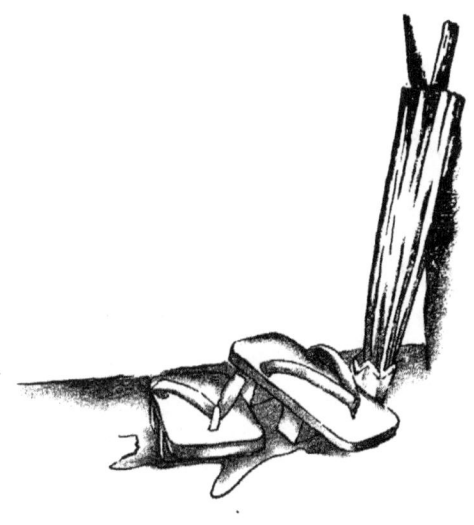

62. THE BEAUTY

Beauty often hides in form,

A mystery we cannot grasp

Neither the why nor the how of it.

A flower blooms amidst the swamp,

As if something stirred

In the dark of a night steeped in desire,

And today, you glow

With the scent of longing,

Intoxicating and pure.

The flowers tremble with emotion,

Swaying in the steam of the earth,

In the thick, tangled grass,

Aware of life's fragility.

Desire rises to the surface,

A thirst beneath a fading sunset

Seemingly distant, yet so near.

And though fleeting, this moment

This offering to the world

Is eternal in its devotion.

63. LITTLE OF HAPPINESS

From now on, I'm committed to focusing on the unexpected joys that find me every day. Those little moments that catch me off guard and the secret feelings that linger in the quiet spaces of my heart.

Yesterday, I made my way to the beach to visit some old friends. I almost didn't go - worried there'd be too much alcohol, too much music, and too many emotions to handle. But after a whirlwind of a week, filled with work and a shareholder meeting that (thankfully) went smoothly, I figured, why not?

Before heading out, I stopped by to see my father. We had a good chat, and I encouraged him to keep up his exercises. I even helped him call the grandchildren and daughter-in-law who were far away - it was a small gesture, but it felt good.

With that done, I hit the road. I popped in a CD I had tossed in the car without much thought, and to my surprise, the music was unexpectedly good. Just me, the lyrics, the open highway, passing fields, the blue sea stretching endlessly alongside mountains. It felt like the world was wide open and mine to explore.

When I arrived, I was greeted by familiar faces - partners, employees I hadn't seen in ages, and a few strangers who quickly became less strange after a few hugs and warm smiles. The best moment, though? Sitting on a hill, overlooking the shining sea, the perfectly trimmed green of the golf course, watching people swing their clubs with such focus and precision. My heart stirred, reminding me of how much I missed it. It's been over three years since I last played golf, but something in me sparked, and I promised myself I'd be back out there soon.

Later that night, after more hugs and farewells, I lay down, my mind still flashing with images - the smooth green grass, the endless sky, the white clouds lazily drifting by...

Each leaf holds the kiss of Heaven and Earth,

And I long to taste the sweetness of those loving lips.

64. WAVES OF DESIRE

Every night, she returned to him like a wild cat seeking comfort, longing for the intimacy only he could provide. She craved the magic they shared, waiting for love to wash over her like waves breaking against the shore.

She carried with her the scents of spring - fresh grass after the rain, the delicate fragrance of lilies, orchids, jasmine, like a garden blooming under the moon. She was soft, vibrant, dewy, her eyes wide with desire, shining like drops of morning dew.

His hands explored her body, gentle yet hungry. She moaned, her body arching and bending to his touch, surrendering to the waves of passion that surged between them. The intensity grew, enveloping her, each wave stronger than the last, sweeping her deeper into the tide of love.

Her skin was smooth and fragrant, as soft as fresh milk. Her hair fell around her face like a halo in the candlelight, as she lay back, welcoming the sensations that rolled over her, shivering from the cold only to burn with heat moments later.

She bit into the pillow, trying to stifle the cries that rose from deep within her, her hands grasping at the sheets, wet with the warmth and vitality of their passion. Suddenly, she became aware of him - his scent filling her senses: hot sunshine, rain-soaked earth, the musk of oak and coffee, blending with the smoky sweetness of a cigar and the salty tang of the sea. He was primal, wild, like a beast barely contained.

She panicked, her body trembling as she clung to him, her nails digging into his shoulders, his back slick with sweat. His kiss, long and suffocating, left her gasping for breath, her desire drained, only to be reignited again.

He sank deeper into her, and she lost herself, diving alongside him into the depths of lust. She swallowed, bent, squeezed, floating in the ocean of their desire. But soon, she grew tired, disoriented. She couldn't find her way back - frantic, dizzy, consumed by it all. She had given herself over completely.

She remembered how he once told her he wanted to devour her. No, she thought, not tonight. Tonight, she would devour him. Like a wildcat leaping from the shadows, she pounced, covering him, tearing into him with an intensity that left her aching and satisfied.

In the end, she felt herself shatter, like glass crashing to the floor, scattering in a thousand pieces. Her body swayed, shook, and rolled like fireworks lighting up the night sky, bursting and fading, until finally, she plunged into the quiet abyss of exhaustion, wave after wave of pleasure leaving her feeling empty and alone.

As the sea of passion calmed, she found herself in the silence, the soft music of their lovemaking fading into the background. His whispers and gentle touch carried her away, floating among the endless, empty waves of nothingness.

When dawn came, she quietly slipped away, leaving behind the warmth of his embrace. Like a breeze carrying the scent of love, she disappeared into the light, taking with her only the memory of their fleeting moments.

EPILOGUE: The Journey Within

Where do we go?
What do we seek?
Who are we searching for?

Where do we go,
Through the mindless school,
Through the silent street,
Through the forgetful rain?

Where do we go,
Through the blank pages,
Through the white paper,
Through the tiles of time?

Where do we go,
Through the faded photo,
Through the scars of war,
Through the hallowed mausoleum?

Where do we go,
Through the green forest,
Through rustic provinces,
Through the humid air?

Where do we go,
Through the moonlit sky,
Through foggy clouds,
Through the bustling crowd?

Where do we go,
Through the sunny day,
Through the rainy night,
Through gardens of flowers and leaves?

Where do we go,
Through the bamboo groves,
Through the village pond,
Through the graceful dresses?

Where do we go,
Through the crimson dawn,
Through the pale sunset,
Through the cold embrace?

Where do we go,
Through the crowded train,
Through the lost city,
Through the lonely mountain?

Where do we go,
Through the roaring ocean,
Through fickle hearts,
Through the fortunes of love?

Where do we go,
Through buds in the wind,
Through birdsong's echo,
Through the call of distant nostalgia?

Where do we go,
Through lighted streets,
Through empty roads,
Through the lonely monument?

Where do we go,
Through the pages of history,
Through scripture's text,
Through the falling petals?

Where do we go,
Through the wet walls,
Through the green moss,
Through the smoke of the kitchen fire?

Where do we go,
Through the eyes of dogs,
Through children's smiles,
Through the hugs of our parents?

Where do we go,
Through the greening grass,
Through the old library,
Through the last ray of sunshine?

Where do we go,
Through the body's desire,
Through the cup of wine,
Through the passionate kiss?

Where do we go,
Through the shadowed silhouette,
Through suffocated dreams,
Through the cold silence?

Where do we go,
Through the growing pines,
Through trembling flowers,
Through screaming memories?

Where do we go,
Through the ruined temple,
Through the silent pagoda,
Through flickering candles?

Where do we go,
Through the pandemic's grip,
Through the deserted tomb,
Through beauty's fragile bloom?

Where do we go,
Through the months and years,
Through familiar roads,
To witness the passing of a lifetime?

Where do we go,
If tomorrow,
We keep wandering
In this fleeting world?

Where do we go?
Stop, just stop.
Put it down, let it go -
Be empty, be free.

Where do we go,
To melt away sorrows,
To reignite our faith,
When our hearts begin to sing?

We have gone through
The narrow door of life,
To the vast, formless realm,
To see Him manifest in us,
To know we are Him,
The One we've been searching for.

JOHN